THE U.S. MILITARY AND HUMAN RIGHTS PROMOTION

THE U.S. MILITARY AND HUMAN RIGHTS PROMOTION

LESSONS FROM LATIN AMERICA

Jerry M. Laurienti

PRAEGER SECURITY INTERNATIONAL
Westport, Connecticut • London

Library of Congress Cataloging-in-Publication Data

Laurienti, Jerry M.
The U.S. military and human rights promotion : lessons from Latin America / Jerry
M. Laurienti.
    p. cm.
   Includes bibliographical references and index.
   ISBN-13: 978–0–275–99938–4 (alk. paper)
   1. United States–Military policy.   2. United States–Foreign relations–Latin
America.   3. Latin America–Foreign relations–United States.   4. Human
rights–Latin America. I. Title.
  UA23.L325   2007
  323.098–dc22   2007016226

British Library Cataloguing in Publication Data is available.

Library of Congress Catalog Card Number: 2007016226
ISBN-13: 978–0–275–99938–4
ISBN-10: 0–275–99938–6

First published in 2007

Praeger Security International, 88 Post Road West, Westport, CT 06881
An imprint of Greenwood Publishing Group, Inc.
www.praeger.com

Printed in the United States of America

The paper used in this book complies with the
Permanent Paper Standard issued by the National
Information Standards Organization (Z39.48–1984).

10 9 8 7 6 5 4 3 2 1

For Kelly

Contents

Acknowledgments

I owe a debt of gratitude to many individuals whose support was invaluable in completing this work. While all named here were helpful, I alone am responsible for any factual mistakes or errors in judgment. I am particularly grateful to my advisor, Dr. David Goldfischer, who over several years fought for my academic career and provided guidance when others were unwilling. Dr. Goldfischer apparently saw in me an ability that was not evident to others. I only hope that this book can meet his expectations. I am thankful to Dr. Paul Viotti and Dr. Peg Sanders for their helpful comments and interest in this work.

Bill Prillaman provided years of critical encouragement and analytic mentoring that I appreciate. Dan Lambert, David Pacelli, and Dale Avery were helpful in making sure I had the opportunity to complete my research. Several U.S. and foreign military and civilian officials across Latin America were willing to interview for this book. Leana Bresnahan of U.S. Southern Command was particularly helpful. Sarah, Chad, and Michael also provided critical backing during the research phase of this work. General Barry McCaffrey, Adam Isacson, and Dr. Richard Downie deserve thanks for their committed interest in the topic. I credit Pat and Mary Laurienti for unending encouragement and support. Finally, I am indebted to Kelly Laurienti, who served as my first line editor, has read multiple drafts of this book, and provided critical feedback and urging that significantly improved the final product.

1

Introduction

The U.S. armed forces were vigorously engaged in nudging their Latin American counterparts to recognize the strategic imperatives of respecting human rights on the battlefield many years before the U.S. military had to deal with the repercussions of abuses at Abu Ghraib prison in Iraq. Before Iraqi accusations of massacre at Haditha forced the U.S. military to again scramble to defend its honor and reputation, U.S. forces in Latin America were more than a decade into repairing their image in Latin America after taking the blame for numerous human rights crises. Indeed, U.S. military relations with Latin America are at the center of numerous academic and policy debates, particularly regarding U.S. military assistance and its impact on human rights and broader democratic development. No work, however, has focused on determining whether the U.S. military could serve as a primary source of human rights promotion around the region. Meanwhile, U.S. military human rights promotion efforts in Latin America have become central to the Department of Defense Strategic Engagement Plan since the end of the cold war.[1]

U.S. Southern Command (SOUTHCOM) boasts a collection of human rights centered policies and programs that are unique among U.S. military commands. SOUTHCOM's human rights promotion efforts include:

- Mandatory training for all U.S. personnel assigned to the Command
- Mandatory human rights training for all recipients of military-related training in host countries

- Programs for training Latin American military and civilian officials to serve as human rights trainers in their own countries
- Mandatory human rights training for any attendees at the Army's Western Hemisphere Institute for Security Cooperation (WHINSEC)[2]
- A human rights division in the Command responsible for managing the region's Human Rights Initiative (HRI) geared toward implementation and evaluation of human rights standards in training, doctrine, enforcement, and civil-military relations.

These efforts are worthy of increased attention, at a minimum, to determine their value to an overall regional policy that emphasizes democracy and human rights as part of a broader goal of fighting terrorism. With little more than a decade of human rights promotion behind it, the Department of Defense (DoD) is faced with the question of whether human rights policies, rooted in democratic enlargement, now serve the overall U.S. counterterrorism strategy.

A NEEDED ASSESSMENT

An evaluation of U.S. military human rights promotion efforts in Latin America is long overdue. The centrality of human rights promotion to U.S. military strategy in the region, the lack of literature and knowledge about U.S. military efforts in this area, and the possible positive implications of finding some common ground between militaries and human rights groups all contribute to the need for such an assessment. This assessment will critically assess DoD's human rights promotion efforts in the region and determine the factors that help and hinder those efforts. This book will outline how human rights promotion became a DoD priority in the region and will aim to provide an objective assessment of U.S. military efforts in this area. One objective is to make a valuable addition to the current literature on Latin American security issues, leaving advocates and critics of U.S. policy better informed of the current facts and environment. Lastly, I will try to make relevant policy recommendations and attempt to bridge the often-heated, and also somewhat overstated, divide between human rights advocates and the U.S. and Latin American militaries.[3]

This book also comes at a critical juncture for the U.S. military as it faces a daunting war on terror with human rights implications at every turn. The author recognizes that it is improbable that the U.S. military can take a leading role in human rights promotion unless that priority is shared and advocated by elected civilian officials. Chapter 6 offers a discussion of this very challenge and argues that U.S. military human rights promotion today finds itself at a crossroads between achieving prominence as a critical element of the war on terrorism and losing significant ground to a narrowly defined, civilian-guided security policy. Chapter 6 also fleshes out the critical reality that, at least in Latin America, U.S. military officers are more attuned to human rights than their civilian superiors, a fact that has implications well beyond the region. This assessment also broaches the critical reality that, without doubt, the U.S. military as a whole has not incorporated human rights promotion into its core business. The objective here is to determine whether a regional approach to human rights promotion can become a model for the larger force. Indeed, while focused on one region, this book offers broader, far-reaching implications for U.S. security policy. Finally, this book tries to explain how military human rights promotion fits into the larger landscape that makes up human rights awareness. As Chapter 2 details, the expansion of human rights awareness in Latin America and elsewhere is not simply a product of U.S. influence, but the fruit of historical events, including the end of the cold war, increased human rights activism by civilians and human rights groups, and the spread of democracy. Admittedly, military human rights is a small part of a much larger picture, and it is this small but important piece of a complex puzzle that this book hopes to bring to the fore.

THESIS

The overarching thesis of this work is that U.S. military human rights promotion can serve as a positive influence in foreign armed forces, particularly as Washington searches for a balance between counterterrorism and democratic growth in its broad military engagement strategy. In an effort to prove this thesis, I have employed four working assumptions, all derived from relevant literature and field research.

The first assumption is that the success of human rights promotion efforts depends on consistency in U.S. policy. Looking for inconsistencies in U.S. efforts and the impact of those shifts should help to measure the effectiveness of military human rights promotion. Measuring performance against consistency will also help to answer the key question of whether U.S. human rights promotion efforts are largely symbolic, an argument that this work's thesis contests. A body of literature surrounding the debate over whether human rights plays a role in decisions regarding levels of U.S. military assistance has led many to conclude that U.S. emphasis on military human rights performance in Latin America is no more than rhetoric.[4] Perhaps the most direct statement to this effect is Poe, Pilatovsky, Miller, and Ogundele's assertion that "US efforts to promote human rights through economic and military assistance can be seen as only symbolic."[5] In addition to the academic reasoning for my first assumption, dozens of U.S. military officers have communicated to me that they see their duty as one of promoting U.S. values of democracy and human rights, not detracting from them. Hence, this work is obligated to test their convictions.

My second assumption is that the status of overall U.S. bilateral relations, specifically military-to-military relations with a country tends to have a positive impact on that country's military awareness and respect for human rights. This assumption is a reaction to and argument against a body of literature that assumes and often asserts that U.S. military relations with, and assistance for, Latin American countries correlate directly with increased human rights abuses.[6] As cited above, much of this literature is focused on the question of whether human rights considerations play a role in U.S. assistance decisions. At the foundation of these studies is the assumption that the tradeoff between punishing human rights abusing states by eliminating assistance and ignoring human rights abuses for other strategic reasons is absolute, with no middle ground. In other words, human rights considerations can only take the shape of suspension of assistance, not provision of aid to influence or help improve the record of human rights abusing countries. My assumption runs counter to the above, in a sense flipping it on its head in assuming that military relations with, and aid for, abusing countries can prove a critical variable for change. The argument that U.S. involvement in Latin America leads to a poor human rights record comes from an era when human rights was a more systemic problem in Latin America and was not a primary strategic concern of U.S. policy, so the assertion is due for reexamination.[7]

The third assumption focuses on a host country variable in asserting that the level of democratic development of a particular country affects the level of success that human rights promotion has in the armed forces of that country. Even if U.S. relations are shown to have a positive impact, one must account for other independent variables in the success or failure of such efforts. As a body of literature has asserted that human rights are linked with democratic development, the author found ample reason for the assumption.[8] Second, the work of DoD and the U.S. State Department (State) in promoting human rights in foreign militaries is largely done in the name of supporting democratic growth, so the assumption also has valid policy relevance.

The fourth and final working assumption is that military human rights promotion tends to play a positive role in military counterterrorism strategy and operations. The Bush Administration's National Security Strategy lists human rights and the promotion of human rights as critical aspects of its counterterrorism policy.[9] Thus, the real value of human rights awareness in the military and its impact on counterterrorism efforts deserve attention. Second, fears are emerging—and after the Iraq prison abuses are being realized—among activists that human rights will suffer much as they did during the cold war, falling by the wayside when fighting terror is made the priority.[10] In essence, observers fear that the tradeoff of the cold war—anticommunism in sacrifice of human rights—will rear its head today in the form of counterterrorism at the cost of human rights. Therefore, the staying power and relevance of human rights promotion is of key interest.

Four Working Thesis Assumptions

1. The success of human rights promotion efforts depends on the consistency in U.S. policy.
2. The status of overall U.S. bilateral relations, specifically military-to-military relations with a country, tends to have a positive impact on that country's military awareness and respect for human rights.
3. The level of democratic development of a particular country affects the level of success that human rights promotion has in the armed forces of that country.
4. Military human rights promotion tends to play a positive role in military counterterrorism policy.

KEY FINDINGS

The assessments included in this book, based upon country case studies of Bolivia, Colombia, and Venezuela, largely support my thesis that U.S. military human rights promotion efforts can serve as a positive influence in Latin American militaries. Indeed, weighing the four key assumptions outlined above against my case study findings shows that U.S. military human rights promotion has been critical to the performance of the respective militaries in this area. The consistency of U.S. human rights awareness application and the status of military-to-military relations proved to be critical factors influencing human rights performance. Democratic development, or more specifically a lack thereof, proved to be a critical obstacle to human rights promotion efforts. The final assumption that U.S. military human rights promotion can be key to a counterterrorism strategy emerged as the least testable of the assumptions based on the cases employed; hence, the second element of my thesis, resting on this assumption, holds up less well. The work does draw out the conclusion that some counterterrorism policies, such as discounting civil liberties or encouraging internal military roles, are detrimental to human rights promotion. While not perfectly testable against my case studies, the findings based on this assumption are perhaps among the most interesting, revealing the area most in need of future research, and worthy of a concluding chapter.

Assumptions 1 and 2 Prove Strong

The consistency of U.S. human rights promotion and the status of military-to-military relations emerge in the three case studies as the most consistent factors affecting human rights performance of the host country militaries. The strength of this assumption is perhaps best displayed in contrasting the findings in Venezuela—where an increasingly poor human rights performance is emerging as U.S. efforts to promote human rights and the military-to-military relationship wane—with that of Bolivia and Colombia—where U.S. engagement and signs of improved human rights awareness are moving in the same direction. Short-term improvements in Bolivia and Colombia appear linked to U.S. efforts and the overall relationship. These trends also are likely easily reversed and depend on a persistent mix of carrots and sticks from Washington. All of these examples signal a short-term weakness of U.S. efforts, but buttress the idea that consistent application can be critical to improved human rights performance.

Assumption 3 A Critical Factor

Democratic development, specifically the lack of development or retrenchment in some areas, proved to be the most prominent variable in hampering human rights performance in all three case studies. Troubles with basic democratic developmental issues emerge as central hurdles to military human rights performance. In Bolivia, where U.S. application is strong and consistent, democratic civil-military shortcomings are keeping human rights awareness from fully taking root because of simple doctrinal hurdles to understanding and implementation of human rights standards. In Colombia, retrenchment of civil rights in the name of security seems to open the door for lax military attitudes toward human rights. Retrenchment of democratic norms in Venezuela appears to be threatening to overwhelm the human rights standards that previous close ties with the United States helped instill. Finally in all three countries, judicial ineffectiveness and impunity emerge as a common problem blocking progress of U.S. military human rights promotion efforts.

Final Assumption Proves Least Testable, Among the Most Interesting

Counterterrorism and its intersection with human rights emerges less often in the case studies than expected in the initial stages of this work, and therefore proves less testable than the other assumptions. The expectation that U.S. counterterrorism policy would be an ever-present element of the military-to-military landscape proved incorrect, and appears to have only taken shape in a handful of countries based on specific counterterrorism funding. The overarching strategy geared toward counterterrorism so far in Latin America is an ideal, but has not significantly changed how militaries interact with the U.S. armed forces. Only in Colombia, where the military uses counterterrorism as a term to justify use of U.S. resources to battle insurgents, to limit civil liberties, and to expand military authorities, is counterterrorism policy somewhat operational in the case studies.

Still, more broadly, counterterrorism as a strategic objective appears to have resonated with regional and U.S. military officers in a way that is critically linked with human rights. Latin American and U.S. military officials are thinking critically about counterterrorism as a topic that will be a central guiding element of future policies, operations, roles, and missions, regardless of a country's posture toward the issue. Perhaps most important for this assessment, the dozens of interviews I conducted revealed some important common ground among military, civilian government, and NGO officials in thinking about human rights and counterterrorism. Further, Latin America, as highlighted in Chapter 2, has emerged more so than any area of the world as a focal point for human rights activists to observe U.S. and foreign military human rights performance, raising the likelihood that counterterrorism policies in the region will fall under the microscope. Finally, just as Latin America grew to represent a key battleground during the cold war, certain factors, such as inequality and the lack of government control over territory, make the region vulnerable to terrorist infiltration.

RESEARCH METHODOLOGY

I conducted the bulk of research for this book in the field through dozens of interviews in nine countries, including Argentina, Bolivia, Brazil, Chile, Colombia, Mexico, Peru, Venezuela, and the United States. In an effort to produce a balanced assessment of U.S. military human rights promotion, I tried to gain access to a wide variety of individuals, such as U.S. and foreign NGOs, think tanks, and military and government officials. While scholarly literature has provided some of the background and context for this book, the majority of my findings were derived from my travels to Latin America and several areas of the United States, including SOUTHCOM and the Western Hemisphere Institute for Security Cooperation (WHINSEC). This approach asks much of the reader in trusting my findings as a legitimate primary resource. I can only assure the reader that in synthesizing and evaluating hundreds of pages of interview notes, my goal was always to achieve an informal assessment of whether and how U.S. military programs were effectively promoting human rights. Some findings are surprising and largely fall in the realm of unexpected common ground between adversaries or re-freshingly balanced accounts from individuals whose reputations suggested they might present slanted views.

In each interview I sought to ask a standard set of fifteen questions about U.S. policy, DoD's strategy, military human rights promotion, and the relationship between military human rights issues and counterterrorism. Some participants gave prepared briefings that I tried to supplement by asking questions that they did address. While I did not engage in any precise empirical exercise to find conclusions, the underlying goal of the interviews was to draw out information critical to evaluating my thesis assumptions.

In detailing my findings, I rely on the case study chapters to tell the cur-rent story surrounding the military and human rights issues. No two chapters will follow a precise formula for assessing the current environment. Rather, I try to allow each case to tell its own story. Each case study chapter, how-ever, is geared toward finding generalities and determining the validity of my thesis assumptions. I rely on additional primary sources, such as govern-ment reports and data, to give the reader a basic guide for understanding the current situation in the case studies. One objective is to stay away from narrow empirical analysis with an eye toward shedding more light on the substantive questions surrounding military awareness of human rights.[11]

Defining Human Rights

For the purposes of this book I have chosen to use a State Department definition of human rights that has become the standard for scholarly works that examine military-related human rights issues.[12] When discussing human rights, and unless otherwise indicated, this book will be referring to *respect for the integrity of the person*, which includes freedom from:

(a) Arbitrary or unlawful deprivation of life
(b) Disappearance
(c) Torture and other cruel, inhumane, or degrading treatment or punish-ment
(d) Arbitrary arrest, detention, or exile
(e) Denial of fair public trial
(f) Arbitrary interference with privacy, family, home, or correspondence
(g) Use of excessive force and violations of humanitarian law in internal conflicts (Attribute g is an optional State Department section used in the Colombia human rights report)

The State Department also uses other definitions for categories of hu-man rights that are typically less directly related to military human rights performance, but that I will refer to in this book when they have im-portance for the topic. These categories include: *respect for civil liberties*, which encompasses freedom of speech and press, freedom of peaceful assembly and association, freedom of religion, and freedom of movement; *respect for political rights*, including the right of citizens to change their government.

Defining Democratic Development

Like human rights, democratic development has numerous definitions. For the purposes of this book I have opted to use a categorical definition that applies more directly to military-related issues. Here I will borrow from Mark J. Ruhl's work on Central American civil-military relations that employs a comprehensive set of criteria for evaluating democratic development.[13] Building on previous works by Stepan and Fitch, Ruhl defines *democratic civil-military relations as political subordination of the armed forces to civilian authorities*, to include:

(a) Military compliance with all legal orders issued by the democratically chosen chief executive and refraining from interference in civilian policymaking
(b) Armed forces acceptance of an organizational framework of civilian supervision over their internal activities via a civilian-led defense ministry and appropriate congressional committees
(c) Civilian courts must be able to hold military personnel accountable to the rule of law

Case Studies

In choosing case studies for this book I selected three countries that I hope will serve as relevant for assessment of current U.S. military human rights promotion efforts and that have a current problem with human rights abuses. After traveling to eight Latin American countries, it became readily apparent that U.S. human rights promotion varies in its consistency and focus across countries and is currently much less prominent in Southern Cone countries, such as Argentina, Chile, and Brazil, that tend to view themselves as having moved beyond the problem and are in an era of reconciliation.[14] Thus, I selected three countries—Bolivia, Colombia, and Venezuela—that have recent or current records of working closely with the U.S. military and can help draw out general conclusions about the effectiveness of U.S. military human rights promotion.

Bolivia

Bolivia's recent and ongoing political instability and the associated charges of military human rights abuse make the country a perfect case for assessment of current U.S. efforts to promote human rights. Moreover, Bolivia is at the forefront in implementing specific human rights standards agreed upon by the regional militaries and detailed in a consensus document drafted in human rights seminars sponsored by SOUTHCOM. Bolivia's status as a top recipient of U.S. military assistance also makes it a key candidate for evaluation of U.S. efforts.

Colombia

Colombia is an almost obvious and required case study for any assessment of military-related human rights issues in Latin America today. Steeped in civil war for some 40 years, the country's military and associated combatants are the region's worst violators of human rights. The country is by far the top recipient of U.S. military assistance in the region, surpassing all other countries by several hundred million dollars. Colombia's war and U.S. support for the government, now in the name of combating terrorism, or more specifically narcoterrorism, has also attracted the greatest amount of attention and criticism from local and international human rights groups. U.S. funding to Colombia is unique in that it is subject to certification by the U.S. Congress based on the country's human rights record, making U.S. efforts to promote human rights all the more relevant. While Colombia's human rights record is poor, the country, with U.S. assistance, has been at the forefront in indoctrinating human rights norms in military training and operations. Thus, the question of whether these efforts are effective is of central importance.

Venezuela

Venezuela is an appropriate case study for this assessment because it serves as a sort of control model, allowing for assessment of U.S. efforts over time and amid significant interruption. The Venezuelan case allows us to ask whether U.S. programs and influence persisted after bilateral relations cooled and whether the absence of U.S. human rights promotion efforts leads to notable changes in human rights performance. Venezuela was among the top recipients of U.S. military assistance in the 1990s and has since fallen to the bottom of that list, receiving little U.S. military aid (see Table 1.1). Having served as one of the first countries to utilize U.S. assistance to develop and implement a military judge advocate corps, the country is well suited for longer-term evaluation. Moreover, with military-to-military relations at a historic low, following an era of strong bilateral ties, we are able to assess the enduring impact of overall military relations and the importance of consistency in human rights promotion.

Table 1.1. 1996–2005 U.S. Military and Police Assistance to Bolivia, Colombia, Venezuela, and Selected Latin American Countries

	1996	1997	1998	1999	2000	2001	2002	2003	2004, est.	2005, req.
Bolivia	13.3	19	33.8	41.9	49	35.1	51.3	57.3	59.6	58.5
Colombia	54.2	88.6	112.4	308.8	765.3	224.7	371.7	605.1	551.3	574.2
Venezuela	13	5.8	7.2	4.1	6.5	3.2	5.4	3.7	4.1	3.6
Argentina	9.5	1.6	6.1	7.8	1.4	2.1	3	3.4	2.9	2.9
Brazil	0.2	3.5	5.8	2.2	5.2	20.7	6.8	7.7	11.5	10.4
Chile	0.6	0.5	17.5	0.9	0.9	1.4	1.3	1.8	1.4	1.4
El Salvador	0.5	0.6	0.8	0.6	4	2.9	8.9	5.5	6.1	5.5
Guatemala	1.5	2.2	2.9	3.1	3.3	3.3	3.6	2.7	3.2	2.9
Honduras	0.5	0.7	2.9	0.9	0.9	1.2	1.1	1.5	3.6	3.1
Mexico	3.4	79	26.1	21.2	16.6	27.5	54.2	28.9	53.6	59.3

Source: CIP, Just the Facts (www.ciponline.org/facts). All numbers in millions of U.S. dollars.[15]

REFOCUSING THE DEBATE

Before delving into the evolution of U.S. military human rights promotion and selected case studies, it is worthwhile to highlight some relevant works on Latin American military-related human rights issues that I argue need a shift in focus. The majority of the written work in this field contains a strong bias, either condemning U.S. actions or condoning them, but rarely offering a fair and impartial assessment. Human rights advocates have been slow to recognize even the existence of U.S. military human rights promotion efforts that are well intentioned and may produce valuable change. Similarly, evidence of U.S. military collaboration with, or tolerance of, human rights violations in the region is conspicuously absent from armed forces publications. Both sides of this debate have clouded the issue with polemical studies designed largely to support a particular position.[16] I will briefly discuss the literary record in three areas: (1) the debate over whether U.S. foreign assistance promotes or is inherently linked to human rights abuse; (2) works that focus on the question whether some military roles and missions, often promoted by the United States, are more conducive to human rights abuses; (3) exploring the question of whether human rights considerations play a role in U.S. decisions to provide military assistance to Latin American countries. The substance of the three sections overlaps somewhat, and some key works are representative of more than one debate.

The Impact of Military-to-Military Relations

The debate surrounding whether U.S. military assistance has an inherent negative or positive impact on host countries in many respects is the foundation of the field. The question has come to represent a movement among NGOs as much as a literary subfield. This debate has influenced the other debates surrounding U.S. military efforts in Latin America, and I believe, is in need of a rigorous reevaluation based on current policy and events. The bulk of literature in this genre assumes the negative—that U.S. military assistance to Latin American countries leads to human rights violations or antidemocratic behavior. Arguments to the contrary are typically put forward by government officials and are significantly overshadowed by more academic accounts.

This debate emerged largely as a reaction to atrocities in Latin America during the 1970s. The vast majority of early assessments pointed to the negative impact of U.S. military assistance to the region. These works were also well grounded, based on U.S. military involvement or relations with several armed forces that committed human rights abuses, particularly in Southern Cone countries of Argentina, Brazil, Chile, Paraguay, and Uruguay during the 1970s. Rampant human rights abuses throughout Latin America spurred critique and criticism of U.S. military policy and congressional review of the impact of U.S. military assistance to the region.

While debate raged in Congress during the 1970s, the canon of literature found its roots in a 1981 publication by Lars Schoultz entitled *Human Rights and United States Policy toward Latin America*.[17] This comprehensive assessment of U.S. policy toward Latin America proved at the time to be the most influential in the field and survives today as perhaps the most commonly cited work on the region concerning military assistance and human rights. Schoultz's goal of assessing the role of human rights considerations in U.S. policy toward Latin America spurred a genre of literature built largely on the assumption that U.S. assistance to militaries is a cause of human rights problems. Schoultz comes across more balanced than perhaps some of the literature that followed his work, stating more than once that just because U.S. military support was used or manipulated for bad ends, does not mean that it must be, or that it is inevitable that it would be used for this purpose.[18] Subsequent literature seems to have lost this tenor, seizing upon Schoultz's more negative conclusions:

> Lamentably, it is not possible for even the best intentioned US administrations to pursue the goal of access and influence without simultaneously increasing coercive power of the military....
>
> ... To provide military aid to a government that bases its existence on the repression of its citizens' human rights is to support the repression of human rights, since any government sustained primarily by threats of physical force is obviously strengthened by the acquisition of greater amounts of force or, in the case of military training, by the acquisition of the skills necessary to employ coercion.[19]

These sentiments fed a frenzy of publications that asserted, for the most part, that U.S. military assistance to Latin America leads to human rights violations, or more precisely, that the United States in providing military assistance often gives short shrift to human rights. Much of this literature, cited here and detailed further below, falls within the debate over the role of human rights in the foreign assistance policy process and has spanned the last two decades.[20] Additional literature based on the argument that U.S. military assistance is linked to, or often ignores human rights abuses, grew dramatically in the 1990s and was primarily published by human rights groups and NGOs. The same groups that led the way in promoting greater awareness of human rights at home and abroad became the primary producers of documentation and literature that critiqued U.S. military assistance.

For example, the group School of the Americas Watch (SOA Watch) has as its primary purpose the closure of the Western Hemisphere Institute for Security Cooperation (WHINSEC), formerly known as the U.S. Army School of the Americas and associated with Latin American officers that have committed human rights abuses. SOA Watch publications argue that WHINSEC should be permanently closed and that the 2000 closure of the School of the Americas and opening of WHINSEC in 2001 was no more than the perpetuation of negative U.S. influence on human rights in Latin America.[21] The Center for International Policy (CIP) recognizes the importance of some U.S. military assistance while listing limitation of U.S. military assistance to the region as one of its primary objectives.[22]

Perhaps the best recent example of the presumed negative impact of U.S. military assistance to the region surrounds the issue of U.S. involvement in Colombia's insurgency and war on drugs. Along with CIP, groups such as the Washington Office on Latin America and The Latin America Working Group have published manuscripts opposing the levels and direction of U.S. military assistance and often point to the U.S. military's past association and influence with human rights abusing countries in Latin America.[23]

Finally, Amnesty International's 2002 review of the human rights dimension of U.S. military training is of note. While the study does give credit to some of the positive trends and programs in U.S. military training for regional militaries, the overarching message is one of warning and leans toward the view that U.S. military influence has unanticipated negative consequences.[24]

Relatively fewer assessments are geared toward arguing the other side of the equation, or at minimum assessing the possible positive impact of U.S. assistance to the region. It is this gap that this book will attempt to help fill. Ramsey and Raimondo put forward a convincing argument of the value of U.S. military training at WHINSEC, but both individuals work with the institution, so academics are likely to paint the work as inherently biased.[25] Addicott and Roberts have detailed SOUTHCOM's legal engagement strategy and its positive impact in Colombia and Venezuela, but again the authors were engaged in the policy they defend, so while a valuable contribution, many may discount it as biased.[26] Along similar lines is Max Manwaring's edited volume on the use of armed forces in Latin America.[27] This collection of essays offers a fairly balanced assessment of U.S. military assistance toward the region and largely assumes that U.S. military influence can be an overriding positive. Of note is Donald E. Schulz's chapter on the role of the U.S. Army in promoting democracy, which offers a positive view of possible U.S. military influence.[28] One refreshing addition to the field is George Vickers's historical timeline of human rights engagement in the region. While not meant as a rigorous analytic piece, it does reveal some positive development linked to U.S. military involvement, written by an individual outside the military and closely linked with human rights awareness and the academic community.

Schoultz, Smith, and Varas offer a collection of fairly neutral essays that often raise the question of whether U.S. military assistance is a positive or negative influence for human rights and democracy.[29] Of particular interest is Nina Serafino's work that specifically explores the debate surrounding the influence of U.S. assistance and its mixed reception in areas meant to encourage democratic norms through training and civic action. Serafino argues that positive influence on the human rights front is likely to come from a low-key, long-term approach, as opposed to explicit training on the subject.[30]

Debating Military Roles and Their Impact on Human Rights

The debate surrounding the question of which roles are appropriate for the military and whether or not these roles are conducive to human rights abuses is an old one, but has seen a resurgence since September 11th. This debate has its roots in the literature cited above, but is more specifically focused on military roles and missions rather than specifically on military-to-military relationships. The debate today shows promise of becoming a central policymaking issue that could affect the types of roles and missions encouraged by the United States and taken on by Latin American militaries. This grouping of literature has emerged largely as a part of the discussion surrounding democratic civil-military development. The military's role in counternarcotics and counterterrorism has also taken centerstage.

Searching for a Civil-Military Balance

Scholars have paid a good amount of attention to the question of how to deal with militaries in Latin American countries that are moving toward democratic consolidation. This grouping of literature has focused on how to include militaries, with past records of human rights abuses and often unpopular with the public, into a democratic society. It is appropriate to introduce the readers to this literature, first because of its importance to the field of Latin American military-related studies, and second to note some of the relevant claims about military roles and human rights records. Since the literature on military roles in democratic development is vast, I will touch here on only those works that bring human rights into the debate and are relevant to this book. A comprehensive review of virtually every piece of literature written on military roles and missions in Latin America can be found in Russell Ramsey's series on strategic reading on Latin America.[31]

An assessment of the bulk of this literature reveals that most authors that have explored the issue of militaries in democratically developing Latin American countries have adopted the basic view that certain military roles and missions, particularly domestic policing, security, and intelligence gathering contribute to poor human rights performances, and therefore are not recommended. These assumptions typically come with little theoretical justification because, for the most part, the historical record convincingly supports the assumption. A vast majority of the human rights abuses in the

Southern Cone countries, for example, which led to tens of thousands of deaths and disappearances of civilians, were carried out in the name of counterterrorism.[32]

Some single author works and a few essay collections are worth mentioning as prominent among the contributors to the field. Alfred Stepan's 1988 work entitled *Rethinking Military Politics: Brazil and the Southern Cone* set a standard for the field in establishing indicators for assessing civil-military relations.[33] Samuel Fitch's 1998 book on the armed forces and democracy in Latin America is one of the most cited pieces in scholarly publications and contributed a useful typology for comparing the status of civil-military relations and democratic control across countries.[34] Indeed, this book, building on recent efforts by Mark Ruhl, relies on elements of Stepan and Fitch's work to measure democratic development as it pertains to civil-military relations and the human rights performance of the armed forces.[35]

Also in 1998, Donald Schulz published his Strategic Studies Institute assessment of the role of Latin American militaries. His analysis looks at the search for new military missions as Latin American countries move toward finding external defense roles.[36] Two earlier works worth mentioning are Paul Zagorski's *Democracy vs. National Security*, and Frederick Nunn's *The Time of the Generals*. Both books deal with the central struggle of incorporating traditionally strong military regimes into society under civilian leadership.[37] Zagorski argues that human rights is a "flash point" that governments must address to promote strong civil-military relations.[38] Also of note here is Wendy Hunter's work on the value of peacekeeping operations in offering militaries a legitimate role and allowing for stronger incorporation into democratic regimes.[39]

Several multiauthor works are worthy of mention. The most recent collection of works to touch on the role of militaries in democratic development is *Civil-Military Relations in Latin America*, edited by David Pion-Berlin. Various authors contributed to this book, focusing on recent cases of military roles and missions under democratic rule, with a strong emphasis on the civilian responsibility to demonstrate interest and competence in military affairs. The collection touches on human rights in several ways, but particularly as it pertains to past abuses and the related impact on civil-military relations in terms of reconciliation and accountability for the abuses.[40]

Earlier important collections include Jorge Dominguez's series on security and democracy in Latin America and the Caribbean published in 1998, and Schoultz, Smith, and Varas's broader look at security, democracy, and US-Latin American relations in 1994. Of note in the Dominguez collection is the concluding assertion that the United States should recognize and support the legitimate external roles of Latin American militaries. This argument, in part, is built on the idea that external missions lead armed forces away from internal security roles that are conducive to human rights abuses.[41] The Schoultz collection, as cited above, takes a broader look at military relations between and within countries, but also lists as a core concern the role of militaries in democratizing countries.[42] Max Manwaring's 1998 Strategic Studies Institute essay collection, cited above, is geared toward policy implementation and debate and is less theoretical in its approach.[43] Manwaring explores Washington's role and influence in fostering military roles and missions. Of note here is Schulz's contribution in emphasizing the need for military doctrines to detail military roles in democratic development and the need for proper human rights training for military personnel.[44]

Finally, David Pion-Berlin and Craig Arceneaux in 2000 published what was then a highly controversial work detailing when it is appropriate for Latin American militaries to engage in internal security roles, such as policing.[45] At the time of publication, the assertion that militaries could legitimately take on an internal security role not only ran against the grain of virtually all academic literature on the topic, it was even considered controversial in military circles. In 2000 the debate surrounding military roles in counternarcotics had already taken a foothold, but it was narrow and limited to a handful of relevant countries. After September 2001, Pion-Berlin and Arceneaux's argument for internal security roles took on new life and has moved to the center of the debate among scholars and military practitioners.

U.S. emphasis on legitimizing internal military counterterrorism roles since September 2001 has helped breathe new life into the old debate between policymakers and academics over roles and missions and their impact on human rights. The Bush administration's almost immediate reaction to the terrorist attacks in redefining narcotics traffickers as narcoterrorists has roiled the human rights community. Former SOUTHCOM Commander General Hill's 2004 testimony before Congress, in which he focused on traditionally nonmilitary issues, sparked further concern among human rights activists and drew Latin America directly into the debate.[46] Further, the General in 2004, in a speech at Florida International University, called on Latin American armed forces to support and cooperate with law enforcement, and he argued that "only military forces have the organization, infrastructure, capabilities, and personnel to deal effectively with sophisticated narcoterrorist groups."[47]

In response, and setting the bar for literature critical of the U.S. emphasis on internal military roles, is the 2004 publication entitled *Blurring the Lines*, which argues in detail that the U.S. military is undermining democratic consolidation and respect for human rights by emphasizing the need for Latin American armed forces to adopt internal security roles.[48] The piece also argues that the U.S. military is militarizing civilian institutions, such as police forces, by training them in military tactics.[49] Haugaard, Garcia, Schmidt, and Anderson preceded *Blurring the Lines* with a similar look at the U.S. counterterrorism focus in Latin America, also arguing that Washington's strategic shift toward focusing on counterterrorism in the region lifted military interaction above diplomatic relations and lowered human rights to a secondary interest in the region.[50] The 2003 publication *Paint by Numbers*, by the same authors of *Blurring the Lines*, helped lay the groundwork for arguments condemning the Bush administration's approach toward funding and oversight of U.S. military assistance to Latin America.

The debate surrounding roles and missions has waxed and waned and is now poised to again envelop the field of Latin American security studies. Whether U.S. military training for nonmilitary entities and the emphasis on internal security roles for militaries is right or wrong in the current setting and in the face of terrorism is yet to be answered. The debate is also in need of some balance since it has been largely a one-sided reaction to policy. What is absent from this renewed interest in roles and missions is a substantive discussion of U.S. military efforts to promote human rights, and whether these efforts are productive, undermined by other operations, or even measurable. It is this gap that this book will attempt to help fill.

Debating the Links between Human Rights and U.S. Assistance Levels

This final section is, in part, an assessment of relevant works and, in part, a critique of the underlying debate assumptions. The question of whether human rights considerations play a role in determining if countries receive U.S. military assistance has emerged as perhaps the most rigorous focused debate on U.S. military relations with Latin America.[51] This debate has contributed many positive developments to the field, including a better understanding and appreciation for policymaking and increasingly sophisticated methodologies. The debate, however, after 25 years has proven largely inconclusive. The various authors leave unexamined the dated assumption that foreign policy tradeoffs between denying assistance to human rights abusers and supporting a country without attention to its human rights performance is an absolute, with no middle ground. Lastly, the empirical bent of the debate has moved assessment of U.S. military policy away from substantive analysis and has largely ignored the substantive shifts in U.S. security policy toward Latin America.

Some Positive Contributions

This debate, also pioneered by Schoultz, was championed by a group of scholars during an era when social scientists were striving for more scientific methodologies to reach more generalized findings.[52] Cingranelli and Pasqaurello, Carleton and Stohl, McCormick and Mitchell, and Poe, as cited above, are just a few authors who produced numerous manuscripts using statistical analysis to determine how U.S. assistance levels correlate with human rights abuse trends in the region. Over two and a half decades, the methodologies for measuring human rights and gauging policymaking have become more sophisticated and have helped academicians better evaluate trends in U.S. policymaking and the region. For example, an early work that became the centerpiece of the debate used only one source to evaluate human rights abuses over a 3-year period and evaluated only 1 year of U.S. foreign assistance.[53] Subsequent evaluations, in critique of the above assessment, increasingly employed numerous years of human rights trends as well as U.S. policymaking.[54] The growth of sophistication in assessing decisionmaking also has been significant, progressing from a narrow focus on presidential preferences to inclusion of congressional processes and numerous independent variables, such as status of democracy, external conflicts, internal war, presence of U.S. troops, trade, and GNP.[55]

An Inconclusive Debate

The debate surrounding whether human rights plays a role in the U.S. foreign policy process appears to have made little progress in finding common ground. Studies of roughly the same time period and region persistently reveal different conclusions based on empirical analyses, and some authors have recognized that the scope and utility of the studies are limited.[56] For example, assessment of some of the most prominent works in the debate between 1981 and 2000 reveals wide differentiation in findings. Of eight selected studies, one of the earliest as well as the latest publications argues that human rights do influence foreign assistance decisions.[57] Four of the studies argue that there is either no correlation or that human rights abusing countries actually received more aid.[58] Two of the works argue that there is a correlation but that it is relatively small compared to other variables.[59] The debate shows little or no trend toward consensus and reveals that quantitative approaches to the issue are no more conclusive or rigorous than case study approaches to the issue. Stephen Cohen's conclusion in one of the field's early works is worth repeating:

> This examination of attempts by Congress to require the Executive to withhold military aid and arms sales on human rights grounds suggests another important issue: whether withholding is an effective instrument for enforcing adherence to international human rights law. . .
> . . . While the impact of withholding security assistance on human rights practices is beyond the scope of this article, it is the logical next question for scholars interested in international human rights.[60]

A number of scholars decided to build on Cohen's work, examining whether human rights is a factor in congressional decisions surrounding

U.S. military assistance. Unfortunately, the field never heeded Cohen's suggestion to examine whether withholding aid is effective, perhaps because the quantitative analyses never settled if withholding based on statistical human rights performance, was actually occurring.

Empirical Focus Based on Flawed Assumptions

A key problem surrounding the assistance versus human rights consideration debate is that it is almost purely quantitative, providing insufficient contextual detail for substantive evaluation. Several authors, including Carleton, Stohl, Cingranelli, Pasquarello, and Poe, to name a few, have engaged in a search for methodological rigor that seems to have turned to a debate over numbers, statistics, and variables that impact the empirical results, with much less attention to substance, the facts surrounding the numbers, and obvious limitations of statistical analysis.[61] The assessments, for example, rarely, if ever, accounted for a real change in the goals of military assistance policy.

The empirical assessments of whether human rights factors weighed on foreign assistance to the region began somewhat on the wrong foot in understanding or considering policy. At the root of the problem is that the empirical assessments assume that any correlation between human rights abuse trends and U.S. assistance must be absolute. In other words, the authors assume that human rights abuses either lead to a cut in aid, or do not; there is often no allowance for aid flowing in the name of human rights promotion, or a middle-ground foreign policy approach in which aid is sustained both to assist and to influence change. To put it simply, this field never accounted for the inclusion of human rights-related assistance in the overall packages for particular countries.

Some of the literature does include two stages of foreign assistance, a gate-keeping stage where recipients are awarded and eliminated, and a second stage, where amounts of aid are decided, and is arguably more applicable to the policy reality.[62] Even in these assessments, however, there is no discussion of assistance as part of an effort to also change a country's human rights performance. The exclusion of this variable, especially as it became increasingly present in military policy, renders the statistical analysis of whether human rights played a role in foreign assistance decisions flawed. For example, if a country that had a high level of human rights abuses received foreign assistance, the positive correlation was assumed automatically to equal bad policy, or more precisely, that human rights was not a consideration in awarding assistance. This assumption ignores that a significant portion of assistance, including military training, increasingly has been geared toward addressing the problem of human rights awareness.[63]

The policy reality is that U.S. military assistance has qualitatively changed, rendering the absolutist assumptions of statistical analyses inadequate. Many readers may generally identify with the assumption that providing military aid to human rights abusing countries is bad policy. While sensible on the surface, this assumption is flawed in the current setting because it ignores the reality that all U.S. human rights assistance is naturally targeted at those countries with problems. If the United States seeks to improve military human rights awareness through aid, that aid must go to a violating country. Indeed, the topic of this book rests on the reality that human rights promotion is central to U.S. military engagement in Latin America. Certainly aid to a country that is a gross violator of human rights, denies the problem, and is unwilling to address the issue would be poor policy. On the other hand, a violating country with civilian leaders that recognize a problem and with a military that is willing to take on human rights awareness is naturally a good candidate for increased aid and human rights assistance.

Some literature does highlight DoD's efforts to target human rights–violating militaries for human rights awareness training and programs. Nina M. Serafino has argued that, at a minimum, human rights has served as a rationale for U.S. military engagement in Latin America. She notes, "US military support for democracy in Latin America has been a historical rationale for US military activities there, and it is a strong component of SOUTH-COM's rationale for continued involvement in Latin America."[64] In other words, one could convincingly argue that military assistance in the region flows to the countries because they have problems with democratic norms, such as human rights, and with an eye toward promoting change. Examples of this shift in policy can be found in U.S. government's justifications for foreign assistance. The State and DoD's foreign military training joint report to Congress in 2004 listed promotion of democracy and teaching human rights standards as primary objectives.[65] SOUTHCOM's vision statement lists respect for human rights as a top goal of its engagement strategy.[66] It is debatable whether these objectives are real or rhetorical, and if they are effective. The point here is that the United States often allocates money using human rights promotion as a justification, so the scholarly questions should assess sincerity and effectiveness, not mere correlation of funding with human rights abuse records.[67]

Lastly, and perhaps the most troubling problem with the debate surrounding human rights performance and its impact on U.S. assistance is that without recognizing the changes in policy noted above, the authors never made an attempt to identify and assess the positive impact of their own studies. Indeed, the purely empirical approach to the issue fails to consider that the subfield's early findings were part of an overall movement, recognized by civilian and military officials alike, that helped nudge U.S. policymakers toward a more holistic approach to security cooperation and the inclusion of human rights promotion as a strategic objective in Latin America.[68]

BOOK STRUCTURE

The next six chapters will attempt to detail and assess whether the recent shift in U.S. military policy toward promoting human rights in Latin America can serve as a positive force. The objective will be to introduce the reader to U.S. military human rights policy in the region, assess the policy and its impact in three countries, and draw out some general conclusions weighed against my thesis.

Chapter 2 will offer a largely historical account of how and why U.S. military human rights promotion evolved. The chapter will bring together earlier assessments of congressional and military developments in the human rights arena, forming a single comprehensive review of how current policies became practice. An objective of the chapter will be to place U.S.–Latin American relations in historical context and show how a mix of influences and events between the early 1970s and the end of the cold war helped reshape U.S. military policy toward Latin America and diminish the problem of an absolute tradeoff between supporting human rights and defending national security.

Chapter 3 will include an assessment of the current instability and the related military human rights performance in Bolivia. The chapter will assess the current civil-military environment in Bolivia and U.S. military efforts to promote human rights in the country. Chapter 3 will also include an assessment of institutional hurdles that emerged as impediments to human rights promotion.

Chapter 4 will briefly outline the current civil war environment in Colombia. The chapter will focus on U.S. military assistance geared toward human rights promotion, the ongoing debate surrounding the country's human rights record, and the military's mixed record in approaching human rights awareness. The chapter will include a discussion of the problem of measuring democratic development in Colombia.

Chapter 5 will detail the current political problems in Venezuela. The chapter will detail the changed state of United States–Venezuela military relations and an assessment of the current military human rights performance in the country. Chapter 5 will assess democratic retrenchment in the country, its impact on human rights generally, and its spillover to the armed forces.

Chapter 6 will examine the role of U.S. military human rights promotion in the age of counterterrorism. Drawing on the case studies and additional information from research on the same topic around the region, the chapter will assess the importance, status, challenges, and opportunities for U.S. military human rights efforts under the guise of counterterrorism. This chapter will pose implications for U.S. military human rights policy and counterterrorism more broadly, noting current and past lessons learned from Latin America.

Chapter 7 will serve as the concluding chapter and will include a general summary of the findings while outlining some more general implications for the field of Latin American security studies. This chapter will offer concluding assessments of, and recommendations for, U.S. military human rights promotion efforts. The case studies should provide some context for broader debates surrounding military assistance, training, and civil-military relations. The conclusion will also include some general conclusions about democratic development and its impact on military human rights performance.

2

The Evolution of U.S. Military Human Rights Promotion in Latin America

The U.S. Department of Defense's (DoD's) efforts surrounding human rights promotion in Latin America grew out of a series of pressures and reactions, culminating in what today is part of an overall foreign policy approach and a model for U.S. military engagement. I will show how multiple overlapping factors over three decades helped move DoD toward its current Latin American human rights focused posture. I will also detail how DoD's efforts became part of a broad policy approach toward national security and human rights. Some of the events that I will discuss, which helped create outside pressure for change at DoD, include human rights violations in Latin America and the U.S. role in those events in the 1970s and 1980s; NGO and congressional reactions and pressures following these events; global political change, and a shift in U.S. policy toward the region. A single factor that emerged from within DoD—the timely and fortuitous rise of enlightened leaders to key positions in DoD's Latin America Area of Responsibility (AOR)—was also key to ushering in a period of change.

This chapter will first briefly establish the historical context of U.S.–Latin American relations and detail how human rights abuses became synonymous with Latin American military dictatorships. The second section will detail the importance of military human rights promotion as a part of overall U.S. foreign policy. Three additional sections will outline relevant events during the 1970s, 1980s, and 1990s that culminated in a mixture of pressures, and reactions to those pressures, and helped shape DoD's human rights promotion policy toward the region.

FOUNDATIONS OF U.S. DISREGARD, LATIN AMERICA'S CHECKERED PAST

U.S. foreign policy toward Latin America grew out of early American unilateralism and was based on dealing with Europe and the rest of the world, rather than actually building a relationship with Latin America. During the first two centuries of U.S. relations with Latin America, Washington's approach to the region paid short shrift to human rights and included only a brief period of mutual, friendly relations. U.S. independence up until the Great Depression saw the birth and development of U.S. dominance of the Western Hemisphere under the Monroe Doctrine (1776–1929). The period from the Great Depression through the beginning of the cold war saw some U.S. efforts to cultivate greater cooperation between Washington and Latin America (1929–1954). Finally, the deepening of the cold war ushered in an era of U.S. interventionism that was characterized by fear of communism and disregard for integrity of the person (1954–1973).

In 1783, U.S. victory in its war of independence led to a policy toward Latin America that was built on the common interests of opposing European colonial rule and supporting the revolutionary drive for liberty. Indeed, the United States gave diplomatic and moral support to countries around the region that sought independence from European rule and was the first country to recognize the independence of several Latin American countries.[1] Whatever mutual interests the United States shared with Latin America, however, fell by the wayside with the declaration of the "Monroe Doctrine" in 1823. President Monroe—reacting to continued European influence in Latin America and growing Russian influence to the north of the United States—announced that the United States would not allow outside interference in the countries of the Western Hemisphere. Historians agree that the Monroe Doctrine carried little weight in 1823, since the British Navy controlled the high seas and the United States lacked the military strength to back up Monroe's threat.[2] However, one scholar correctly notes that "The Monroe Doctrine was a document rather of the future than of the time of its utterance...The significance in 1823 of the Monroe Doctrine is that it served as a capstone to a very positive structure of American foreign policy that had been built up from a half-century of independent dealing with foreign nations. It proclaimed in strong Republican tone an American system for the New World."[3]

In the context of human rights in Latin America, the Monroe Doctrine set important precedents. First, the Doctrine was the first of what would be many policies toward other regions of the world on how the United States would deal with Latin America; it was not a policy with or toward Latin America. Second, it established the foundations of U.S. intervention in the region, intervention based on defending U.S. security and economic interests, usually at a cost to the human rights of Latin American citizens. The

U.S. refusal to consider almost immediate Latin American pleas to make the Monroe Doctrine the basis of an inter-American security alliance was perhaps the most telling signal that the Doctrine would give lax consideration to the interests of Latin American citizens.[4] Latin American leaders were perhaps naïve in initially applauding and seeking to expand a doctrine that in practice relegated the region and the rights of its citizens to secondary status.

Monroe's policy paved the way for what became known as "Manifest Destiny," the ideological identity and economic drive behind the territorial expansion of the United States, including the annexation of Texas in 1845, and the U.S.-Mexican war, which ended in 1848 with expansion of the continental United States to California, Nevada, Utah, New Mexico, Arizona, and parts of Colorado and Wyoming. Manifest Destiny also saw U.S. economic expansion with private investment staking significant natural resource claims in Latin America, including copper in Mexico and Chile, sugar in Cuba, oil in Mexico, and meat in Argentina. In 1896, the military component of the Monroe Doctrine began with President McKinley's rise to power. By 1898, the United States was embroiled in the Spanish-American war over the Caribbean, which ended with Cuba becoming a U.S. protectorate and U.S. ownership of Puerto Rico.[5] The United States also intervened in Panama on several occasions, until that country achieved independence from Colombia in 1903.

In 1904, President Theodore Roosevelt took McKinley's activism a step further with his "Roosevelt Corollary" to the Monroe Doctrine. Roosevelt's addition to the Doctrine explicitly justified United States "police power" over Western Hemisphere nations that suffered internal "chronic wrongdoing, or impotence."[6] This pronouncement further downgraded Latin American sovereignty and independence from the U.S. perspective. Over the next two-plus decades the United States would intervene in domestic upheavals in several countries including Cuba, the Dominican Republic, Haiti, and a more than two-decade long military presence in Nicaragua.[7]

The Great Depression and the early signs of World War II helped usher in a brief respite in U.S. interventionism in and disregard for Latin American interests. The disenfranchised working class in Latin America began to mobilize while the U.S. resources needed to maintain its interests in Latin America—including through military force—diminished. For the first time since the Monroe Doctrine, the United States began to look to Latin America as a strategic partner as opposed to a protectorate. In 1933, Franklin Roosevelt adopted the "Good Neighbor Policy" geared toward convincing Latin American leaders of Washington's good intentions in the region. While abusive U.S. business and government policies continued around the region, the tenor of overall bilateral relations appeared to shift. In 1947, the United States had joined with Latin American nations in signing the Rio Treaty, a document that reflected century-old Latin American collective security goals and committed all signatories to defending any party of the treaty against armed attack. In 1948, the United States joined in the creation of the Organization of American States, which explicitly forbids interventionist policies.[8]

Many of Roosevelt's policies toward individual countries also differed significantly from those of his predecessors. For example, in the 1930s, he reacted largely sympathetically to the expropriation of U.S. oil interests in Bolivia and Mexico.[9] In 1934, the United States withdrew its Marines from Haiti and gave up control of the county's national bank.[10] As one historian has characterized it, the Good Neighbor Policy was "a repudiation of the 'Roosevelt Corollary.'"[11]

By 1954, Roosevelt's Good Neighbor Policy had given way to the pressures of the cold war, and a long, detrimental U.S. record of lifting anticommunism above all other foreign policy priorities, particularly integrity of the person, and in many cases, even democracy. The Monroe Doctrine and the Roosevelt Corollary had laid the foundation for a broad U.S. policy geared toward blunting any revolutionary behavior that threatened the status quo in the region, irrespective of whether U.S. actions had a negative impact on human rights. In 1954, U.S. President Eisenhower backed a coup against democratically elected President Jacob Arbenz of Guatemala, after Arbenz gave some communists low-level government positions and expropriated land from the United States-based United Fruit Company. Arbenz's ouster led to the installation of a military dictatorship and numerous human rights violations in Guatemala. Guatemala was thrown into a civil war that lasted until 1996, claimed the lives of more than 100,000 people, and displaced some 1 million.

In 1959, the communist revolution in Cuba led the United States to become fully entrenched in its interventionist posture toward the region. In 1961, the failed U.S. Bay of Pigs invasion, and in 1962, the Cuban Missile Crisis served to further harden the U.S. posture against communism under President Kennedy, leaving little room for human rights in the foreign policy hierarchy. In 1965, the United States under President Johnson invaded the Dominican Republic under the assumption that the country's revolution was communist-led. Finally, in 1973, the United States backed the military coup against Chile's democratically elected Marxist President Salvador Allende, leading to thousands of human rights violations. As discussed in greater detail below, the Chilean coup helped spur an era of human rights awareness in U.S. foreign policy and significantly increased U.S. political attention to Latin America.

A Checkered Past

While U.S. relations with Latin America were showing almost complete disregard for human rights, Latin American countries were establishing their own poor human rights record. The region's most egregious violations of human rights took place during the 1970s and early 1980s under the guise of what was known as Operation Condor, a clandestine operation between several South American countries geared toward systematically rooting out left leaning opposition to military-run governments. During this period, authoritarian military regimes garnered worldwide attention for their abuses and systematic violations, particularly in Argentina, Brazil, Chile, Paraguay, and Uruguay, with the worst occurring in Argentina and Chile where 30,000 and 3,000 civilians "disappeared" respectively. The Chilean case became a poster child of military authoritarianism because of Washington's association with the military coup against a democratically elected Marxist government.

Serious abuses in Central American countries and most prominently in El Salvador grabbed attention in the early 1980s. Government efforts to quash leftist insurgent movements in several Central American countries led to abhorrent treatment of insurgents and civilians alike. Military officials also suffered widespread abuses, but media rarely publicized these abuses, which played little to no role in spurring U.S. military human rights promotion efforts. The United States, in its effort to back Central American governments' fight against communism, stepped up military assistance and training for the region, setting the stage for a prolonged battle between human rights activists and the U.S. military. In the end, these events would clear a path for change and the policy approach toward Latin America that we see today.

THE DIMINISHING HUMAN RIGHTS, NATIONAL SECURITY TRADEOFF

U.S. military emphasis on human rights in Latin America is a relatively new phenomenon that grew out of a mix of events and outside pressures and now represents a key breakthrough and model for U.S. foreign policy as a whole. Military human rights promotion represents a middle ground between traditional choices of supporting human rights or fostering other foreign policy priorities. Military human rights is at the center of a complex mix of sticks and carrots used to award, influence, and punish Latin American countries for their respective human rights records. While military diplomacy more broadly has existed for decades, the current approach does not have a name, and probably could not be identified by many in the policymaking community.[12] As David Forsythe has appropriately noted, "there remains much ambiguity about where human rights fits in US foreign policy priorities over time, and what specific actions in the name of human rights any US government is likely to pursue."[13]

Still, the idea that human rights is now an institutionalized part of U.S. foreign policy is gaining ground. Kathryn Sikkink is perhaps the most recent and most fervent proponent of the idea, stating "Human rights advocates both in government and outside, in the United States and abroad, succeeded in securing a major shift in US policy and international institutions in the last quarter of the twentieth century. Human rights issues, long seen as moral concerns inappropriate for foreign policy, have become and integral part of US Policy and of international and regional institutions."[14] This book builds on Sikkink's broad contention by delving into specific policy-level actions that reveal the operationalization of human rights on the ground. In the sections below, I will attempt to highlight the recent emergence of a recognizable human rights-centered foreign policy approach toward Latin America, which to a large extent came about by accident, but also as a concerted military leadership effort to respond to external pressures and to promote real policy change.

Before proceeding to the evolution of this policy approach, it is worth detailing here some of the specific arguments surrounding the traditional policymaking tradeoff that I argue, at least in Latin America, is seeing a slow breakdown in the name of military human rights promotion. The idea that there is a fundamental conflict between morality and national security is an old assertion of *Realpolitik* that has slowly lost legitimacy in the scholarly world, and suffered a significant setback with the emergence of significant human rights considerations in the U.S. Congress in the 1970s. As Cohen notes, drafters of legislation constraining military assistance in the 1970s rejected this dichotomy;[15] for them, there was not a natural restriction preventing morality in decisions of national security. In practice, however, the inclusion of moral objectives in foreign policy at times presented the problem of a policy tradeoff, namely that the United States choose between supporting countries that were anticommunist but abused basic human rights and punishing human rights abusing states regardless of their ideological bent or vulnerability to communist influence. Donnelly acknowledges this tradeoff as it pertains to human rights and foreign policy:

> In a world of sovereign states, foreign policy is principally concerned with the pursuit of the national interest, as each country sees it. The national interest may include respect for human rights in other countries, either as an intrinsic value for instrumental reasons (such as the belief that rights-protective regimes are more likely to be dependable friends in international relations). But in no country can the national interest be reduced to international human rights.
>
> The obvious question, then, is *what* place human rights occupy. The best way to tell is to look at what happens when there is a conflict of objectives. Talk about human rights is cheap—often not entirely without cost, but usually relatively cheap. The decisive tests are the costs a country is willing to bear in pursuing human rights concerns and the competing objectives it is willing to sacrifice or subordinate.[16]

Even Donnelly, a well-known human rights scholar and critic of realist theory in favor of constructivism—or approaches that assume that a mixture of material and nonmaterial influences shape foreign affairs—recognizes that, in terms of foreign policy objectives and human rights, often a clear tradeoff of priorities is at stake. Donnelly goes on to show that this tradeoff problem was indeed a policy reality during the 1970s and 1980s and typically favored subordination of human rights to national security priorities of combating communism in Latin America. He states simply, "whether this was good policy or bad, its human rights consequences were disastrous."[17]

When Donnelly published these assertions in 1998, a change in U.S. military foreign policy toward Latin America was underway, a shift that I will depict here as a final step toward eliminating the pressure for absolute subordination or sacrifices in foreign policy when weighing national security and human rights. Donelly's observations are correct in that a tradeoff existed, and proved detrimental to human rights in the region. Yet, as a result of the ever-present tension within this tradeoff, the resulting congressional focus on human rights, interest group pressure, and shift in world dynamics provided an opening to abandon the tradeoff premise for a more substantive and complex policy approach. This approach no longer assumes that you must choose between condemning or condoning human rights abuses.

As listed in the Introduction, and detailed further below, the U.S. military human rights promotion efforts in Latin America are significant, especially when compared to U.S. military policy toward the rest of the world. Moreover, a clear shift in thinking appears to have taken root in military and policymaking circles, diminishing the need to make foreign policy tradeoffs when considering even the most pressing foreign policy issues. For example, virtually every U.S. and Latin American government official interviewed for this book, numbering several dozen and including State, CIA, and retired and current military, and civilian DoD staff, believed that U.S. military human rights promotion efforts help, and rarely if ever hinder, military priorities such as counterterrorism. Moreover, all U.S. and foreign NGO officials had the same sentiment, that U.S. military human rights promotion efforts help, and do not hinder, other operational priorities.[18]

These sentiments, coming from diverse and often opposing groups, suggest that U.S. military efforts to play a central role in promoting human rights have become a legitimate and respected foreign policy tool. The collapse of the Soviet Union appears to have diminished the perceived need for an absolute tradeoff between national security and human rights. Indeed, most of the respondents, including NGO representatives, noted that military human rights promotion can prove a critical element of foreign assistance, particularly to countries dealing with internal wars or terrorist problems. Simply put, field research revealed broad acceptance of the need to ensure military human rights awareness amid security threats, as opposed to simple punishment through removal of all assistance or allowance of abuses based on national security interests.

This sentiment is particularly notable as we move into the era of counterterrorrsim that threatens to pose foreign policy tradeoffs similar to those of the cold war. Indeed, detailing the emergence, and what this assessment poses largely as successes, of military human rights promotion can prove critical to fending off pressures for a return to simplistic, *realpolitick* approaches to foreign policy and the war on terrorism. Already questions are emerging as to whether the United States should support governments that are human rights abusers, but that are at Washington's side in fighting terrorism. The emergence of military human rights promotion as a central element of U.S. foreign policy in Latin America serves as an example that the answer to such questions does not need to be a simple yes or no. As detailed below, the military's role in promoting human rights is an outgrowth of years of conflict and difficult debate that should not have to be reinvented.

Finally, it should be noted that the argument that U.S. military assistance can serve as a part of the effort to improve human rights performance is not entirely new. What is new is the makeup of the efforts that support this argument, including the specific targeted military human rights promotion efforts that are part of assistance packages to the region.

Schoultz and Cohen outline in detail the various arguments that U.S. officials in the 1960s and 1970s put forward in the name of promoting human rights through military assistance. These justifications, however, were weak at best and included almost nonsensical links between assistance and human rights. Cohen notes, for example, that the Carter administration invoked "extraordinary circumstances" to approve provision of spare parts and support equipment to several Latin American countries considered to be "gross violators" of human rights, based on the idea that such provisions were an acceptable inducement for improved human rights.[19] While the sale of such items is arguably justifiable—although not in Cohen's estimation—based on the need to make sure personnel are not placed in harms way because of faulty or dated parts and equipment, there is no basis for linking that policy to inducing respect for human rights, absent a mix of human rights promotion efforts and other sticks and carrots specifically linked to human rights performance.

Schoultz notes that "the notion that military aid increases a nation's sense of security was Nixon-Ford administration's primary argument against reducing military aid to the Pinochet government of Chile."[20] The idea here is that human rights violations are the result of threats to a country's national security. Again, the link between military assistance and a better human rights performance is almost absurd and is far removed from the real efforts of providing human rights training and awareness as part of basic military assistance, as we see today. Indeed, it is my contention that these poorly justified arguments linking military assistance to human rights promotion have served as part of the barrier to greater acknowledgment and promotion of the idea that the military could and should help improve human rights records of violating countries.[21]

THE 1970s: ABUSE AND AWARENESS COLLIDE

The 1970s proved to be a watershed decade for the prominence of human rights in U.S. foreign policy, and is at the root of what today is an activist human rights promotion agenda in DoD's strategic approach toward Latin America. Regardless of one's belief surrounding the effectiveness of the policies that emerged from a greater focus on human rights, it is a fact that the issue gained prominence and influence that is felt in U.S. foreign policy even today.[22] Several authors have detailed the growth of human rights awareness in congressional foreign policy considerations, the most prominent of which are Lars Schoultz, Stephen Cohen, and David Forsythe.[23] Schoultz, in particular, offers an assessment of a combination of pressures and events that raised the profile of human rights in U.S. policymaking circles.[24] Jack Donnelly has added to the earlier literature with a concise account of the ongoing human rights abuses that took place in Latin America during the 1970s, when the issue of human rights was gaining prominence in U.S. foreign policy.[25] Building on these scholarly works, this section will highlight the influence of three events, the 1973 military coup in Chile, increased congressional attention to human rights, and the election of Jimmy Carter as president, as the foundation for change in DoD's posture toward human rights in the region.[26]

Chilean Abuses Stoke Concern

The fall and assassination of the world's first freely elected Marxist President, Salvador Allende, on September 11, 1973, marked a victory for opponents of communism and the beginning of a struggle between human rights activists and U.S. foreign policy practitioners, whose overall objective was combating far left political movements. This event was the first element that contributed to a surge, some 15 years later, of U.S. military human rights promotion in the region. Allende's fall represented more than just the defeat of Marxism in Chile, the victory of a right wing authoritarian government, and increased human rights abuses. It represented the pinnacle of the much more complex problem in U.S. foreign policy detailed above, the struggle between supporting dictators as a means to fight communism and promoting awareness of human rights, namely in the form of integrity of the person.[27]

The military regime in Chile was guilty of several thousand killings and additional human rights abuses during and after the coup. The atrocities coincided with what was already a heated debate in the U.S. Congress over restrictions on military assistance based on human rights. The Chile case helped build consensus around legislation to rein in foreign military assistance, focusing on Latin America more than any other region in the world.[28] Adding to the fervor surrounding the Chilean case was Allende's nationalization of banks and the country's largely United States-owned copper industry. Chile had also been one of the most stable democracies in the region, so the political unrest represented a retrenchment for political stability in the region and signaled that U.S. preferences in defeating communism trumped even support for democracy. After revelations of U.S. military and CIA involvement in the September coup came to light, Chile became the poster child for activists looking to impose restrictions on military assistance, and, as the congressional record shows, Chile's Latin American neighbors were the logical next focal point for increased attention to human rights in the foreign policy arena.[29]

Congress Takes Action

Chile's political instability provided momentum for human rights legislation already under consideration at the time of Allende's fall. Indeed, 1973 marked the beginning of several years of debate and dispute between the presidency and Congress regarding human rights, foreign policy, and issuance of foreign military aid. Moreover, as noted above, Latin American countries, because of their gross human rights violations, their proximity to the United States, and the high profile of the Chilean coup in the United States, garnered the brunt of congressional attention and accounted for almost all military aid withheld for human rights-related reasons.

Congress enacted foreign policy human rights legislation for the first time in 1973. Section 32 of the Foreign Assistance Act (FAA) stated a "sense of Congress" that was not legally binding on the Executive, but that suggested that the president deny military assistance to any foreign governments that practiced internment or imprisonment of its citizens for political reasons.[30] In 1974, Stephen Cohen contends as a reaction to Kissenger and Nixon's disregard for Section 32, Congress voted to enact Section 502B of the FAA, which after several amendments, exists today as the cornerstone of U.S. human rights restrictions on foreign military aid. Section 502B, however, also originally only stated a "sense of Congress," but this time much more specifically targeted toward limiting foreign security assistance, including sales of arms and military aid to human rights abusing nations:[31]

> It is the sense of Congress that, except in extraordinary circumstances, the President shall substantially reduce or terminate security assistance to any government which engages in a consistent pattern of gross violations of internationally recognized human rights, including torture or cruel, inhumane, or degrading treatment or punishment; prolonged detention without

charges; or other flagrant denials of the right to life, liberty, and the security of the person.[32]

Congress one year later removed the "sense of Congress" language to make the section legally binding on the Executive.[33] The 1975 legislation ignited a dispute with the presidency, and in 1976, President Ford vetoed the foreign aid bill containing the amended language. Congress changed the language through compromise with the president and replaced the "sense of Congress" with a statement that denial of security assistance to gross violators of human rights was "the policy of the United States."[34] That same year, Congress created the post of Coordinator for Humanitarian Affairs in the State Department, charged with overseeing all human rights matters in the department.[35]

1977 was a lax year for congressional action on human rights-related legislation, owing largely to congressional leeway for President Carter, who came to office promising human rights top billing on the U.S. foreign policy agenda. The one significant act by Congress that year was to designate a position of Assistant Secretary of State for Human Rights, to take the place and bolster the work of the previously installed coordinator at the State Department.[36] The assistant secretary would head an entire bureau that early on was plagued by controversy and pushback from other State bureaus.[37] In 1978, in an effort to reassert legislative influence in the issue, Congress again strengthened the Section 502B language, making it a binding requirement for the Executive and emphasizing in the congressional Conference Committee report that "it is the intent of the committee of the conference to place renewed emphasis on human rights as a major factor that must, as a matter of law, be taken into account in making security assistance decisions."[38] It was not until 1997 that Congress would again make a significant impact on the foreign policy of human rights with the enactment of the "Leahy Amendment." As an attachment to the Foreign Operations Appropriations Act, the Leahy amendment broadened the required proper verification that no foreign unit receiving U.S. military assistance had committed a gross violation of human rights.[39] The mandate spurred U.S. Embassy human rights vetting of United States-trained and equipped foreign military units worldwide.

While Congress was working to make human rights considerations a permanent fixture of U.S. security assistance decisions, the body was also enacting numerous country specific restrictions on military aid, setting the tone for future restrictions and certification requirements based on human rights, such as those for El Salvador in the 1980s and currently for Colombia. In 1974, Congress limited military aid and arms sales to ten countries, seven of which were in Latin America. Congress prohibited Chile from receiving any military aid in 1975, and in 1976, the legislation imposed an indefinite ban on aid and arms to the country. The following year, Uruguay lost all U.S.

military aid, and in 1978, Congress stripped six additional Latin American countries of military assistance. Congress enacted an indefinite ban on aid to Argentina in 1979. Latin American countries were the only nations that faced total elimination of aid during this period, and only a few countries outside Latin America saw their aid reduced.[40]

Carter Struggles to Provide Momentum

Carter's rise to the presidency provided a critical opening for the human rights movement, but his own frequent ambivalence highlighted the difficulty of balancing security with human rights in foreign policy. Carter's well-known position, that human rights should play a preeminent role in foreign policy, cultivated an environment that encouraged and allowed human rights issues to take centerstage, particularly as the issue pertained to security assistance. Moreover, Carter's record of allowing country specific legislation to limit or eliminate military aid to numerous countries, and the strengthening of Section 502B, were marked departures from the attitude of his predecessors. Carter's appointment of staunch human rights backers to the newly created bureau at State also signaled his commitment to the issue. As Schoultz states, "President Carter legitimized a humanitarian concern in much the same way that John Kennedy had legitimized economic aid through the Alliance for Progress."[41] Indeed, as this chapter shows, the prominent position of human rights in U.S. foreign military policy toward Latin America today, in many respects, found its footing in the Carter presidency.

Even Carter's advocates, however, have noted his hesitance to fully champion the human rights issue. Stephen Cohen has best captured the sentiment:

> The public generally identifies the Carter administration with aggressive pursuit of a human rights oriented foreign policy. Some foreign affairs specialists have charged that its "single-minded" approach seriously overemphasized human rights objectives and failed to consider or pursue other important foreign policy goals, to the detriment of US interests. The general public's impression and the specialists' criticism are attributable, in large measure, to the rhetoric of high administration officials, particularly President Carter himself, who even 2 years into his term declared, "Human rights is the soul of our foreign policy." Moreover, both perceptions suggest that the administration did considerably more than the minimum required by the standards on the law.
>
> Yet a careful examination of actual decisions under section 502B leads to a very different conclusion: that the Carter administration exhibited a remarkable degree of tentativeness and caution, so that its pursuit of

human rights goals was anything but "single-minded." Relatively few governments were considered to be "engaged in a consistent pattern of gross [human rights] violations." Security assistance was actually cut off to even fewer, because other US interests were often found to outweigh human rights concerns under the exception for "extraordinary circumstances." Moreover, in some instances, the Carter administration adopted a highly strained reading of the statute which, although not contrary to its literal terms, produced a result contrary to congressional intent. In other cases, the language was simply disregarded, so that decisions violated even the letter of the law.

Perhaps the most remarkable evidence of the administration's conservative approach to section 502B was its policy never to determine formally, even in a classified decision, that a particular government was engaged in gross abuses.

Ironically, as emphasis on human rights reached its pinnacle in Congress and with Carter's policies and rhetoric, the United States faced the decision of whether to get involved in the brewing civil war in El Salvador, a war riddled with gross military abuses that would spur further human rights activism, exemplify a shift in U.S. policy, and tarnish Carter's record as a purist in promoting human rights in foreign policy. Only days before Ronald Reagan's 1981 inauguration, Carter reinstated military aid to El Salvador that Washington had suspended due to human rights abuses, exemplifying the president's own struggle in dealing with a tradeoff between absolute defense of human rights and combating communism.

THE 1980s: EL SALVADOR'S DUAL IMPACT ON HUMAN RIGHTS

El Salvador's civil war, which spanned the 1980s, served as both a focal point for increased interest group and congressional attention to human rights in Latin America, and as the foundation for what would become U.S. Southern Command's (SOUTHCOM's) approach to human rights around the region in the 1990s. Marxist-Leninist groups united in 1980 to form the Farabundo Marti National Liberation Front (FMLN), throwing the country into an insurgent conflict and attracting almost immediate U.S. attention and economic and military assistance for the Salvadoran government, in hopes of fending off an FMLN victory. Several high-profile military human rights abuses, many against Catholic clergy and some against U.S. citizens, stoked calls to withhold U.S. military aid from Latin American militaries on abuse grounds, based on the view that U.S. military assistance influenced, or at a minimum, was linked to ongoing abuses. U.S. funding for the Salvadoran efforts to combat the FMLN persisted, despite human rights groups' lobby for Washington to cease support. U.S. support for El Salvador, however, was not as cut and dried as some have depicted, and often saw cutbacks imposed or approved by Presidents Carter, Reagan, and Bush. Meanwhile, partly in response to the outcry and to keep U.S. funds flowing, a much less publicized effort to inculcate human rights standards in the Salvadoran military rank and file was taking shape as a part of U.S. military training and assistance.

Abuses Grab the Spotlight

Americans tuned in to the events in El Salvador, first because it represented the first major offensive against communism in Central America, which Washington openly and vigorously backed, and second because the gross human rights violations committed by the armed forces began to capture U.S. headlines. While abuses of government forces by the insurgents were often as bad as those committed by the military, the government abuses drew the ire of the American public. Moreover, the abuses appeared severe relative to other abuses that had taken place in Latin America, particularly due to the murder of religious figures.

In March of 1980, just as the civil war began heating up, government forces assassinated Archbishop Oscar Arnulfo Romero, who had been sympathetic to the leftist movement. In December of the same year, on the eve of what would become the FMLN's so called "final offensive," government forces murdered four American church women. The immediate impact was U.S. suspension of aid to El Salvador. President Carter reinstated the assistance only 12 days later for fear of allowing the FMLN's offensive to bring down the Salvadoran government.

The 1981 "Massacre at El Mozote," as it is now commonly known, became the icon for what would be a decade of high-profile military abuses. Recounted in great detail in a 1993 book by Mark Danner, the massacre is now infamous for coinciding with significant increases of U.S. support for the Salvadoran military as well as congressional requirement of presidential certification that El Salvador was making progress in addressing the human rights abuse problem.[42] The massacre, by some accounts, left just under 800 men, women, and children dead and buried in a small remote Salvadoran village.[43] The details of inhumane treatment ranged from hangings to decapitation. The events hit the U.S. media in late January 1982 and came to dominate debates among U.S. agencies, the FMLN, and human rights groups.

Abuses persisted and resulted in the deaths of tens of thousands of civilians over the decade. The civilian death toll in 1980 stood at 750 per month.[44] High-profile murders committed by government forces overshadowed a gradual decrease in overall violence against civilians. In 1988, the military massacre of ten civilians garnered high-level attention in Washington. Dominating U.S. attention was the 1989 murder of six Jesuit priests, their housekeeper, and her daughter. This murder of Catholic clergy again stoked the ire of human rights groups and shattered any hope that U.S. or Salvadoran officials may have had in highlighting what by then appeared to be a concerted, broad effort to promote human rights in the military. Indeed, the event cast doubt over whether human rights promotion was taking root at all.[45]

U.S. Assistance Balloons, But Human Rights Remain a Factor

U.S. assistance for El Salvador, principally geared toward keeping communist forces from taking hold of the government, shot up dramatically during the 1980s, despite the high-profile human rights abuses and resulting increased pressure from human rights groups calling for cessation of U.S. support. Between 1980 and 1990, the United States provided about $1 billion in military assistance to El Salvador.[46] By 1990, El Salvador was first among all Latin American recipients of U.S. military aid and eighth in the world.[47] El Salvador received nearly half of all U.S. assistance sent to Central America in the 1980s and more than double of any other Central American nation.[48] This assistance helped increase the size of the Salvadoran military from 11,000 to 45,000. The Salvadoran military, with Washington's backing, also significantly bolstered its ability to sustain weapon and equipment inventories, improve training and tactics, and largely contain, although not defeat, the FMLN insurgency.

U.S. backing, however, did not come without starts and stops for human rights reasons. The significant increase in U.S. assistance for El Salvador came during a profound shift in U.S. foreign policy under Ronald Reagan, in which fighting communism trumped human rights as the top priority. Human rights took a back seat to anticommunist efforts, but the record on El Salvador shows that the funding did not come wholly absent human rights considerations by both Congress and the Executive Branch. Certainly human rights activists would argue that nothing short of cutting all military assistance in the face of gross abuses would have been appropriate, and in line with congressional foreign assistance law. Still, the use of some sticks and carrots in the name of human rights persisted, and was important as a part of what became the current overall mix in military and diplomatic policy toward Latin America.

Some notable and rarely reported assistance restrictions took place during the Reagan and Bush presidencies. In November 1983, Congress passed and President Reagan signed legislation to withhold 30 percent of military aid to El Salvador, pending a verdict in the trial surrounding the 1980 murder of four American churchwomen.[49] One month later, Vice President Bush during a visit to El Salvador told the country's military command that Washington would cut military assistance unless right-wing death squad activity declined. The U.S. General Accounting Office indicates that human rights monitors reported a decline in death-squad killings after the vice president's trip. For several years, beginning in 1985, Congress withheld $5 million in military aid annually pending legal resolution of a 1981 murder of two U.S. land reform consultants. In 1990, after Congress moved to decrease overall aid to the country following the Jesuit murders, The State Department refused appropriation of $19.6 million because of slow judicial progress in the case.[50] The 1991 legislation withheld 50 percent of military assistance and mandated suspension of all funds contingent upon specific human rights-related improvements. Fear of FMLN gains in 1991 prompted reversal of these funding restrictions, although some funding was suspended to leave an opening for ongoing UN-supervised peace talks, which eventually brought an end to the civil war in late 1991.[51]

Again, these moves to restrict funding were small relative to the actual flow of assistance, and arguably were mere gestures, rather than real efforts to strengthen human rights. Yet, this use of diplomatic, presidential, and congressional pressures proved critical to encouraging the U.S. military to step up human rights awareness, training, and military diplomacy. Indeed, probably by accident, this mix of political pressure combined with military human rights promotion became the foundation for the approach employed around the region today.

Modern Military Human Rights Promotion Is Born

The human rights abuses, pressure from Washington, and persistent media and human rights activist attention helped nudge the U.S. military into the position as the a promoter of human rights in El Salvador. Several military and civilian individuals have reported to the author that the high profile of human rights abuses in El Salvador helped spur U.S. military human rights promotion efforts.[52] This development in understandable, particularly since U.S. military sensitivities surrounding human rights abuses during the Vietnam War were less than a decade old when the United States began bolstering its military assistance to El Salvador in 1981. Indeed, Vietnam-era worries led to a congressional cap of fifty-five military advisors that the U.S. armed forces could send to the country.

Because Congress capped the U.S. military presence in El Salvador, the Salvadoran military sent several thousand armed forces personnel to U.S.-sponsored training in Panama, and after 1984, to Ft. Benning Georgia, primarily at the U.S. Army School of the Americas. This training included topics such as the treatment of civilians and captured combatants as prescribed by the Geneva Convention, the law of land warfare, and civil-military relations. This training alone was significant because, as the GAO reports, "before 1982, the Salvadoran Army did not include human rights issues in its military training." Over the next several years, with U.S. military assistance, the Salvadoran military expanded human rights training to all officers and most enlisted personnel. U.S. military initiatives by 1989 had given the Salvadoran military the expertise to include human rights instruction in the military academy.

By 1990, the Salvadoran military had established an office of human rights, responsible for monitoring, training, and publishing proper code of conduct related to human rights. The U.S. military also encouraged personnel deployed to incorporate human rights issues into all training materials presented to the Salvadoran military.[53] In 1990, the U.S. military also began an effort to bolster its own awareness by requiring all personnel deployed to El Salvador to receive human rights training. A U.S. major in 1990 was the primary individual who obtained and reported the evidence that the Salvadoran military was responsible for the Jesuit murders, an event that is a small testament to the increased U.S. military vigilance toward human rights abuses.[54]

The stepped-up training and human rights promotion on the part of the U.S. military, and subsequently the Salvadorans, coincided with sharp decreases in human rights abuses during the 1980s. Civilian deaths dropped from 750 per month in 1980 to 17 per month in 1989.[55] That this trend does not equate to full respect for human rights casts some doubt on the importance and effectiveness of U.S. military human rights promotion at the time, especially considering the continued gross abuses, such as the Jesuit murders in 1989. What is clear, however, is that SOUTHCOM saw the Salvador case as a model for what would evolve into a genuine effort to encourage respect and awareness of basic human rights throughout Latin America.[56] Abuses, human rights promotion, and a growing peace process in El Salvador, however, were all overshadowed by the October 1989 fall of the Berlin Wall, which in the next decade would have a direct impact on U.S. policy and military strategy toward the region.

THE 1990s: DEMOCRACY'S VICTORY AND THE RISE OF ENLIGHTENED MILITARY LEADERSHIP

While the Salvadoran war was winding down in the late 1980s, the cold war was also coming to a close. By 1991, with the complete dissolution of the Soviet Union, the U.S. strategic policy toward Latin America began to change. Essentially, the Soviet collapse and the resulting cessation of ideological, material, and economic support to Latin American leftist movements eliminated the pressure for traditional tradeoffs between defending human rights and fighting communism. Presidents Bush and Clinton were able to promote democratization as a U.S. priority in the region. Moreover, Bush ushered in an important change by coming to view democracy and human rights as mutually reinforcing.[57] Meanwhile, human rights groups had fixed their sights on the U.S. Army School of the Americas, providing additional pressure for change during an era of peace and democratic growth.

School of the Americas under Fire

Within months of the 1989 Jesuit murders in El Salvador, revelations that individuals involved in the atrocity had received training at the School of the Americas set in motion a stream of negative media that blasted the School for its connection to serious human right abusers around the region. Over the next decade, a series of events and policies would transform the School's approach toward human rights, eventually lead to its closure, and the opening of the Western Hemisphere Institute for Security Cooperation (WHINSEC) with a mandated focus on human rights.

The Jesuit murders spurred the 1990 establishment of School of the Americas Watch (SOA Watch), an independent organization that listed closure of the School as its primary objective. The group began annual protest marches to the gates of the School's location at Ft. Benning, Georgia, and also started an aggressive lobbying campaign in Congress.[58] Within a year of SOA Watch's creation, the School would begin to suffer a rash of bad publicity.

In 1991, the Office of the Assistant Secretary of Defense ordered a classified investigation into the preparation and use of several training manuals used by School of the Americas officials during 1987 to 1989. The investigation found that two dozen passages in six manuals contained material that was not consistent with U.S. policy. Much of the language included encouragement of coercion and torture. In 1992, then Secretary of Defense Richard Cheney ordered discontinuation of the manuals, recovery of the manuals from Latin American officials, and destruction of all manuals except one record copy for the DoD Office of General Counsel.[59]

In 1993, the public relations battle surrounding the School heated up after the UN Truth Commission on El Salvador released its report. Media seized on the publication of dozens of names of violators that had received training from the School during the Salvadoran conflict. *Newsweek*, in an August 1993 article entitled "Running a 'School for Dictators'" charged that forty-five of the officers identified by the Commission as having committed human rights violations had received training at the School, including nineteen of the twenty-seven officers implicated in the 1989 Jesuit murders.[60] The article listed numerous former Latin American dictators and human rights abusers that had attended the School. While no media discussed whether these individuals had been specifically trained in a manner leading to their indiscretions, the point became somewhat irrelevant, since public and congressional perceptions of the School had already formed.[61]

Over the next several years, the U.S. Army appears to have made an effort to repair the School's image and to institute some changes. The Secretary of the Army ordered the creation of an independent board of visitors to oversee and monitor the School's training and curriculum. The board included former military officers and several civilians, including a top human rights expert as Chairman. The School also began the process of changing its curriculum to emphasize democracy and human rights, including mandatory sessions on human rights for all students.[62] In 1996, in what stoked another salvo of bad press, the Army publicly released the results of the 1991–1992 investigation into training manuals, and the manuals themselves. This release and declassification led to wide press coverage and renewed charges of abuse linked to training. In 1997, the Washington-based NGO Latin America Working Group published a lengthy critique of DoD's handling, investigation, and follow-up concerning the manuals.[63]

Seizing on this momentum, SOA Watch in 1999 successfully lobbied for the introduction of legislation in Congress to close the School; the legislation was narrowly defeated. In 2000, SOA Watch coordinated several protests, including a gathering of some 1,000 people in front of the White House, a two-week national blitz against the School, and a massive protest at Ft. Benning in November that led to the arrest of some 1,700 protestors.[64] In late 2000, Congress passed legislation repealing the legal authorization for the School of the Americas and stipulated that a new entity would open in 2001 under the name Western Hemisphere Institute for Security Cooperation.

The new legislation also called for the Institute to train Latin American officials within the context of democratic principles of the Organization of American States. Congress mandated continuation of previous School of the Americas courses on human rights awareness, including at least 8 hours of human rights instruction for all students. The legislation also opened the door of the Institute to civilian students and codified the practice of utilizing a board of visitors.[65]

Commanders Rise to the Occasion

While U.S. policy toward the region was undergoing change and the School of the Americas was under pressure, key military leaders, primarily at SOUTHCOM, and later at WHINSEC, were already charting a new path. In many respects, military commanders assigned to the Latin America Area of Responsibility went beyond the call of duty in regards to human rights. They set out to make SOUTHCOM human rights policy and regulations that far exceeded any efforts within DoD as a whole. Indeed, these commanders appear to have effectively observed and internalized the pressures and lessons from Congress, interest groups, and the war in El Salvador. The changes instituted toward human rights promotion now make up the center of an overall policy approach toward the region that is often devoid of tradeoffs and employs a complex mix of pressures, inducements, and awareness. Indeed, in interviews with the author, only congressional pressure was mentioned more often than astute military leadership as the key to change in U.S. approaches to human rights in the region.[66]

The changes in SOUTHCOM's approach to human rights began to take shape almost immediately after the Jesuit murders in El Salvador. In 1990, SOUTHCOM Commander General Thurman issued a policy directive requiring all military personnel in the AOR to immediately report any knowledge of human rights abuses and required all personnel deploying to the region to receive human rights training.[67] The training included instruction on the laws of war, international humanitarian law, and U.S. human rights policies. SOUTHCOM supplemented the training with a wallet-sized card detailing standing human rights orders and what Command personnel now knows as the "five Rs of human rights: recognize, refrain, react, record, and report."[68] All deployed personnel were required to carry the card at all times. General Thurman then instituted mandatory human rights training as an element of any military training provided to Latin American personnel.

Succeeding Thurman was General Joulwan, who expanded on the established human rights promotion efforts. The commander produced a 10-minute video that became a standard part of predeployment training and was praised by human rights groups. Joulwan also began the process of significant human rights-related engagement with Latin America. Of particular note was the 1992 legal engagement plan with Peru that helped establish a model for "training the trainer" programs and assisting Latin American countries in establishing their own judge advocate corps schooled in human rights standards.[69]

Perhaps the most important development in SOUTHCOM's approach to human rights came under Joulwan's successor, General Barry McCaffrey. McCaffrey established a dedicated Human Rights Division in 1994, staffed and operated by the Command's Strategy, Policy, and Plans Directorate, or J5.[70] The Human Rights Division, still in existence today, is the only of its kind in the U.S. military command structure and is responsible for ensuring human rights standards are integrated throughout the Command, facilitating human rights working groups and consultation with civil society, and promoting training, awareness, and implementation of human rights standards with Latin American militaries. McCaffrey also stood up a temporary human rights steering group, chaired by a brigadier general, and tasked with ensuring that human rights became a central theme in all Command components, duties it eventually handed off to the Human Rights Division. McCaffrey also reportedly lifted the first Human Rights Division Commander to preeminent status among his counterparts in the Command, frequently taking the human rights officer with him on trips to Latin America.[71]

By 1996, the human rights office began a new phase of international engagement. The division hired a civilian human rights expert to provide expertise and continuity between command changes. The division also began hosting a series of regional conferences on human rights in the military.

The first conference, entitled "The Role of the Armed Forces in the Protection of Human Rights," included defense, NGO, and academic officials from around the region and the United States. The conference was infused with tension between military officials and human rights advocates who had rarely if ever cordially discussed the theme of military human rights promotion, sending a message that achieving Command's objectives in this arena was going to be a hard fight.[72]

General Wesley Clark succeeded McCaffrey and took on the human rights theme with equal vigor. The Human Rights Division held a second conference cosponsored by the Organization of American States (OAS). OAS affiliation was important to attracting key respected human rights groups and activists to the table. Clark then called for an ongoing process of seminars, which became known as the "Human Rights Initiative: Measuring Progress and Respect for Human Rights." The Initiative represented a significant step from debate toward agreement on specific detailed military human rights standards for the region.[73] The first seminar resulted in the initial drafting of a consensus document detailing what are now regional standards in training, doctrine, internal control and prosecution, and civilian cooperation surrounding military human rights issues.[74] In 1998, SOUTHCOM human rights training policies, including mandatory annual human rights awareness education, became a Command regulation.

While 1998 marked progress in the human rights promotion arena, it also marked the end of momentum for 2 years. The new commander, General Whilhelm, saw human rights as an issue that should be part of targeted bilateral programs, as opposed to the previous multilateral seminars and conferences. Thanks to some NGO pressure, and specifically the nudging by a single human rights advocate, George Vickers, then Executive Director of the Washington Office on Latin America, the General found reason to restart the Human Rights Initiative seminars.[75]

Over the next 4 years, several seminars helped strengthen and fine-tune the Initiative consensus document. The Human Rights Division subsequently moved into the process of implementing the document, which has required multilateral and bilateral engagement to maintain the document's profile and to garner memorandums of action from individual countries agreeing to adopt the criteria in the document. Progress in implementation is monitored by a Costa Rican based NGO, ensuring that Latin American militaries can take ownership of the process and that it is not a United States-imposed directive.[76] With only a handful of countries, including Bolivia, Colombia, the Dominican Republic, Guatemala, and Uruguay, now signatories to consensus document memorandums of implementation, the Command's next challenge is to encourage broader and more enthusiastic adoption across the region.

CONCLUSION

Three decades of struggle in Congress, on the battlefield, and within military institutions helped shape what is today a comprehensive approach to military human rights promotion, part of a broader and more complex mix of inducements and levers geared toward bolstering U.S. national security while also improving human rights. The United States—in its approach toward Latin America—now has a model for avoiding the problem of having to choose between backing a government for national security reasons and condemning that government for human rights abuses. Similar to the notion of criminal rehabilitation, as opposed to choosing between simple incarceration and acquittal, today the United States approaches the difficult problem of human rights abuses with something akin to a prescription. The leniency of the pre-1970s era and the congressional condemnation of the 1970s, have grown into a single approach of helping to repair a human rights situation, rather than ignoring or punishing.

Certainly one can envision a case where tradeoffs would still be necessary. A government guilty of gross systematic violations leading to genocide might be beyond the influence of the policy mix discussed above. Moreover, the choice of mere punishment in such a case may be the only appropriate case. If a government is decidedly unfriendly to the United States and unwilling to acknowledge an abuse problem at any level, accept human rights promotion efforts, or bow to threats of condemnation, the problem would clearly require a different approach. Conversely, I can envision no case in which the United States must now choose to support a state that is a violator of human rights without simultaneously insisting on an improved human rights record, conditioning assistance, providing human rights training and promotion for the host country armed forces, and continually vetting military units that use or receive U.S. material and assistance.[77]

A Policy without a Name

If there is a weakness in the argument that a relatively new policy approach or middle ground has emerged with military human rights promotion at its center, it is that this approach often comes together by accident, is intermittently applied, and perhaps most importantly, is unknown to many policymakers. Indeed, it is difficult to pin point an appropriate middle ground between unconditional military assistance and canceling military assistance in the name of punishing human rights abusing states, because the U.S. policy approach as a whole is somewhat erratic. The mix of pressures, inducements, and human rights promotion efforts detailed above often emerges from multiple departments and agencies coming to the table with different responsibilities and concerns. There is rarely an overriding consensus to place human rights promotion at the center of policy, but individual bodies all approaching foreign policy with at least an element of concern for human rights often results in a robust overall focus on the issue.

So, Congress may detail requirements for human rights certification, along with the Leahy requirements for vetting. State may choose to implement and support some efforts, such as funding or assisting in the establishment of a human rights office while simultaneously pressing host country officials on the need to improve human rights. DoD, meanwhile, might work with the war fighters and officers through training, assistance in establishing human rights standards, writing doctrine, and promoting norms among the rank and file. While many of these elements may involve coordination and collaboration across policymaking bodies, to call the process a single policy approach, some might argue, is an overstatement, or perhaps gives Washington too much credit.

The policy approach also is not something that Washington insiders are likely to be able to point to if queried. In other words, this is not an approach that has a name or is recognized as a single approach by many. Because most of the policy comes as individual approaches to a single problem, one is likely to encounter several different answers depending on whom one asks. Congressional staffers, for example, are likely to point to any human rights certification or Leahy recommendations. State personnel are likely to point to their Department's efforts, and some may name the Leahy requirements if they work around vetting.

The exception to this is DoD staff, or more specifically, SOUTHCOM personnel. Military officers and the DoD civilians working in the region are the officials most likely to be able to detail and discuss human rights-related elements of U.S. security policy toward the Latin America. In dozens of interviews, for example, SOUTHCOM personnel in host countries and in the United States typically knew more about all U.S. human rights policy efforts with a country than any other government officials, a testament to my assertion that DoD's human rights promotion is the driving force behind U.S. human rights awareness in the region. Moreover, it is U.S. military officials that seemed to envision the different elements of the overall policy as a single approach. Leahy vetting for example, while viewed by many as cumbersome and in need of streamlining, was also listed by military officers as a tool toward reinforcing SOUTHCOM's own human rights message and a gauge for the seriousness of the host country.[78]

The assertion that the U.S. military is now at the center of a complex policy approach toward Latin America that promotes human rights, but that is rarely identifiable by civilians, also conjures the enduring debate over whether the U.S. military is isolated from the civilian population, and raises questions about the staying power of military human rights promotion. Those that back Samuel Huntington's argument—that there is little to no civil-military integration in the United States—would probably point to the lack of civilian recognition or knowledge of the policy approach that I have detailed above as evidence of military isolation from civilian influence.[79] On the other hand, the Morris Janowitz school, which asserts that the military is influenced and integrated with civilian concerns and public interests at various levels, could almost certainly point to the growing importance of U.S. military human rights promotion as evidence of armed forces attuned to issues outside of war fighting and likely imported from society.[80]

At a minimum, the military evolution that I argue has taken place—from disregard, to checking the box, to serving as a primary advocate for human rights—raises a variety of questions that have civil-military integration at their core. How deep is the human rights focus, and does military leadership on an issue typically championed by civilians signal a fundamental institutional flaw in the approach? Has the evolution of military human rights promotion been dependent upon enlightened military leaders, leaving the approach vulnerable to leadership turnover and retrenchment, absent broad civilian buy in? Is it healthy, even if the shift in U.S. military attitudes toward human rights promotion is deep and permanent, to rely on human rights promotion from an institution with a primary goal of fighting wars; is the military even the right institution for the job?[81]

This book hopes to frame a variety of questions in its effort to highlight a relatively unknown U.S. military priority in dealing with Latin America. This chapter has detailed the evolution of U.S. military human rights promotion, arguing that the efforts today are at the center of a complex policy approach that in many respects eliminated the pressure of choosing between supporting a government and condemning it for human rights abuses. The case studies in the chapters that follow will detail some of the specific efforts that DoD has put forward to promote human rights in Latin American countries. While military human rights promotion has become part of an overall approach to security engagement efforts, the case studies will draw out some obstacles in the road ahead. In particular, a concluding chapter on human rights in the era of counterterrorism will show that this very policy approach is at a critical juncture, and absent strong resilience from military practitioners and human rights activists, is likely to suffer significant setbacks in the name of national security. The approach has diminished the tradeoff between human rights promotion and national security, but now faces a test in deflecting efforts to subordinate human rights to post-9/11 counterterrorism goals.

3

Bolivia: Human Rights Promotion Yields Mixed Results

U.S. military human rights promotion efforts in Bolivia are likely to prove critical to the armed forces' long-term understanding and respect for human rights. In the short term, however, poor military doctrine and civil-military relations could hamper public security and diminish the value of U.S. efforts. The Bolivian military has been on guard about human rights since 2003 when violent demonstrations lead to then President Sanchez de Lozada's resignation, emergency military policing, numerous civilian deaths, and a backlash by human rights groups against the armed forces. Driven by U.S. influence, and fear of repeating the past, the military has responded by stepping into the forefront in the region in implementing military human rights objectives facilitated by U.S. Southern Command's (SOUTHCOM) Human Rights Initiative (HRI), geared toward the implementation and evaluation of human rights-related training, enforcement, doctrine, and civilian relations standards.

Military-related human rights issues are a central driving factor in Bolivian public policy today, and U.S. engagement is paramount to the government's strategy of fostering military respect for human rights. Former President Carlos Mesa—Mesa succeeded Sanchez de Lozada in 2003 and resigned in 2005—numerous government ministries and offices, and civil society elevated human rights to the top of the policy discourse. Any visitor to Bolivia that takes an interest in public policy currently would find it impossible to avoid the military human rights topic.

While the unfortunate events in 2003 had the positive impact of fostering greater military human rights awareness, these events also brought several aspects of Bolivia's democratic weakness to the surface. Former President Sanchez de Lozada's resignation and the inability of Bolivian police forces to handle social unrest were apparent vulnerabilities of the Bolivian system. Below the surface, the armed forces' lack of doctrine emerged as a central stumbling block to promoting public security and human rights in a country that faces the real prospect of future unrest and political instability. Indeed, upon writing this chapter in 2005, the former Carlos Mesa government fell under pressure from internal opposition groups, ultimately leading to the election of opposition leader Evo Morales to the presidency and opening the door to continued instability down the road and a possible cooling of United States–Bolivia ties.

Military human rights instruction, meanwhile, has moved ahead, encountering problems in military institutional development in areas such as rules of engagement and use of force, complicating the armed forces' understanding of when and how to provide public security.[1] Confusion between human rights standards and proportional use of force could lead to a spike in violence, inadequate public security, and further abuses during any future social unrest.

Unlike the cases of Colombia and Venezuela, assessment of U.S. efforts alongside data of human rights abuses would prove unproductive and inappropriate in this case. Due to the events in 2003, and a clear drop in military human rights performance during that year, U.S. efforts beforehand would appear as an all-out failure, while efforts since could be hailed an enormous success. While the 2003 violence signaled a weakness and challenge for U.S. human rights promotion, the events also revealed that more factors were at play in influencing military behavior. For that reason, I will try to assess the current environment, placing U.S. efforts in a broader context. The goal here is to explore whether U.S. efforts currently can play a role in helping the military move beyond the 2003 abuses, draw out the factors that positively influence U.S. efforts, and reveal the obstacles that could nudge the already volatile environment toward a return to violence.

This chapter is divided into five sections, including a scene setter, offering a review of the current events in Bolivia and background on why the country is a good case study for evaluating U.S. human rights promotion efforts. Second, I lay out the U.S. military human rights promotion efforts in Bolivia, the elements that compromise perhaps the most comprehensive military human rights engagement effort in the region, and the drivers behind Bolivian receptiveness to this program. Third, I assess the current ambivalence of the military when faced with tensions between human rights and public security. Fourth, I discuss the institutional hurdles that are feeding the military's uncertainty and complicating human rights promotion, tying these problems to Bolivia's lagging democratic growth. Lastly, the conclusion will focus on Bolivia as a regional model for lessons learned in the human rights promotion arena.

SCENE SETTER: FROM HYDROCARBONS TO HUMAN RIGHTS ABUSES; UNREST SPARKS CIVIL-MILITARY UNCERTAINTY

A close look at recent civil-military tensions in Bolivia is necessary to place human rights concerns in context. February and October 2003 marked two of the most violent incidents in recent Bolivian history, leading to former President Sanchez de Lozada's resignation and leaving between 91 and 111 people dead and hundreds injured, according to the U.S. State Department.[2] Lozada's push for a new hydrocarbons law to allow greater private exploration and export of natural gas was a central catalyst in uniting indigenous and leftist opposition groups and igniting the social unrest that ultimately lead to the president's demise. Perhaps more troubling for Bolivians than the political instability, which has been ever-present in the country's history, was the level of associated violence, lack of public security, and resulting casualties, which have been relatively rare, even during Bolivia's recent turbulent past.

The February 2003 violence broke out when a group of high-school students began stoning the presidential palace. Palace guards engaged the students and attracted the ire of police. An eventual exchange between the students, palace guard, and police culminated in 2 days of rioting and a presidential request for military units to provide public security in place of the incapable Bolivian National Police.[3] Subsequent confrontations left 17 civilians, 9 police, and 5 soldiers dead, and approximately 200 injured. The Bolivian Attorney General indicted eleven police officers and four military officers on human rights abuse-related charges, but reported the investigations stalled in November 2003 citing a lack of funds.

The February events likely provided a precedent and, at a minimum, momentum for the uprisings in September and October 2003. A federal congressional deputy helped spur protest when he began a hunger strike in response to the president's push for a hydrocarbons law that allowed for private export of Bolivian natural gas. Opponents of the hydrocarbons law followed the congressman's lead by blocking a roadway to the popular tourist destination, Lake Titicaca, trapping some 800 tourists in the area. The government ordered the military to undertake a rescue operation, and peasants ambushed the operation leading to several deaths.

The violence sparked the emergence of what the U.S. State Department calls a loose coalition of the opposition, comprised unionists, coca farmers (cocaleros), students, NGOs, and indigenous peasants.[4] These groups began blockading key access points to La Paz and attacking fuel convoys en route to the capital. Violence ensued, leading to rioting, confrontations between the military and civilians, resignation of the president and his cabinet on October 17, and the rise of then Vice President Carlos Mesa to the presidency. Mesa, in a far less violent fall from office, resigned under political and social pressure in June 2005.

Against this backdrop, Bolivia became the focal point of national and international human rights groups, and already ongoing military human rights promotion became a public policy priority for the armed forces and the Mesa government, which all but forswore the use of lethal force against civilians. Moreover, human rights seized the public spotlight. U.S. Embassy officials claimed that NGOs and human rights groups had formed strong press and lobbying networks. This conglomerate of media and activists plugged into the most influential NGOs in Washington and had sympathetic ears on Capital Hill, overwhelming any public relations efforts that the Byzantine military institution may have tried to put out to counter abuse accusations.

The Mesa government, meanwhile, garnered mixed reviews from both NGOs looking for major improvement in the military's treatment of civilians, and the armed forces searching for a balance between human rights awareness and their now unwanted public security role. Mesa, upon taking office, decried the use of lethal military force for policing, and in 2004, issued a decree mandating the creation of a federal human rights commission to ensure the implementation of human rights standards across government ministries.[5] The move, a clear message to the armed forces for their aggressive actions in 2003, pleased human rights groups while roiling the military leadership. U.S. officials indicate that military personnel are now wary about presidential willingness to appropriately defend soldiers whom he orders to enforce stability, and that may face more, and in the military's opinion, likely unwarranted abuse charges. Mesa's inability to assert full civilian control over the military also drew criticism from human rights activists.

This environment, combined with high-level U.S. engagement on the military human rights issue, provides a ripe setting for asking key thesis questions: Whether the level of U.S. commitment to military human rights is a factor; if the status of bilateral relations matters; if the level of Bolivia's democratic development is a factor in promoting greater respect for human rights from within the military? The military's treatment of U.S. assistance and how human rights promotion is applied in Bolivia's situation should also offer an opportunity to assess whether this case tells us anything valuable about the relationship between military human rights practices and an overarching U.S. strategy geared toward counterterrorism.

TIMELY U.S. EFFORTS FIND AN AUDIENCE

Already established human rights promotion efforts suffered a setback in 2003, but the violence served to encourage more awareness, as opposed to abandonment of U.S. assistance. U.S. military human rights engagement with Bolivia in 2004 moved forward at an unprecedented pace for the region. As unrest wracked Bolivia and the military fell under hardened scrutiny, SOUTHCOM was transitioning its HRI from the consensus building phase to implementation. The events in Bolivia made the country a top candidate for pushing forward with a plan for adopting the key elements of the HRI. With the Bolivian military looking for an avenue to help assuage and to some extent deflect NGO concerns and charges, the HRI was a good vehicle for the United States to better engage the country and try to make a positive impact during a turbulent time in the country's history.[6] Even amid some military-to-military tension surrounding the U.S. American Service-Members' Protection Act that cut State Department assistance to the Bolivian armed forces, Bolivia was among the first countries to sign a memorandum of action committing it to full implementation for the HRI.[7]

The Bolivian military, with the assistance of civilian ministries and backing from the U.S. Embassy, began formation of a detailed plan for adoption of all the Initiative's key components, with a special focus on military code and justice to address pending concerns from the 2003 violence. U.S. civilians in the embassy also began to play a central role in facilitating the follow through of the HRI through meetings with the Ministry of Defense Human Rights Office, various defense officials, and the Ministry of Justice. A Bolivian national working for the U.S. Embassy served as the central point of contact on the HRI and continues to help the Bolivian military with technical and legal questions on the implementation plan. The Bolivian national also served as a key proponent of the HRI, nudging the military to persist in its adoption of the consensus document, a fortunate and uncommon asset for SOUTHCOM and its human rights effort.[8]

Bolivia Showing Honest Effort

Evidence that the United States-sponsored Initiative has been more than just window dressing in Bolivia, as is often the problem with U.S. assistance, can be found in the high-level interaction and in-depth knowledge of the HRI amongst government agencies. For example, the federal prosecutor's office has in-depth knowledge of the program and is engaged in working to facilitate a working relationship with the military on the issue. The Ministry of Defense provided the author with a description of key goals with a timeline for completion of specific objectives, including helping institute better civilian justice protocol detailed in the HRI, a rare sign of close civil-military cooperation.[9] Moreover, the justice officials told the author that their superiors were enforcing implementation of key objectives by issuing individuals charged with such duties disciplinary sanctions for failure to meet deadlines. Further, the military's human rights office claimed that a critical component of HRI implementation was his office's efforts to engage civilian experts, NGOs, and the Bolivian Defensor del Pueblo, or human rights ombudsman.

Strong Desire, Significant Incentive

Perhaps the most striking element of Bolivia's adoption of the HRI was the genuine sense of desire displayed by all involved, a sentiment likely driven by a mix of carrot and stick approaches from the United States and a fear of repeating the events of 2003. The author's numerous meetings with Bolivian government officials, civilians, and the U.S. Embassy revealed a consistent view that the military wanted to do, and was trying to do, the right thing by taking on the HRI and fostering a better understanding and respect for human rights within its ranks. Even questionable military behavior that signaled some reticence to move forward with HRI elements, largely related to military justice issues and discussed further below, appeared more rooted in a broader civil-military context and a tradition of military autonomy than a lack of desire to improve the human rights environment.[10]

While difficult to prove, Bolivia's reliance on the United States for significant U.S. military funding and assistance likely helped drive the willingness to implement the HRI. Bolivia is the fourth largest recipient of U.S. military aid in the region—in 2004 security assistance from the United States stood at just under $60 million—after Colombia, Peru, and Mexico, and receives significantly more U.S. military training than all Latin American countries except Colombia.[11] Having seen significant cuts in assistance and funding around the region because of human rights-related circumstances in the past, as detailed in Chapter 2, the Bolivians likely are kowtowing to the United States on the human rights side to keep the assistance flowing. Bolivia suffered its own significant cut in military assistance because the government would not sign an "Article 98" agreement with Washington, geared toward ensuring that U.S. military personnel in Bolivia at any given time would not face extradition to the International Criminal Court if accused of human rights abuses in the country.[12] As the authors of a recent publication on U.S. military assistance entitled *Blurring the Lines* note, foreign military assistance from the United States has increasingly shifted from the State Department to DoD, which is not subject to Article 98 restrictions.[13] Bolivian military officials likely see HRI as a window for encouraging additional nonhuman rights-related DoD funding. Implementation of the HRI, at a minimum, would signal Bolivia's positive posture toward the U.S. military and U.S. priorities of democratic growth in the region, keeping the country competitive for DoD funding that is not subject to Article 98 restrictions. Even without the draw down in aid to Bolivia under Article 98, the country's heavy reliance on U.S. military assistance is likely a key inducement encouraging the military's willingness to tackle key problems, such as human rights.

Lastly, one might argue that the military's enthusiasm can be accredited to bolstering its credentials as a professional force in order to fend off future charges of human rights abuse, as opposed to acknowledging a problem and actually improving the force's human rights performance. In other words, if assessed on the surface alone, military human rights enthusiasm could be dismissed as a façade, or an exercise in checking the box. The time and energy devoted to this issue by Bolivian officials and their detailed knowledge of the military's human rights program, however, suggest that this is not the case, or is minimally true at best.

HUMAN RIGHTS DYNAMICS COMPLICATING PUBLIC SECURITY

The military's positive approach to human rights promotion, in part, runs counter to its predominant view that human rights activism has harmed the armed forces. While the fear of repeating the 2003 events and the prospects of future prosecutions helped drive military human rights promotion, the rancor surrounding the human rights issue has also clouded the armed forces posture toward its public security role, increasing the possibility of future unrest, shoddy policing, and a worsening human rights environment. The charges against the military for human rights abuses during 2003, apparent NGO skewing of human rights claims—as reported by U.S. and Bolivian officials—and civilian officials' approach toward subsequent security incidents have the military on edge about fulfilling its public security role.[14] Military concerns surrounding fair treatment of the human rights issue, whether legitimate or self-serving, could instill reticence in the ranks and dissuade the armed forces from defending public security amid chaos. In essence, military fears of human rights activism could serve to disarm the force in a key time of need.

Military concern over charges against soldiers in 2003 is part legitimate and part denial of wrongdoing. It is rational for a military to shun a role that would almost certainly lead to legal proceedings against its rank and file. Still, the military leadership appears to be in complete denial of any wrongdoing during the 2003 unrest and wants to avoid what they would view as undue claims of abuse in the future. Military officers, for example, have consistently avoided civilian attempts to charge and try soldiers.[15] U.S. State Department reporting and NGO accounts agree that there is credible evidence that military personnel were guilty of human rights abuses in 2003.[16] Moreover, even the most strident backers of the military's position on the human rights issue have noted that the most high-profile case of soldiers shooting an innocent bystander, an individual trying to help him, and a nurse that came to their assistance was likely a clear-cut case of an abuse of lethal force.[17]

While the military appears to be taking an unreasonable stance based on past charges, its position on the matter is bolstered and the issue is complicated by uneven NGO and civilian law enforcement treatment of human rights abuses. Multiple officials and State Department reporting, for example, have noted that organized government opposition groups—typically including workers' union members and coca farmers or "cocaleros" seeking retribution for antidrug policies and capitalist economic policies that they blame for endemic unemployment and inequality—have beaten or tortured government officials in public without legal reprisal and with little to no NGO denunciation of such actions.[18] Cocaleros looking to stem government coca eradication and who are generally opposed to government antidrug efforts that limit the legal distribution of their crops, have been particularly violent. Indeed, in one case in 2003, coca farmers beat a mayor to death in public and on live television as he pled for his life, and none of the assailants faced arrest or charges.[19] In 2002, cocaleros kidnapped a police colonel and his wife. They forced the police officer to watch the torture and murder of his wife and then murdered the officer. The assailants in this case have not faced prosecution and human rights activism in the name of the officer and his wife has been rare to nonexistent. Indeed, the largest Bolivian human rights NGO, faced with pleas from the families of the murdered, asked the U.S. Embassy to take the case off its hands.[20]

This lack of enforcement against violent actors that the military has faced, and probably would again confront in the streets during any future unrest, grants the armed forces an unfortunate but real justification for the fear that the human rights issue does not favor public security and that the government and NGOs are promoting a dual and inconsistent standard of human rights enforcement. Poor enforcement against civilians in such publicly egregious violations of the law stokes emotions that feed a negative perception of how the human rights issue is playing out and would take shape in future circumstances.[21]

U.S. military and civilian officials reported that the Bolivian armed forces' other top concern in taking on any future policing role is that the president would send soldiers into harms way without the authority or equipment to properly defend themselves or public security. Military officials openly complained to U.S. officials that Mesa was on edge about the possibility of human rights abuse accusations under his watch. As a result, military officials judge that the president was at best hesitant to use "proportional force" for fear of having to step down from office, like his predecessor, following civilian deaths, even if legitimate.[22]

The military has sound reason for concern based on precedent during a smaller security-related event in 2004. In June 2004, the government called on the military to disburse a road blockade using only nonlethal means. In the U.S. context, nonlethal force to clear a roadblock seems appropriate, but in Bolivia in 2003 the roadblocks proved to be highly volatile venues.

In this case the military was ambushed with lethal force as cocaleros fired upon soldiers with live ammunition, injuring and killing several personnel and some of their own members with friendly fire.[23] U.S. officials point to this event as a smaller-scale example of what the military fears could take place in a future large-scale event.[24] In essence, the impact is that civilian vigilance to prevent military abuses could lead to orders for military policing without appropriate orders or equipment for a particular situation, leaving solders ineffective and disproportionately vulnerable to injury or death.

United States Sending Mixed Messages on Human Rights and Justice

While the U.S. military emphasizes human rights in Bolivia, Washington's push for "Article 98" agreements—a bilateral exception to the International Criminal Court (ICC) mandates that allow extradition of foreign troops from a host country to the Court in cases of human rights abuses—is sending a message of hypocrisy. Since 2002 the United States has vigorously implemented the American Service-Members' Protection Act, which places restrictions on provision of military assistance to governments that are parties to the ICC and that refuse to sign an Article 98 agreement exempting U.S. personnel from the Court's jurisdiction.[25]

The U.S. efforts to impose its own immunity from the ICC, and specifically international standards for enforcing International Humanitarian and Human Rights Law, has spurred blowback against U.S. efforts to promote human rights in Bolivia and around Latin America, particularly in the justice realm. At the same time that legislation moved through the Bolivian Congress to clarify civilian versus military jurisdiction of human rights-related cases, the legislature faced debate surrounding granting U.S. soldiers assurances that they would not be extradited to the International Criminal Court.[26] Moreover, U.S. military and civilian officials note that the Article 98 issue has stoked some resentment among the Bolivian military leadership who see the U.S. push for immunity of its own soldiers as contradictory to U.S. human rights promotion efforts. Indeed, the SOUTHCOM Commander has gone on record noting his judgement that Article 98 sanctions are detrimental to military-to-military relations.[27]

POOR MILITARY PROFESSIONALISM STOKING CONFUSION AND DISAGREEMENT

Inadequate institutional foundations and lack of respect for civilian authority are obstacles to assuaging military ambivalence toward human rights. The military's lagging professionalism as a whole is a source of internal armed forces confusion and spurs debate and disagreement with civilians and the human rights community. Indeed, if we examine Bolivia through the lens of criteria detailed in Chapter 1 for evaluating a country's democratic civil-military relations, the country appears critically flawed. A clear organizational framework for civil-military authority, military respect for civilian orders, and armed forces acceptance of civilian judicial jurisdiction are all central obstacles to a better military human rights performance in Bolivia. In essence, if graded against these standards, Bolivia fails.

One central problem in the military's institutional failings is a lack of modern armed forces doctrine. U.S. Embassy officials in 2004 indicated that Bolivia lacked a military code defining use of force and rules of engagement, and that if any related doctrine exists the military has no understanding or knowledge of it.[28] In October 2004, at a U.S. SOUTHCOM-sponsored seminar for the armed forces on rules of engagement and use of force, senior Bolivian military officials were quick to understand the basic tenets of the issues, but clearly lacked any previous exposure to the topic. The absence of these most basic of military operational standards serves to confuse and often strike fear in the military rank and file, especially when simultaneously exposed to human rights standards meant to go hand in hand with use of force doctrine.

In 2003, Bolivia experienced what happens when soldiers are ordered to police with neither clearly delineated, previously agreed upon rules of engagement nor exposure to human rights awareness; aggressive tactics and human rights abuses are likely. Conversely, strong emphasis on human rights without clear rules of engagement risks amplifying soldier reticence to act with appropriate force for fear of committing abuse.[29] In other words, military personnel in harm's way and with a clear mandate and requirement to use proportional force against violent individuals may shy away from their duties because of uncertainty over whether enforcement action violates human rights or falls under their legal enforcement authority. In the latter case, soldiers certainly err on the side of human rights, but a lack of balanced knowledge between human rights and use of force could lead to an even worse scenario, including mass unrest and chaos with little hope of enforcement or security for the innocent.

While the inadequate military code breeds confusion within the military, poor standards of military justice and an armed forces' refusal to recognize civilian judicial authority undermines civilian control, breeds hostility toward the military, and gives credence to even the most extreme charges by NGOs and opposition figures. The lack of effective and respected judicial treatment of military human rights abuse cases is the top concern consistently mentioned by Latin American and U.S. NGO officials, and is of particular concern in Bolivia.[30] Indeed, an Amnesty International official opined that the key problem with U.S. military human rights promotion efforts was that they are more focused on preventing abuses, while the larger problem today is the inability of justice systems to fairly, promptly, and effectively treat these cases.[31]

The Bolivian military's justice system and the armed forces' posture toward civilian justice are inadequate and unprofessional at best. U.S. Embassy, NGO, and Bolivian justice officials all noted that the military system is insular, bogged down, and unable to treat human rights cases judiciously.[32] The Washington Office on Latin America, a leading U.S. NGO that monitors the region, notes that the military courts failed to prosecute a single official for violations during 2003, despite strong evidence of abuse.[33] State Department reporting indicates that "the military justice system generally was susceptible to senior-level influence and avoided rulings that would embarrass the military."[34]

Senior officers' recalcitrance and insubordination toward civilian authorities regarding judicial jurisdiction issues has deepened the problem. The military has failed to cooperate with civilian judicial authorities investigating the human rights abuse claims from 2003.[35] Moreover, after an unappealable Constitutional Tribunal ruling in 2004 that four military officers, accused of killing two civilians during the February 2003 unrest, must stand trial in civilian courts, military commanders publicly denounced the decision and arrived at a meeting with the president on the issue dressed in battle fatigues.[36] As late as February 2005, federal prosecutors had to issue judicial orders compelling military officers to testify under the civilian justice system after eight senior officers ignored subpoenas connected to ongoing investigations of the 2003 violence.[37] Such actions clearly violate the norm of civilian rule and cast doubt over any genuine military effort or desire to better promote human rights.

A REGIONAL MODEL FOR LESSONS LEARNED

This case serves as a single affirmative example toward proving my overall thesis that U.S. military human rights promotion can play a positive role, that the status of military-to-military relations is an important factor, and that democratic development is critical to success of U.S. efforts. The Bolivia case has proven U.S. military human rights engagement to be an ever-present and critical element in Bolivian military policymaking. The status of bilateral relations and the influence and leverage of U.S. assistance also proved critical sources of positive change. However, the status of Bolivian democratic growth, specifically the lack of military institutional development in terms of doctrine and civilian control, emerged as a critical obstacle to change.

The prominence of U.S. efforts in Bolivia today and the positive attitude toward implementing human rights standards with U.S. backing suggest that the efforts are helpful, if not critical, to improvement in Bolivia's human rights performance. Although fear of future human rights abuse charges and desire for continued U.S. assistance are significant factors driving Bolivian interest, it is clear from bilateral and interministerial collaboration that there is serious interest in military reform. Without close military-to-military relations and the resulting U.S. efforts on the human rights front, the Bolivian armed forces probably would revert to deeper insularity, increased aggressiveness toward civilian criticism, and less attention to human rights. Indeed, as the possibility of cooling United States–Bolivia relations looms large with the rise of the radical and often anti-United States President Evo Morales, Bolivia's improving military human rights awareness is at risk of an almost immediate decline. In summary, any achievements in terms of positive Bolivian military growth on the human rights front, are likely linked to or the result of U.S. military assistance.

That said, employing the criteria defined in Chapter 1 for gauging democratic civil-military relations reveals several lingering problems in Bolivia, such as the lack of an accepted organizational framework—in terms of doctrine, rules of engagement, and use of force—military disrespect for civilian authority, and lagging civilian judicial jurisdiction. The first problem appears to have been at the root of the 2003 abuses and is unlikely to improve significantly in the near future. While the U.S. military is engaging the Bolivians on the very issue of use of force through seminars and legal education, and although doctrinal development is a central element in SOUTHCOM's Human Rights Initiative that Bolivia is implementing, the needed level of change and collaboration with civilians in delineating clear rules of engagement has not happened.

The military's distrust for the president and a glaring lack of clarity on when, why, how, and with what authority the president would call for military policing leaves little doubt that neither the military nor the civilians have taken the necessary steps to prevent future social volatility. The president simply stating that he will not use lethal force, as Mesa had rhetorically promised, is not enough, and as we have seen, leaves the military distrustful, unsure, and even unable to fully appreciate the human rights awareness that the United States is trying to imbue.

The second problem of lacking military respect for civilian authority is an obstacle that could not only tarnish but also obliterate the value of U.S. human rights promotion efforts. Military decisions to ignore civilian justice and clear insubordination toward the president, regardless of whether the presidential positions or attitudes are spurring such action, is inexcusable behavior in the eyes of human rights activists and Washington, which aspires to promote the growth and strength of democracy around the world. History has shown, and particularly in Latin America, that insubordinate militaries also tend to be human rights abusing militaries.[38]

So, while U.S. efforts have proven useful and could be critical to Bolivian awareness of human rights, some larger problems—while identified as critical developmental areas by U.S. military programs—are going largely untreated and risk diminishing or even tainting U.S. efforts in the country and region. Certainly one can see the signs of a more human rights conscious armed forces developing in Bolivia, but no matter the level of human rights awareness, an action such as a military coup or significant intervention in the currently unstable political environment would render most, if not all, human rights training moot. Even the norms that may be currently taking root would be discounted by observers as insignificant.

The answer then to the Bolivian problem is a call for even greater engagement. Bolivia is a prime example of the new approach to foreign relations detailed in Chapter 2, which includes a mix of carrots and sticks and military human rights promotion as a key element of engagement, as opposed to complete disengagement because of the military's recent poor record. This case suggests that U.S. military human rights promotion can be central to U.S. foreign policy in a host country, but it cannot stand alone.

U.S. military encouragement perhaps should be feeding into the justice reform process, but should not always serve as the primary U.S. influence in such areas. Indeed, the Bolivia case gives partial credence to the arguments detailed by the authors of *Blurring the Lines*, who assert that U.S. assistance to civilian institutions should come from sister establishments in Washington, not the military.[39] Unlike the authors of *Blurring the Lines*, I commend the U.S. military on its efforts and think the Bolivia case argues for continued and increased engagement, but certainly the U.S. military could benefit from greater civilian participation, particularly in the realms of justice and executive authority.[40] Why put forward fruitful military human rights efforts if they are vulnerable to being overcome by events and behavior that clearly run counter to such efforts? Why leave costly and important U.S. military efforts to promote human rights at the mercy of poor civilian institutions, unable to command the military's respect? Ultimately, military human rights promotion, I believe, will prevail because of the genuine desire and efforts detailed above, but the path toward full military human rights awareness in Bolivia will be tough and full of setbacks as long as institutional development and democratic growth lag.

Implications for Counterterrorism

While the Bolivia case did not reveal direct links between U.S. military human rights efforts and the broader DoD strategy of countering terrorism in Latin America, some related lessons did emerge. Most prominent is the problem in Bolivia of charging the military to take on a domestic policing role, something that SOUTHCOM, as noted in the Chapter 1, has begun to encourage as a part of its counterterrorism campaign in Latin America. The Command's priorities in this regard run counter to its efforts to promote human rights. The Bolivian case clearly shows the problems associated in asking an underdeveloped military to take on a domestic policing role, and while the incidents in La Paz had nothing to do with counterterrorism, the link is easy to draw. Human rights promotion is already up against significant obstacles in Bolivia because of poor civil-military institutions and standards. A domestic counterterrorism role for the country's military any time in the near future would be problematic for human rights promotion, at a minimum.

Washington's attempt to press for an Article 98 agreement also brings a lesson to the forefront. Although none of the events in Bolivia were terrorism related, the Article 98 issue, its link to larger U.S. goals of counterterrorism in the region, and its negative impact on military-to-military relations was an ever-present issue while the author was in La Paz in late 2004. Bolivians likely see U.S. military efforts to promote human rights as hypocritical given the U.S. effort to free its own soldiers from any international scrutiny for human rights abuses. While practitioners on the ground fight a tough battle to improve human rights awareness and performance in Bolivian military circles, the larger priorities of the U.S. government detract from and diminish these efforts. Indeed, the Article 98 push in many ways is reminiscent of the cold war trend of subordination of human rights that I have argued is significantly diminished today. If U.S. military human rights promotion in Bolivia is to succeed, it cannot come with a simultaneous message of "do as I say, not as I do."

4

Colombia: A Complex Mix of Victories and Lessons for U.S. Military Human Rights Promotion

The Colombian case is perhaps the U.S. military's greatest human rights success story in Latin America, while also serving as the top challenge and problem for U.S. military human rights awareness in the region. Human rights promotion has proven a critical factor influencing the armed forces' extensive human rights awareness and training, which is unmatched in the region. Other factors, however, such as lagging government respect for democratic civil-military standards, armed forces collusion with paramilitary groups guilty of widespread human rights violations, and military impunity from prosecution for abuses taint the military's human rights record and hinder U.S. efforts to instill greater awareness.

One difficulty that U.S. military human rights promotion faces is that the Colombian case is by far the most politically charged and complex of any country in Latin America, is wrapped in an ever-changing civil war, and is steeped in a heated public relations debate fraught with skewed arguments and data. Indeed, unlike the other two cases in this book, Colombia presents numerous situations that often are not as they seem on the surface and are easily distorted by one-sided interpretations on both sides of the debate. For example, the Colombian government is promoting vast civilian involvement in the country's civil war, is pushing for extensive legal immunities for paramilitary fighters guilty of human rights abuses, and has significantly increased the military war effort, all signposts of a worsening human rights environment. The human rights situation, however, is undeniably improving, with violations as a whole down across the board, security around the country significantly bolstered, and democracy showing some signs of growth. In a sense, the facts surrounding the Colombian military human rights situation are often a conundrum in themselves, frequently lending apparently equal credence to opposing arguments. As this chapter will show, proving the utility of U.S. military human rights promotion is exceedingly complex in an environment where government policies appear to simultaneously improve and threaten human rights.

This chapter is divided in five sections, each with the goal of fleshing out the complexities surrounding the Colombian human rights debate and shedding light on the real impact and obstacles to U.S. military human rights promotion. The first part is a scene setter that offers a brief overview of Colombia's turbulent domestic security environment that stems from 40 years of civil war. The second section will attempt to make some sense of the vast Colombian human rights data, highlighting what appears to be a real decrease in human rights abuses by armed groups in the country and an ongoing debate surrounding military's recent record. The third section will detail the close United States–Colombia military relationship, highlighting the extensive U.S. human rights promotion efforts and their impact. The fourth section will detail the current complexities of Colombian democracy and put forward the argument that amid recent growth of political rights and institutions, democratic civil-military standards are still suffering and military impunity plagues the country's judicial system and the war in general. Lastly, the conclusion will attempt to draw on the previous sections to highlight successes and failures of U.S. military human rights promotion, and will also detail lessons learned for the U.S. war on terrorism.

SCENE SETTER: FOUR DECADES OF CIVIL WAR AND HUMAN RIGHTS ABUSES

Colombia's changing civil war, shifting political landscape, and abhorrent human rights record have made it perhaps the most complex and intriguing case study for academics and human rights activists. Colombia has been mired in a civil war since 1964, a war that has changed from an ideologically driven conflict between the state and leftist revolutionaries, to a dispute that has lost much of its ideological tenor and is dominated by illegal combatants trying to protect crime and narcotics networks. The internal conflict now pits the Alvaro Uribe government against multiple parties. Illegal paramilitary groups claim allegiance to the government against insurgents but are saturated in crime and corruption and increasingly find themselves in combat against government forces. Two primary insurgent guerrilla groups, the National Liberation Army (ELN) and the more prominent Revolutionary Armed Forces of Colombia (FARC), still burnish their Marxist roots but are more concerned with sustaining narcotics trafficking syndicates (see Table 4.1 for the number of personnel in each armed

Table 4.1. Colombian Military Balance

Group	Number of Personnel
Colombian Armed Forces	374,125[a]
Revolutionary Armed Forces of Colombia (FARC)	12,500–23,000
National Liberation Army (ELN)	3,500
Paramilitaries—United Self-Defense Forces of Colombia (AUC)	10,600 (2005 est.)[b]

[a] Projected number by the end of 2005.

[b] The AUC since a large-scale demobilization during 2005–2006 is widely seen as disbanded and the current number of remaining AUC members varies widely. Government sources typically list a lower number based on AUC members killed, captured, or demobilized. Private sources note that the AUC continues to replenish its ranks through recruitment. Smaller, decentralized paramilitary groups still occupy territory and hold arms.

Source: Economist Intelligence Unit, Country Profile Colombia 2004/2005 Main Report (September 2004).

group). Adding to the complexity is a now widely recognized reality that the paramilitaries and insurgents share their top objectives of maintaining control of criminal and narcotic networks, which makeup the world's largest source of cocaine.[1] For these illegally armed groups, the Colombian conflict is now less about ideology than about access to illicit power and resources.[2]

Under President Uribe, who took office in August 2002, paramilitaries and insurgents have found themselves increasingly on the defensive. Uribe rose to the presidency on the heels of failed government-insurgent peace talks that had spanned nearly 4 years and were characterized by record-level insurgent violence. Uribe's promise to his constituents was to take the war to the insurgents through a plan he terms "Democratic Security," which includes an underlying goal of providing security for all citizens, increased military spending—with large portions funded from foreign sources, including the United States—the military's "Patriot Plan" offensives against insurgent-held territories, increased civilian participation in the security effort, deployment of soldiers in local municipalities termed "hometown soldiers," peace negotiations with the United Self-Defense Forces of Colombia (AUC), and a renewed focus on promoting human rights. Uribe's approach has spurred wide-ranging local and international responses, including praise from the U.S. government and significant criticism from human rights groups. The president's policies garner broad support at home where he maintains an approval rating of around 75 percent and is credited, even by some of his toughest critics, for significantly improving domestic security around the country.[3]

While criticism from human rights groups has spiked, the human rights problem in Colombia is nothing new. Colombia has an exceptionally violent history spanning the past century. The country's "One Thousand Day War" in 1899–1902 claimed 100,000 lives and an undeclared civil-war period in 1946–1958, known by Colombians as "La Violencia," left an estimated 300,000 dead. The latest conflict over the past 40 years has been no different in terms of violence and the toll on Colombian society. The U.S. State Department reports that in just the past decade violence has displaced more than 2 million people.[4] The Colombian Commission of Jurists (CCJ), a local human rights NGO, has recorded just fewer than 65,000 combined extra-judicial deaths, sociopolitical homicides, and forced disappearances during 1997–2003.[5] The total number of homicides of all types in Colombia over the past decade is more than 250,000, according to government statistics.[6] The same sources show kidnappings at an annual average of more than 3,000 since 1998, the highest level in the world. This abhorrent human rights environment, albeit improved in recent years, is among the worst in the world and has attracted some 60,000 registered human rights and civil society NGOs to Colombia. [7]

MILITARY STEEPED IN HUMAN RIGHTS DEBATE

The Colombian military's human rights record is a small part of a much larger and more complex debate surrounding the deplorable human rights situation in Colombia as a whole, and the armed forces' performance varies from moderate improvement to recent worsening, depending on the data source. Nearly all observers, government and NGO alike, agree that the overall human rights situation in Colombia has improved under Uribe's watch. Still, the same individuals concur that the human rights situation remains very poor and is far from resolution. Disagreement continues over which trends deserve greater emphasis—the improvements or the continued violations—how and why the overall picture has seen improvement, how to record violations, and whether the Colombian military deserves accolades or condemnation for its own record.

Human Rights Gains amid Heightened War

Discussing military human rights in Colombia is nearly impossible without recognizing the larger human rights problem and recent improvements in many areas. First and foremost, as already noted, the human rights situation in Colombia is among the worst in the world, even with some recent considerable positive changes. Still the improvements under Uribe in critical areas, such as homicides and kidnappings, have been impressive, particularly considering that the government has increased its war effort, putting security forces increasingly in the line of fire and in situations conducive to human rights violations.

The gains under Uribe are published widely and touted by the U.S. State Department, which has used the numbers as one factor to encourage continued U.S. assistance. According to State, during 2004 violent crime in Colombia was at its lowest level in 16 years.[8] Since 2002, the year Uribe took office and the most violent year in the country's recent history, homicides have fallen by 30 percent, massacres—the killing of three or more people at one time—by 61 percent, and kidnappings by 51 percent.[9] Further, the CCJ, typically an ardent critic of the Uribe government, indicates that extrajudicial killings, sociopolitical homicides, and forced disappearances *outside combat* fell steadily between 2000 and 2003, with a total reduction of 20 percent.[10]

With paramilitaries adopting a self-imposed ceasefire since Uribe's rise to power—albeit with hundreds to thousands of violations—and with ongoing government-AUC peace negotiations having led to some 30,000 paramilitary troop demobilizations, human rights abuses by the paramilitaries are falling.[11] The CCJ notes a significant drop in violations by the paramilitaries, traditionally the worst violator of all warring factions and known for close collusion with the Colombian military. The average number of paramilitary kidnapping victims dropped from a high of six per day in 2001–2002 to below three per day in late 2003.[12] The decline in extrajudicial killings, sociopolitical homicides, and forced disappearances *outside combat*, as cited above, is largely due to a drop in those categories by the paramilitaries, which decreased such violations by one-third during 2000–2003.[13] Finally, the CCJ shows the paramilitaries as the only group achieving significant declines in such abuses committed *during combat*, with violations falling 30 percent in the same time period.[14]

While the improvements are impressive to the point of surprising, the overall abuse numbers are still quite troubling. Government statistics show homicides still at an alarming rate of fifty-two per day.[15] The same source notes that guerillas and paramilitaries kidnap an average of three Colombians every day, and the CCJ lists daily kidnappings at closer to five per day.[16] Further, nearly 140,000 Colombians were displaced by civil-war violence in 2004, according to the government.[17]

Government and NGO sources show several indicators worsening and that many previous gains may have been aberrations. Government data show violence against public officials spiked in 2004 after a dip in 2003; warring factions killed more than a dozen mayors and nearly 60 teachers during the year. Attacks on the general population, which dipped significantly from thirty-two in 2002 to five in 2003, were up sharply to fifteen in 2004, according to the government. Arbitrary detentions committed by the government—a source of heated debate between the Uribe administration and human rights activists—also may have significantly increased, depending on the data source. The government admits no wrongdoing in conducting mass arrests it claims to be legal, while the CCJ argues that from mid-2002 to mid-2003 the government arbitrarily detained 4,362 people compared with 2,869 such detentions during the previous 6 years combined.[18] Finally, the CCJ notes that the number of individuals tortured has increased sharply from 242 during 2001–2002 to 340 during 2002–2003.

This mixed picture of significant critical gains amid continued high level of abuses, and arguable increased abuses in some areas, has stoked debate among human rights activists, the Colombian government, and foreign governments that assist Colombia, namely the United States. The debate has deteriorated into an argument about what deserves greater emphasis, the recent gains or the continued problems. Various sources, including numerous studies published by Human Rights Watch, the Center for International Policy, the Washington Office on Latin America, and the Latin America Working Group Education Fund have been critical of the Colombian government's human rights record while acknowledging improvements only in passing. To their credit, these institutions in the past year have given more attention and credence to human rights gains in Colombia while calling on pro-Colombian government sources to do the same in looking at the continued shortfalls.[19] The CCJ, while largely accurate in its statistical analyses, gives little to no acknowledgment of improvements under Uribe. The Colombian government, meanwhile, is largely transparent and accurate in releasing its data, but dedicates the bulk of its energy to touting human rights gains while paying short shrift to shortcomings. The U.S. State Department, for its part, appears to be the most balanced of all sources in its annual country report on human rights in Colombia, recounting in great detail the gains, shortfalls, discrepancies, and disagreements surrounding the debate. State in public testimony, however, typically highlights gains while giving only slight recognition to lingering problems and the fact that the overall situation requires vast improvement.[20]

Can Heightened War Improve Human Rights?

It is intriguing that Colombia's aggressive approach to the civil war may actually be critical to the improvements in human rights across the country. The author expected a natural increase of abuses resulting from Uribe's more aggressive "Patriot Plan" of pushing into FARC held territories and even increasingly taking on paramilitary fighters. To the contrary, it appears, as noted above, that most key human rights abuses are on the decline while at the same time war efforts are at an all time high. While U.S. military human rights promotion efforts cannot claim credit for this seemingly inverse relationship of war and human rights abuses, the trend certainly is encouraging and shows that even with significantly more fighting and war-related death, human rights can thrive.

A recent study by Jorge Restrepo and Michael Spagat suggests that Uribe's military offensive has been highly successful in both weakening the enemy and in lowering attacks on civilians. Using data from a local respected human rights group collected over the past 16 years, the authors examined the number of violent clashes between the warring factions, and the results reveal "abundant good news" about the war in general. The data of their study strongly suggest that guerrilla and paramilitary attacks are dropping sharply, the rate of military engagement against guerrillas is at an all-time high, government to guerrilla casualty ratios in clashes are falling, and government clashes against paramilitaries are still uncommon, but increasing. As a result, civilian *injuries* are at long-run high levels because of shifting guerrilla tactics toward indiscriminate attacks, yet civilian *killings* are dropping to historic lows. Further, paramilitary performance in the war is proving to be poor and worsening, and clashes between nongovernment warring parties are dropping sharply.

A list of military achievements shows that the state's war effort is proving successful, supports Restrepo and Spagat's thesis, and helps explain why human rights may be seeing some positive effects:

- Paramilitaries killed by the military increased from 187 in 2002 to almost 350 in 2003 and 558 in 2004
- Paramilitaries captured have more than tripled with 1,356 caught in 2002, 2,825 in 2003, and 4,772 in 2004
- The number of guerrillas killed has seen a modest increase from just less than 1,700 in 2002 to more than 1,900 in 2003 and more than 1,800 in the first 11 months of 2004.[21]

In effect, the government's war efforts appear to be eliminating many of the worst human rights violators from the field of battle. Even the most ardent human rights activist have given note to the fact that the FARC for the first time is in retreat under the current offensive.[22] Indeed, perhaps Uribe's greatest justification for his continued war effort is its positive impact on the human rights environment. The question remains, however, whether such a track record is sustainable?

Military Record a Small but Important Part of the Debate

Perhaps the most unclear aspect of the human rights debate in Colombia and a source of ongoing division surrounding the Uribe administration's record is the military's own human rights performance. By all accounts, military abuses make up a small percentage of overall abuses, ranging from 2–5 percent, depending on the source. While a small percentage of overall abuses, the real numbers are still troubling and NGOs claim they are on the rise. Further complicating the military's record are the credible charges of military collusion with the paramilitary forces, linking government forces to even larger numbers of abuses.[23]

The Numbers Debate

CCJ data suggest that military human rights violations resulting in death *outside combat* increased by 50 percent under Uribe, with a total of 184 such violations in 2003, the highest number in at least 7 years. The CCJ contends that the military's overall percentage of abuses has increased, noting that armed forces abuses resulting in death accounted for 4.71 percent of all such *violations outside combat* in 2003, up from 2.81 percent in 2001.[24] Further, the CCJ counts extrajudicial killings, sociopolitical homicides, and forced disappearances of military forces while *in combat* and notes that this number reached a record high of 2,109 deaths in 2002.[25] Even a slight dip to 1,906 such violations in 2003 represents a 65 percent increase under Uribe. Abuses by the military *in combat* now make up 30 percent of the total, up from 17 percent in 2001, according to the CCJ.[26]

While these numbers augur quite poorly for the military, the government disputes their veracity. Much of the problem surrounds the significant increase listed by the CCJ for abuses *in combat*. The government rejects this category outright because it considers deaths in combat to be casualties of the conflict, not human rights abuses. Indeed, the government would likely see these same increases as a positive sign of its increasing war effort, as opposed to proof of significantly increasing abuses. Complicating the government's case, however, is the fact that abuses by the military is the single human rights statistic that the government's Presidential Human Rights and International Humanitarian Rights Program does not publish, leaving the armed forces vulnerable to criticism, raising suspicion of the government's objectives behind this practice, and giving observers little choice but to use only readily available statistics. Indeed, the U.S. State Department Country Report on Colombia cites only that NGO statistics show military abuses on the rise with no mention of official data in this category.[27]

Perhaps the only publicly available government source acknowledging the existence of military human rights abuses comes from the Inspector General and Prosecutor General, responsible for suspending military officials and criminal investigations of alleged human rights abuses, respectively. In the first 8 months of 2004, the Inspector General suspended thirteen military officials for human rights violations.[28] The Prosecutor General during 2003–2004 ordered the preventive detention of twenty-one military officials for such abuses.[29] While indicative of the state's recognition and vigilance toward military abuses, the number charged falls significantly short of allegations and likely present only a partial picture of the official violations taking place. Moreover, while the State Department, in its congressional certification of human rights conditions in Colombia, lists these figures as proof of progress against human rights violations in Colombia, the Department offers no discussion of NGO statistics on military abuses and the Colombian government's failure to publish data on official abuses.[30]

Differing Approaches to Human Rights Data

Much of the debate surrounding the human rights abuse data stems from differing approaches to collecting, counting, and reporting abuses. The Colombian government reports annual totals for homicides, but does not break this down into which homicides were common crimes and who committed the homicides. Further, as noted above, the CCJ reports abuses by type but also includes those committed in combat, which the government contests as inaccurate. The differentiation of how data collectors classify abuses makes close comparison nearly impossible. Only a few categories, such as kidnappings, present a parallel data set for comparison. Most data collectors also use irregular time frames, often starting in July and ending in June, or use only portions of a year, making annual comparisons difficult. The data in Tables 4.2–4.6 show that the approaches by the government and CCJ are vastly different in category and timeframe. The reader will see that the data are mixed, with many key abuses on the downswing and others apparently up. The data, in a sense, are so muddy that one cannot draw a concrete conclusion, absent substantive analysis.

Table 4.2. Colombian Government Data on Human Rights Abuses by Insurgents and Paramilitaries 2003–2004

Abuse Category	Jan–Nov 2003	Jan–Nov 2004
Homicides	21,570	18,579
Victims of Massacre	459	238
Number of Massacres	84	43
Homicides of Mayors and Ex-Mayors	8	14
Homicides of Teachers	41	57
Kidnappings	2,111	1,250
Civilians Forcibly Displaced	210,459	124,284

Table 4.3. Colombian Commission of Jurists Data on Extrajudicial Killings, Sociopolitical Homicides, Forced Disappearances, and Deaths *in Combat* 2002–2003

Responsible Party	Jan–Dec 2002	Jan–Dec 2003
Government Security Forces	2,109	1,906
Paramilitaries	1,774	1,719
Guerillas	1,770	1,058
Unidentified or Under Investigation	2,150	1,652
Total Deaths	7,803	6,335

Table 4.4. Colombian Commission of Jurists Data on Extrajudicial Killings, Sociopolitical Homicides, Forced Disappearances, and Deaths *Not in Combat* 2002–2003

Responsible Party	Jan–Dec 2002	Jan–Dec 2003
Government Security Forces	123	184
Paramilitaries	1,655	1,642
Guerillas	764	542
Unidentified or Under Investigation	1,841	1,537
Total Deaths	4,383	3,905

Table 4.5. Colombian Commission of Jurists Data on Torture by All Parties 2001–2003

Abuse Category	July 2001–June 2002	July 2002–June 2003
Total Torture Victims	242	340

Table 4.6. Colombian Commission of Jurists Data on Arbitrary Detentions by Government Forces 1996–2003

Abuse Category	July 1996–June 2002	July 2002–June 2003
Total Arbitrary Detentions	2,869	4,362

The Military-Paramilitary Collusion Problem

Perhaps the greatest complication to evaluating the military's human rights performance is the institution's history of assisting, tolerating, or at a minimum failing to stop vast paramilitary human rights abuses. Military-paramilitary collusion is nearly impossible to quantify, but it is well documented and is acknowledged by Colombia watchers as a key human rights challenge.[31] Without doubt, the problem of collusion has declined significantly since the demobilization of more than 30,000 paramilitary forces during 2004–2006. Still many observers have noted that the problem is endemic and difficult, if not impossible, to stop.[32] Moreover, the problem persists even amid numerous and strong public orders by the president for military rank and file to desist from collusion. Specific incidents of collusion include military compensation for paramilitary offensives, assistance with offensives that left numerous civilians dead, passive resistance or mere disregard of paramilitary actions against civilians, and reliance on paramilitaries as a primary strike force in military operations.[33] NGOs and media report numerous cases of collusion each year, including charges—now recognized by the United States as credible—that sympathizers infiltrated the Prosecutor General's office.[34]

Much of the impetus behind the collusion is explained by the paramilitaries' history. A fact often overlooked, or merely glossed over, is that the paramilitaries were formed and equipped by the Colombian government during the first years of the civil war. An executive decree in 1965 allowed for military recruitment and use of civilian militias and the arming and equipping of such groups with government resources.[35] This statute became law in 1968 with legislation promulgating military and police support for "self-defense groups."[36] The paramilitaries grew in strength and size and enjoyed legal status for nearly 25 years until declared illegal by executive decree in 1989 after the groups' abusive behavior was condemned by the Inter-American Court of Human Rights, which directly condemned the Colombian State for establishing and supporting the paramilitaries. The Colombian government has since classified paramilitaries as illegal armed groups and considers it a crime to equip or train any such groups.

In spite of the shift in Colombian government attitudes, an increasing acknowledgment of the collusion problem, orders by the president to halt all collusion, and heightened government and military action against the paramilitaries, the collusion problem continues to taint the military's overall human rights record. Further, while the Uribe government has a record of demanding military officials desist from collusion, a wholehearted acknowledgment of the problem is lacking. For example, government officials have strongly condemned other countries at the UN for noting continued government-paramilitary ties.[37] Government officials even take issue with a rather balanced account of the problem put forward by the State

Department annual Country Report, which cites vast human rights improvements amid continued allegations of collusion.[38]

The discussion of collusion and ongoing fissures over the issue is nothing new for Colombia observers. What is new is the debate surrounding whether the military deserves some credit for the significant decreases in paramilitary abuses. Before overall abuse numbers began to trend down in late 2003, the military's greatest human rights liability was that significant collusion was seen by most observers as a fact, and—with paramilitary abuses by far the worst—the military had little room to tout its low direct responsibility for human rights violations. As paramilitary abuses decline, however, the military's record arguably improves accordingly. If the military was at worst helping and at a minimum allowing paramilitaries to commit abuses, certainly these phenomena have also seen significant declines. Indeed, a sign of a shifting human rights environment is that for the first time we see human rights activists turning greater attention toward actual military abuses, rather than focusing almost entirely on the problem of collusion and paramilitary abuses.

U.S. ASSISTANCE FOSTERS HUMAN RIGHTS FOCUS

While the human rights record in Colombia is complex, mixed, and at times unclear, the tangible impact of U.S. military human rights promotion is undeniable. U.S. military human rights promotion has been central to overall massive U.S. security assistance to Colombia and has helped cultivate numerous programs geared toward breaking down a culture of violence and tolerance for abuse and impunity. The broad military-to-military relationship is currently the closest in the region and, through a mix of sticks and carrots, fosters abundant attention to the human rights problem. While U.S. leverage in promoting human rights is clearly maintained through extensive funding and the congressional human rights certification linked to that funding, Colombia's military appears to be on the brink of turning the corner in terms of genuine understanding and respect for human rights.

Extensive Funding Governs Relationship

Total U.S. assistance to Colombia during 2000–2005 reached $4 billion with some 80 percent—$3.2 billion—going to security-related outlays.[39] The U.S. General Accounting Office reports that Colombia during 2002–2004 was the fifth largest recipient of U.S. assistance outstripped only by Iraq, Israel, Egypt, and Afghanistan. Indeed, Colombia, as the largest recipient of U.S. assistance outside the Middle East and with Washington's designation of the illegal armed groups in Colombia as terrorists, represents the United States' second front in its war on terror. Military assistance to Colombia over the past several years has hovered at around $600 million annually, and

Congress is considering a similar budget for 2006. U.S. military assistance to Colombia by far surpasses such funding for any other country in the region; Colombia receives two-thirds of all U.S. security assistance to the Western Hemisphere and eight times that of the next highest recipient, Peru, with a recent annual average of about $70 million.[40] Further, U.S. security assistance to Colombia is 160 times that received by Venezuela and nearly ten times that received by Bolivia, the other two case studies in this book.

The military-to-military personnel relationship is equally extensive. The U.S. military between 1999 and 2003 trained more than 28,000 Colombians, accounting for nearly half of all military personnel in the region trained by the United States and more than five times that of Bolivia, the second highest recipient.[41] The United States since 2002 has maintained 400 U.S. troops in Colombia to train and advise military officials, and Congress increased this number to 800 for 2005.[42]

Human Rights a Critical Element of Funding

While U.S. military assistance to Colombia is significant, particularly considering the country's numerous human rights problems, the aid flows in a manner that both encourages improved human rights and condemns ongoing abuses. Indeed, U.S. aid to Colombia is a model of the policy approach outlined in Chapter 2; Washington funds a country's efforts to combat internal conflict while also applying an extensive mix of carrots and sticks aimed at improving human rights. Colombia is the modern test case for a policy approach that has rejected the idea of a tradeoff between supporting a country's military for security interests and condemning it because of its human rights record. A current statistical model juxtaposing U.S. assistance to Latin America against respect for human rights would reveal a skewed picture that paints the bulk of U.S. funding in Latin America as ignoring human rights records simply because the bulk of funds are flowing to Colombia, a country with a poor human rights record. A substantive review, however, reveals that the U.S. effort to assist Colombia is central to instilling a new respect for human rights. A policy in favor of human rights is not simply a policy that denies assistance; it is a policy that uses its leverage to promote positive change.

Weighty Human Rights Restrictions

The restrictions on U.S. aid to Colombia's military carries perhaps the most rigorous human rights restrictions and requirements of all U.S. military aid. In addition to the required Leahy human rights vetting for all units receiving U.S. training or assistance and the standard human rights stipulations attached to any foreign assistance, as discussed in Chapter 2, U.S. law requires that the Secretary of State certify that the Colombian military takes steps to significantly improve its human rights performance. Specifically, the law allows appropriation of 75 percent of funds prior to a determination and certification by the Secretary of State with the remaining 25 percent dependent upon the Secretary's certification that Colombia is meeting several human rights-related criteria, including:

- Suspending members of the Armed Forces, of whatever rank, credibly alleged to have committed gross violations of human rights or to have aided or abetted paramilitary organizations
- Vigorously investigating and prosecuting members of the armed forces, of whatever rank, credibly alleged to have committed gross violations of human rights or to have aided or abetted paramilitary organizations, and promptly punishing those found to have done so
- Cooperating with civilian prosecutors and judicial authorities in such cases
- Severing links with paramilitary organizations
- Dismantling paramilitary leadership and financial networks.[43]

This certification process, while yet to lead to withholding of significant funds, has served as a primary source of leverage on the Colombian government. Further, while NGOs rightly and vigorously protest that the certification process has been demeaned by continued funding, despite less than convincing certifications by the Secretary of State, the policy process and mere existence of the congressional requirements prove to be critical conduits for input from key observers. It is the certification process that has served as a window for NGOs to voice discontent, add to the debate, and ensure that pressure on the Colombian military remains rigid. In a sense, it is the U.S. policy process that provides the greatest angst for the Colombian armed forces.[44]

Complimented by Robust Human Rights Promotion

While human rights activists argue that the Colombian military has failed to meet congressional criteria on numerous occasions, it is undeniable that the U.S. military has played a role in helping the Colombians significantly improve human rights awareness. The U.S. military's human rights engagement efforts with Colombia include $2.5 million, dedicated to standing up a military penal justice system and a military human rights school. The impact, while certainly not a total success, as noted briefly below, is by most accounts impressive and serves as a model for military legal and human rights reform in Latin America.

The Colombian military's legal and human rights infrastructure and capabilities far outstrip what was almost a nonexistent legal human rights framework prior to the influx of U.S. assistance in 2000. Since 2000, the

Colombian armed forces, relying almost completely on U.S. assistance, advice, and training stood up the military's first Judge Advocate General Corps or Military Penal Justice Corps (MPJC). The MPJC is home to 320 lawyers, including 90 human rights and military justice instructors. Complementing the MPJC, the military has established 288 legal offices around the country and human rights offices at multiple levels of command.[45] The MPJC has a direct impact on the armed forces' human rights performance by deploying human rights advisors in the field. The MPJC is working toward greater deployment in the field, transitioning from advisors to full operational planning support to ensure operations are legally sound and abide by all human rights and international humanitarian law standards, while also providing rank and file with operationally oriented training, such as Law of War and rules of engagement. MPJC lawyers also contribute to armed forces human rights offices and assist in human rights vetting.[46] The MPJC officers also focus on accountability for human rights abuses and are charged with investigating cases and collecting evidence in the field.[47]

The MPJC is moving toward providing increased military defense counsel for armed forces personnel charged with human rights abuses. Currently a military official charged with a human rights violation receives no basic defense counsel. Indeed, many officers purchase defense counsel insurance for this reason.[48] The provision of some type of defense counsel is a critical need in the Colombian military; both the State Department and a leading human rights activist have identified the lack of basic rights of rank and file officials as a critical stumbling block to better human rights awareness and performance.[49] As State notes, the lack of appropriate legal defense for those charged leads to a rallying around the troop syndrome in which the institution tries to insulate anyone charged, rather than defend them legally. In other words, leaving military officials with no defense counsel exacerbates impunity. Further, the human rights activist cited notes that legal rights for rank and file are critical to broad human rights awareness because it is difficult, if not impossible, to encourage strong human rights practices in the military if soldiers do not enjoy such rights themselves.[50]

The legal human rights impact of U.S. assistance is equally impressive in the military's establishment in 2003 of a JAG school known as the Colombian Armed Forces School of Human Rights, International Law, and Military Penal Justice. The school serves as the home for the MPJC and is the primary source of military human rights training for civilians, soldiers, and military officers charged with improving the overall armed forces human rights performance.[51] By the end of 2004, the school had trained more than 6,000 personnel.[52] In 2004 the Defense Ministry announced that the school would serve as the primary facilitator in designing and implementing human rights policies for the entire military.[53]

Working with SOUTHCOM's Human Rights Division, the Colombian Military has also worked to set a regional standard for human rights doctrine, training, monitoring, and enforcement. By 2006, the military will have rewritten all service, academy, and war college manuals to reflect regionally agreed upon standards of human rights and international humanitarian law.[54] The military's Human Rights Office Chief has also played a central role in promoting and facilitating SOUTHCOM's Human Rights Initiative as the single military official that has headed key panels along with three civilians during regional conferences. The Defense Ministry's commitment to broad human rights awareness in 2004 saw investment of nearly $650,000 to hold various training workshops on human rights and international humanitarian law.[55]

While institutional growth and investment in human rights awareness are notable, perhaps the best measure of Colombia's progress on the human rights front is the anecdotal evidence of the force's strong reputation. U.S. military and civilian officials across DoD and around the region consistently list Colombia's military as the most advanced, serious, and committed force in the region in regard to human rights.[56] SOUTHCOM officials have noted that Colombia is already doing nearly everything in the human rights arena that the Command would like to encourage the rest of the region to adopt.[57] Indeed, some U.S. officers note that Colombian officials likely are exposed to more human rights awareness than their U.S. counterparts.[58] Perhaps the best and most striking compliment comes from the International Committee of the Red Cross (ICRC)—which, in an effort to maintain neutrality, rarely will endorse a country for its human rights performance—in its contention that Colombia is among the top countries in the region in respecting and training for human rights and International Humanitarian Law.[59]

Strengthened Civilian Human Rights Programs Buttress Military Efforts

A critical and unique element of U.S. engagement with Colombia is that Washington appears to be taking a holistic approach to human rights promotion. Indeed, although many human rights activists call for greater balance between military funding and assistance for civilian justice, development programs, and democracy building efforts, the already significant outlays in these areas are proving critical to change in the Colombian human rights environment.

Colombia receives an annual average of about $150 million in U.S. assistance for economic and social programs, by far the highest amount of any government in the region.[60] Indeed, this funding far outstrips military funding for any other country in the region. Moreover, a large portion of these funds goes toward promoting human rights awareness and enforcement, complementing the already robust military programs.

The U.S. Agency for International Development (USAID) during 2004 committed almost $25 million to Colombian programs for human rights, justice, local governance, transparency, and peace initiatives and has sent Colombia similar funding for such efforts over the past several years.[61] Nearly one quarter of the allocated money goes toward human rights abuse prevention, protection, and response.[62] Funds also helped establish a human rights abuse early warning system in twenty regions of the country, allowing effective response during 2004 to 195 alerts and potentially preventing massacres, forced displacement, and other violations.[63]

The Department of Justice (DoJ) has also committed significant resources to the civilian efforts. As of 2004, DoJ had funded more that $40 million in judicial reform, security, and training, with more than half of the appropriations dedicated to establishing human rights units in the Colombian National Police and Prosecutor General's Office.[64] DoJ's efforts are central to Colombia's current transition from an inquisitorial to an oral accusatorial justice system. The Department, along with USAID, has held numerous training sessions and by the end of 2006 will have trained 3,000 prosecutors, 1,000 judges, 10,000 police investigators, and 1,500 defense attorneys. DoJ has also helped establish eleven satellite human rights units in the Prosecutor General's office in an effort to better coordinate and streamline human rights caseloads.[65]

Human Rights Promotion Still Faces Obstacles

While the general consensus among military, civilian, and NGO officials is that the Colombian military's efforts in the human rights arena have been vast, effective, and significantly bolstered if not dependent upon U.S. assistance, Colombia's military is not yet over the hump of fully consolidating human rights standards. Several interviews revealed that Colombian officials still push back on some human rights initiatives and that cultural bias, corruption, and institutional shortfalls linger.[66] For example, U.S. military officials reported that commitment to human rights at the lowest officer level is now a given, but that reticence at the mid to upper level remains, and uneducated conscripts complicate awareness efforts.[67] Indeed, the Minister of Defense fired the second commander of the MPJC in 2004 for what U.S. officials note was poor commitment to the mission.[68]

It appears that violence and conflict is such a way of life in Colombia that fully inculcating human rights will take time; the military as a whole has moved past simply seeing human rights awareness as box checking, but still is not to the point of seeing human rights as critical to victory on the battlefield. For example, field commanders continue to push back from transitioning from human rights advisors to full operational JAGs in the field, forcing U.S. officers to help devise internal lobbying plans for this effort.[69] Further, even while the military in 2005 signed a memorandum of action committing the force to all SOUTHCOM Human Rights Initiative standards, a top U.S. officer in Colombia noted that the effort seemed to have few teeth in Bogota because the Colombians assigned an officer of too low a rank to the program to enforce full military commitment.[70,71] Finally, institutional shortfalls, such as constitutional prohibition against a military defense counsel, leave the rank and file without their own rights and hamper full appreciation for human rights more broadly.

MODEST DEMOCRATIC GROWTH AMID ATROPHY AND OBSTACLES

As suggested in the thesis to this book, democratic growth and related civil-military trends have a critical impact on human rights in Colombia and U.S. military efforts to promote human rights in the country. Colombia's democratic stability, despite 40 years of civil war, appears to be strong and developing, allowing for human rights awareness to gain momentum and take root. At the same time, efforts to win the military battle and a long-standing culture of protecting wrongdoers that are on the side of the government hamper U.S. military human rights promotion and in some cases fully negate U.S. training and awareness.

The good news for U.S. human rights promotion efforts is that the Uribe government, in some key areas, is doing and saying the right things to help overcome what are major obstacles to consolidating justice and political openness in the country. Unfortunately, however, the same U.S. military forces that are on the ground promoting human rights also find themselves supporting military strategies that bode poorly for human rights, even if they are well suited for ultimately winning the civil war. In a sense, Colombia is grappling with its own tradeoff between promoting military policies that are critical to national security and respecting human rights in their entirety. Moreover, many of Uribe's policies have a dual impact of helping democracy in one respect while hurting it in another, or bolstering one category of human rights while damaging another.

Experiencing New Political Openings

On the purely political side of democratic development, Colombia in just the past few years appears to have made headway toward moving past a rigid political makeup toward a more inclusive political system. Uribe's victory in 2002 as an independent was a watershed moment for Colombia, which had been dominated by two parties for decades—the Liberal Party (PL) and Conservative Party (PC). While Uribe's victory as an independent arguably symbolizes a potentially unstable proliferation of political movements and parties creating the balkanization of Congress, his rise to the presidency also represents a break from a previous two-party monopoly on power that for years was maintained by the PL and PC though power sharing arrangements and has been at the center of the country's violent civil war. Colombia's political opening is also highlighted by the fact that in the past four elections neither major party has been able to win the mayoral seat in the capital, Bogota, and a far left-leaning candidate won the mayoral race in 2003. Further, the State Department and the *Economist* note that electoral victories of independents in local-level elections signal a further widening of the political arena.[72]

Political growth under Uribe is also taking place in his approach to governance. His disavowal of the traditional wide use of executive allocation of resources and political posts to gain legislative support is notable.[73] Uribe's reputation for transparency in dealing with Congress, along with his ability to bolster security around the country, has helped the president maintain his high approval ratings of around 75 percent, gain approval of a constitutional amendment to allow his reelection, and ultimately win reelection in early 2006.[74]

Political safety may also be on the rise. Violence has traditionally plagued Colombia's political system with numerous local level candidates murdered in the run up to elections and hundreds of mayors trying to govern their cities from satellite offices outside their constituent territory.[75] Under Uribe, this environment appears to be shifting with the number of mayors having to govern in exile declining from 340 in 2002, to only 3 in 2004.[76] Moreover, the Colombian government for the first time in decades has established a presence in all of the country's 1,098 municipalities—similar to U.S. counties. In other words, Colombia under Uribe has succeeded in overcoming what was a failure of the state to implement the most basic requirement of governance, government control over territory. When Uribe took office in 2002, 157 of Colombia's 1,098 municipalities had no federal government or police presence.[77]

Ratcheting Back Civil Liberties and Democratic Norms

While Uribe has arguably moved to adopt a more democratic, transparent governing style, his actual policies have been detrimental to some civil liberties, democratic growth, and civil-military norms, leaving little room for progress on human rights. A series of security-related efforts, including designating special emergency security zones, granting the armed forces special powers, using a network of 2.5 million civilian informants, and deploying so-called "hometown" or "peasant" soldiers have helped President Uribe bolster security, but at a clear cost to democratic norms. These policies have garnered accolades as necessary moves to increase security around the country while also attracting harsh criticism from human rights groups.[78]

Uribe is making a value judgment that sacrificing some civil rights and democratic norms over the short term will help win the civil war. Regardless of the value of these policies in winning the war, the president has undeniably sent a message that he is willing to walk back many basic rights. Indeed, some of his policies geared toward bolstering the government's war effort, while having proved successful thus far in improving the security environment, risk long-term damage to overall civil-military relations, could prove detrimental to a prolonged war effort, and ultimately undermine democracy and U.S. efforts to encourage human rights awareness in the rank and file. His policies are somewhat self-defeating and lack a balance that could bring victory in war with little damage done to human rights in general.

Promoting Special Military Powers

The president's efforts have included designation in 2002 of twenty-seven "special combat zones" around the country in which the military was able to conduct warrantless searches and restrict civilian movement, decreeing special military powers for arresting, wiretapping, and communications interception with only informal judicial approval, and passage of legislation amending the constitution to allow all such special powers without any judicial authorization.[79] Uribe's first effort to extend these powers by decree was ruled unconstitutional by Colombia's Constitutional Court, which also stripped the president of his special decree powers.[80] The president's subsequent effort, which led to congressional approval of special military powers as part of an "antiterrorist statute" that amended the constitution, also fell victim to the Constitutional Court, which struck the legislation down on a procedural technicality.

Regardless of the fate of these measures, or the perceived special need for these special powers during a time of civil war, the president set a tone for lifting the military above the law, undermining civilian judicial authority. Even if such measures proved critical to the war effort, they almost certainly would hamper military human rights promotion efforts, which have at their core respect for civilian authority, subordination to civilian judicial power, and unequivocal respect for civil rights. Numerous human rights groups have also condemned these measures as walking back basic rights, and the UN Human Rights Commission called the emergency powers a "step backwards."[81] One NGO study has captured the duality of Uribe's policies that seek to defend democracy while simultaneously damaging democratic

foundations by noting that "such measures erode the very democratic institutions that officials have committed to protect."[82]

Finally, these emergency policies in the name of fighting terrorism fly
in the face of historical lessons around the region. Certainly many readers will dismiss the above argument as ignoring the civil war environment
and security needs in Colombia. To the contrary, the point here is not
to diminish the strategic value, public desire, and perceived need for such
measures, rather, it is to point out a historical reality that such measures
have the lasting negative impact of blurring the lines between civilian and
military authority and nudging armed forces toward greater human rights
violations. An entire genre of scholarly work, as cited in the Introduction
to this book, has listed military mission creep and usurpation of civilian
authorities as key elements leading to past human rights abuses in Latin
America. Indeed, in several countries, including two of the worst violators during the 1970s, Argentina and Chile, military use of intelligence and
broad arrest powers as "antiterrorism" prerogatives were critical factors
in human rights violations, leading armed forces and civilian officials after the restoration of democracy to strictly foreswear such authorities and
practices.[83]

Employing Hometown Soldiers and Civilian Informants

The same dichotomy of defending democracy and stability through policies that run counter to democratic norms is ever-present in the Uribe administration's extensive expansion of military policies enlisting and using
civilians. So-called "hometown" soldiers are recruited, trained, and serve in
their local municipalities and appear no different than regular military personnel. As the State Department notes, they are "soldiers in every sense of
the word, who wear the same uniforms, use the same equipment, and report
through the same chain of command as regular soldiers." To their credit,
this now 21,000-strong cadre of hometown soldiers and 2.5 million civilian
informants appear to have played a significant role in bolstering security,
reclaiming government presence in municipalities, and have been completely
free of credible human rights abuse allegations. Still, these policies impose a
cost on civil-military standards.

While the hometown soldiers look like regular military soldiers, their
treatment, their role, and the mere tenor of their deployment is far from the
same. Hometown soldiers are paid only $20 per month, far less than their
professional counterparts and one-seventh the national minimum wage of
$140 monthly, which even falls short of providing a decent standard of living
for a worker and family, according to the State Department.[84] Further, the
soldiers have no regular military accommodations, often sleep in shelters
with no beds, and have no place for personal amenities.[85] State has called
their living conditions "Spartan," and one NGO report indicates that many

of the soldiers return home to sleep at night and work second jobs while off duty.[86] The soldiers' role as a true military official is dubious as the units are charged with enforcing public security and assisting local police, again blurring the lines between civil-military authority and encouraging mission creep. Further, as the Colombian Inspector General has noted, the hometown soldier program "made one sector of the civilian population more visible as a military target of the insurgency: the family members of the peasant soldiers."[87]

Use of civilian informants also raises the question of whether the president values the division between civilians and combatants. Certainly in civil war, like all of Uribe's extraordinary security measures, one can imagine the utility and argue the need for civilian vigilance and participation to secure the state. Again, however, regardless of the justification or effectiveness of this effort, it encroaches on internationally accepted standards of war.[88] A primary concern that this practice raises is the possible increased vulnerability of civilians to retribution and abuse. As backers of the policy note that the 2.5 million-strong informant network has yet to encourage abuses against the civilian population, and in fact, has helped the government reduce such attacks by making key intelligence available to military units. Uribe's administration even tried to tout the policy by running televised programs known as "Reward Mondays," during which hooded informants received cash for their participation in the program, a practice scrapped because of wide criticism.[89] Regardless the policy effectiveness in bolstering security, the practice risks breaking down the wall between combatant and civilian, leaving military and civilian indistinguishable to insurgent or paramilitary forces.[90]

Colombia's Geneva Protocol Conundrum

Part of Colombia's problem surrounding the human rights question is how the country has chosen to deal with the classification of its civil war as something less than an "internal armed conflict." The Uribe government's decision to essentially ignore or reject international humanitarian law on this subject helps explain many of the president's controversial internal security policies, particularly use of civilians. Protocol II of the Geneva Conventions is quite clear in defining an internal armed conflict as taking place in the territory of a country and "between its armed forces and dissident armed forces or other organized groups, which under responsible command, exercise such control over parts of its territory as to enable them to carry out sustained and concerted military operations..."[91] Further, the Protocol notes that it does not apply to "situations of internal disturbances and tensions, such as riots, isolated and sporadic acts of violence, and other acts of a similar nature, as not being armed conflicts."[92]

Any fair-minded observer can see that the Colombian conflict qualifies as a Protocol II-type internal armed conflict. The conflict is certainly more than simply an internal disturbance. The Colombian military is engaging dissident armed forces that are under responsible command, control vast areas of Colombian territory, and carry out sustained military operations. Indeed, while Washington has not pressed Bogota on this issue, even the State Department labels the civil war an "internal armed conflict."[93]

So why does Colombia not adhere to UN and human rights activist demands that the government declare its conflict a Protocol II conflict? In many ways this is a perplexing question. First, as noted above, the ICRC has praised the Colombian military's record in training and respecting international humanitarian law, suggesting that the force largely adheres to the Geneva Conventions. Second, if the conflict is not a Protocol II-type conflict, then international humanitarian law is trumped by regular human rights law, meaning that only the government can be responsible for human rights abuses, and that insurgent or paramilitary abuses are common crimes. In other words, the Colombian government can only reasonably and internationally condemn the FARC, ELN, and AUC for their gross human rights violations—which far outstrip violations by the armed forces—if the government agrees to hold its internal conflict to Protocol II classification and standards.

The answer to why Colombia holds out on the Protocol II question is essentially found in the policies detailed in this case study, those policies that skirt the edge of abuse of international norms in employing civilians and utilizing the country's armed forces. At a minimum, Uribe must realize that his extensive use of civilian informants would fall under scrutiny of Article 13 of the Protocol, which notes:

1. The civilian population and individual civilians shall enjoy general protection against the dangers arising from military operations. To give effect to this protection, the following rules shall be observed in all circumstances.
2. The civilian population as such, as well as individual civilians, shall not be the object of attack. Acts or threats of violence the primary purpose of which is to spread terror among the civilian population are prohibited.
3. Civilians shall enjoy the protection afforded by this part, unless and for such time as they take a direct part in hostilities.[94]

Certainly number three above would affect Uribe's 2.5 million-strong civilian informant network and those informants arguably would be seen by the Protocol as no longer enjoying protection afforded to civilians because they could be taking part in hostilities. Uribe has apparently concluded that his use of civilians in the civil war is more valuable as a security tool than is the ability to condemn illegal armed groups under the Protocol. Without doubt, Uribe's use of civilians is working as military intelligence policy, but this posture also flies in the face of international humanitarian law. Ironically, Uribe's decision may undermine his long-term security goal as those forces he fights to defeat enjoy the ability to reject the Geneva Conventions.

If nothing else, the president's use of hometown soldiers and extensive civilian informant networks raises the question of whether Uribe has learned from his country's own history and the possible negative impact of using soldiers and civilians in a way that skirts the line of officially sponsoring militia. As noted earlier, the paramilitaries were originally formed and equipped by the state in an effort to defeat the insurgency, a policy that went awry and has resulted in the government fighting a war against two enemies. The deployment of unprofessional hometown soldiers and maintenance of civilian informant networks is not far from the very practice that backfired some 40 years ago. As one NGO notes, "given the historical legacy of similar previous efforts, both programs present could result in the strengthening of existing illegal paramilitary groups."

The U.S. State Department dismisses such fears as mere misunderstanding. State's contention that the programs have been effective is well taken, but the Department's one-sided defense of Uribe security polices contradicts decades of U.S. military efforts to promote strict lines between civilian and the military roles and keep the military from engaging in domestic police functions. Indeed, even the most ardent supporters of U.S. military policy in the region question the virtue of encouraging military roles and missions that encroach on traditional civilian authorities.[95] Lastly, one only needs to look at Venezuela—covered in depth in the next chapter—to find U.S. condemnation of very similar security policies to those in Colombia. While Washington has championed Uribe's special security measures, it has vigorously and rightly noted that Venezuelan President Hugo Chavez's use of civilians for his national security plan is a threat to democratic norms.[96]

A Plague of Military Impunity

While the status of Colombia's democratic growth is mixed and Uribe's security policies pose a classic struggle between security and civil rights, the problem of military impunity in Colombia is a reality that all observers recognize as a critical stumbling block inhibiting the armed forces human rights performance. A sampling of key statements on impunity drives home the fact that the problem is paramount among Colombia's struggles to achieve peaceful democracy and almost certainly hinders U.S. military human rights promotion efforts.

According to the State Department in 2004, "Impunity remained at the core of the country's human rights problem. The civilian judiciary was inefficient, severely overburdened by large-scale backlog, and undermined by corruption and intimidation. Despite prosecutions and convictions of some members of the security forces, no high-ranking officers were convicted of human rights offenses." State further notes that "Impunity for military personnel who collaborated with members of the paramilitary groups remained a problem. Impunity remained the greatest challenge to the credibility of the government's commitment to human rights."[97] In congressional testimony in mid-2004, State commented about Colombia's failure to prosecute two high-profile human rights abuse cases, stating that it "remains troubling" that "the Government has not taken the opportunity to send a clear message regarding impunity for human rights violations and collaboration with the paramilitaries . . ."[98]

A major NGO publication in 2005 stated, "Colombia has made no progress toward ending widespread impunity for human rights abusers. In fact, the problem seems to be getting worse." The Latin America Working Group Education Fund in 2003 noted that "The military continues to reject human rights advocacy against impunity, often characterizing it as a politically motivated campaign against them." Commenting on the imperative need for judicial improvement in Colombia, the Inter-American Commission on Human Rights (IACHR) notes that "The high levels of impunity and ineffectiveness of the administration of justice in Colombia—which have been the subject of repeated pronouncements and recommendations by the IACHR and the Office of the United Nations High Commissioner for Human Rights—demand that the future investigation of the crimes perpetrated by the parties to the conflict be supported by clear provisions that are consistent with the international obligations of the State." Human Rights Watch, Amnesty International, and The Washington Office on Latin America have stated that "Colombia's military tribunals have established a virtually unbroken record of impunity."[99]

Rarely do U.S. government, multilateral institutions, and NGOs so closely agree on issues concerning human rights and justice. Indeed, the problem of impunity in Colombia is so widely recognized as prohibitive to the country's development and improvement of human rights generally that the government has gone out of its way to highlight the issue as a primary target of its "Democratic Security" strategy. President Uribe's national security strategy lists impunity as a key obstacle to winning the civil war.[100]

Uribe has gone on record stating in a letter to several U.S. Senators in 2004, "impunity and the shortcomings of the judicial system are a major concern of this administration."[101] Moreover, Uribe deserves credit for condemning military-paramilitary collusion and ordering it to cease. His government has made strides toward implementing judicial changes to reduce a massive backlog of more than 100,000 cases. With U.S. advice and funding, as noted above, Uribe's government has bolstered its Prosecutor General's human rights office. The Colombian Army Commander in 2004 dismissed 500 members of the service, many of whom were accused of human rights abuses or of ties to paramilitaries.[102] Finally, Uribe has accepted responsibility for human rights violations under previous administrations, agreeing to pay $725,000 in reparations to the families of eighteen civilians killed in an Air Force bombing in 1998 and $6.5 million, awarded by the IACHR to relatives of victims of a 1987 paramilitary massacre of nineteen civilians.[103]

A Shoddy Record of Justice

Despite what appears to be willingness, at least publicly, on the part of the Uribe administration to accept responsibility for impunity and the challenge of combating the problem, the judicial record casts doubt on the veracity of this commitment. Moreover, in spite of the major continuing judicial reforms, as one Human Rights Watch official has noted, it is not the judicial system or case load that is causing impunity, rather it is a lack of clear desire and commitment by individuals that perpetuates the problem.[104] Numerous accounts of lagging progress on cases with clear evidence of abuse or collusion leave little doubt that the impunity problem is still critical. Moreover, former Colombian Attorney General Osorio's own record is questionable in terms of his approach to key human rights-related cases.

The judicial record from 2003–2004 shows clear signs of lagging prosecutions, lenience toward high-ranking military officials, and lingering impunity in the courts.[105] For example, the Inspector General's office during the first 8 months of 2004 suspended only thirteen military personnel for human rights abuses or collusion and charged nineteen military officials with human rights abuses, which paled in comparison to NGO reports of several thousand military and paramilitary abuses during this same timeframe. The Prosecutor General's Human Rights Unit between July 2003 and August 2004 detained only twenty-one military officials for human rights violations or collusion, again a mere fraction of the total reported by NGOs. During 2004, the Prosecutor General sentenced no military officers and reached only one significant verdict, sentencing two sergeants to 40 years in prison for the kidnapping and murder of two former guerillas. Meanwhile, prosecutors dismissed a trial against General Rito Alejo Del Rio who was charged with establishing paramilitary groups, a move that the U.S. State Department notes as raising questions about Colombia's commitment to fighting impunity, given that the evidence against the accused was well documented and by most accounts vast. A trial against another general for omission of duty causing aggravated homicide and kidnapping remains conspicuously bogged down. Further, the primary witness against the general has been indicted for his role as the whistle blower in the case and remained in exile in the United States. The charges in a third case were dropped on appeal, and a fourth detainee escaped from prison. A total of thirty-nine military abuse cases remained ongoing as of August 2004.

Perhaps most discouraging in Colombia's battle against impunity is the poor record of the man that for several years was in charge of fighting the problem, former Attorney General Osorio. Osorio has earned a reputation as being soft on military criminals, particularly high-ranking officials alleged to have committed human rights abuses or collusion. The Attorney General's record has been the subject of much literature including an entire manuscript by Human Rights Watch denouncing Osorio's overt disavowal of cases against military officials, dismissal of and negative behavior toward prosecutors investigating abuse cases, and a general cultivation of fear surrounding pursuit of military human rights abuse cases.[106] During 2001–2002, for example, Osorio fired nine prosecutors working human rights cases and another fifteen resigned, including the lead prosecutor responsible for bringing charges in the above mentioned Del Rio Case, as well as prosecutors in the midst of key investigations against military officials.[107]

Beyond what Human Rights Watch has called a personnel purge of the Prosecutor General's office, their numerous interviews revealed a high penchant for allowing impunity. Employee's reported a general lack of support or resources to pursue human rights cases.[108] Several prosecutors reported that Osorio had failed to provide adequate security and protection for personnel who received death threats while pursuing military abuse cases, forcing them to flee the country.[109] Finally, remaining officials appear to have been demoralized. Human Rights Watch notes that several prosecutors reported a general lack of willingness in the office to pursue human rights cases.[110] One official reported that an employee, looking to avoid a situation that he judged might cost him his job, shelved a key case against Army officers.[111]

While the Attorney General and his backers—including the U.S. Department of Justice, which funds the Human Rights Unit—refute the above charges, serious problems and ongoing impunity are undeniable. Indeed, perhaps exemplifying the problem of impunity, little more than a year after the Human Rights Watch publication local media revealed corruption and paramilitary infiltration of the Prosecutor General's office, forcing Osorio to engage in another major personnel shakeup and institute new policies on internal vetting and employee investigations.[112]

Paramilitary Demobilization: Another Struggle between Security and Rights

Like most issues in Colombia, the issue of impunity has brought its own tug-of-war between security and democracy. Perhaps the most heated debate surrounding impunity during Uribe's tenure has been over his efforts to promote a legal framework to guide peace talks and demobilization of the paramilitary forces. The president in June 2005, after nearly 2 years of heated debate and various versions of legislation, won congressional approval for a framework package that grants certain immunities to paramilitaries willing to demobilize. The legislation includes the following provisions: paramilitaries guilty of crimes against humanity must demobilize and face a maximum of 8 years in prison; paramilitaries relinquish contact information, including name and place of origin; prosecutors must investigate and charge demobilized paramilitary personnel within 60 days of surrender; membership in a paramilitary group shall be deemed a political crime.

Again, we see a move by the president that he judges can significantly improve security by removing a key enemy from the battlefield, while human rights groups charge that his efforts bolster impunity and crime and do little if anything to dismantle the paramilitary structures. In this case, however, critics have charged not only that the legal framework pays short shrift to human rights but also that it risks worsening security in the country. For Uribe's part, the demobilizations thus far, even with no previous legal framework as a guide, have contributed to a major decline in the country's most worrisome human rights abuses. Indeed, the demobilization has been so large that it has significantly changed the dynamics of Colombia's internal war. Further, as even human rights activists have noted, offering zero impunity for the paramilitaries is not a realistic option, since such a strict requirement would effectively end peace talks.[113]

Still, NGOs worry that Uribe's legislation fails to achieve key requirements in several areas. For example, paramilitaries do not have to give up assets, reveal past crimes, or divulge the structure or workings of what was until 2006 the largest paramilitary group, the AUC. Human rights activists argue that with a maximum of 8 years in prison, these other immunities add up to near impunity. Indeed, several human rights experts list complete formal dismantlement of the AUC structure, rather than mere demobilization of individuals, as the single most critical factor in the demobilization process, which many argue is unlikely to take place under the approved legal framework.[114] Further, observers charge that the 60-day requirement for prosecutors to bring charges against demobilized paramilitaries nearly ensures impunity because it is short to the point of being preventative of any substantive investigation, particularly with hundreds to thousands of likely cases emerging out of demobilization. One prominent human rights activist opines that Colombia's recent record of declining human rights abuses will evaporate under a lenient demobilization framework.[115] The Center for International Policy's Adam Isacson has dedicated his recent assessment of the demobilization and peace process to arguing that no immunity deal at all is better than the current formula, which he sees as consolidating the transition of paramilitaries to Mafia-style organizations.[116]

Additionally, some have charged that the penalties against demobilized paramilitaries will be so lenient that the process has already lured common criminals to the table, claiming that they are paramilitaries and looking forward to light sentences with no requirement of relinquishing illegally procured assets.[117] The fact that thousands more paramilitaries actually demobilized than most observers originally thought existed—30,000 demobilized compared to 12,000–23,000 estimated actual forces prior to demobilization—lends credence to this argument. The UN has reportedly documented several cases of narcotics traffickers previously operating outside the AUC now claiming paramilitary membership.[118] Perhaps most troubling for the Colombian government is that the statutes allowing AUC members certain immunities could block some U.S. assistance; Washington has officially declared the AUC a terrorist organization and U.S. law restricts funding for programs that might assist terrorist groups. Further, the legislation's provision declaring membership to a paramilitary group a "political crime" could complicate extradition of criminals facing charges in the United States. According to a recent Congressional Research Service report, Congress in the 2005 appropriations bill mandated that State "not request funding for demobilization until the Department of Justice determines that the process is consistent with US antiterrorism laws, that the demobilizing groups are respecting a cease-fire and cessation of illegal activities, and that the legal framework eventually adopted not prevent the extradition of suspected criminals to the United States."[119]

CONCLUSION: BEST AUDIENCE, DUBIOUS ENVIRONMENT FOR HUMAN RIGHTS PROMOTION

Without exception, Colombia represents the greatest success story for U.S. military human rights promotion, as shown in the extensive implementation and cultivation of human rights awareness programs, policies, procedures, and institutions in the armed forces over the past several years. Without doubt, Colombia also drives home the reality that these human rights promotion efforts will be hindered, have minimum real impact, and perhaps even be undermined by lagging democratic civil-military standards and civil rights. In almost every respect, Colombia represents the worst and best of U.S. human rights efforts. The key thesis assumptions of this book that U.S. military human rights promotion can facilitate change, that bilateral relations—particularly military-to-military relations—can prove critical to human rights promotion, and that democratic growth—particularly in civil-military relations—is a critical factor for successful human rights promotion, find both their greatest supporting evidence and their weakest foundations in the Colombia case. Even the thesis assertion that human rights can prove critical in the U.S. war on terrorism finds a mix of contradictory evidence emerging from the facts of Colombia's own war on internal terror.

The military's embracing of legal human rights reform paints a picture of undoubted U.S. impact. In fact, the establishment of an entire institution around the promulgation of human rights awareness and the legal defense and support of such standards suggest the U.S. programs and assistance will have long-term impact beyond simple training and exercises, efforts that have limited value without institutional support. Expansion of the legal human rights promotion to the field of battle has been a key achievement, and would be significantly bolstered if U.S. efforts to install operational JAGs in the field of battle prove successful. Promotion of a defense cadre to help rank and file defend their own human rights also appears to be taking root and will prove critical to breaking down the syndrome of "rallying around the troop," which exacerbates impunity.

The Colombian abuse numbers, meanwhile, provide reason both to celebrate and to reflect on U.S. human rights promotion efforts. While Colombia deserves wide praise for significantly reducing overall abuses by illegal armed groups, selected data suggest that military abuses have risen and now make up a greater share of the total. Still, the worst abuses by paramilitaries have significantly dropped, and traditional accusations placed the blame for such abuses squarely on the military, suggesting some credit is due to the armed forces for this decline.

Even if one gives U.S. human rights promotion credit for modest to significant advances in Colombia, the challenges presented by failure to live up to strong democratic standards appear likely to hamper or even undermine such efforts. If we review the criteria set out in the Introduction for measuring democratic civil-military relations, two significant problems stand out; the armed forces do not fully comply with the orders of the president on the collusion issue, and civilian courts are grossly inadequate at holding military officials accountable to the rule of law.

Human rights promotion will be difficult if not impossible as long as rank and file defy the president's order to cease collusion with paramilitaries. Not only does collusion undermine the president's civilian authority, it has a direct impact on human rights, bolstering the ability of the country's worst abusing force. If military officials are unwilling to follow their president's orders to desist from helping the nation's worst human rights abusers, not only have U.S. efforts shown a critical weakness, but they face an almost insurmountable obstacle. Even if the military deserves credit for reductions in paramilitary abuses and the recent large paramilitary demobilization proves permanent, any future small-scale collusion leading to abuses would be a high-profile blemish on Colombia's record of human rights awareness.

With the president expanding military authority to include hometown soldiers, wide use of civilian informants, and special powers of search and seizure, military human rights promotion is also being rolled back. Uribe's orders in these areas, regardless of their positive impact on security, lift the military above the rule of law and blur the lines between civilians and combatants as well as between military and civilian roles and missions. U.S. human rights promotion has at its core the diffusion and implementation of stringent standards of doctrine, including roles and missions and use of force intended to keep the military out of situations conducive to human rights abuses. Uribe's policies, at a minimum, run counter to these efforts and threaten to confuse the division between civilian and combatant, a basic requirement for preventing abuse.

The problem of impunity, outlined in detail above, represents a blatant failure to fulfill the civil-military criteria of judicial authority over the armed forces and leaves Colombian military personnel with little to no impetuous or motivation for embracing human rights promotion. Indeed, the U.S. threat to withhold large amounts of assistance at this point far outstrips any domestic motivation for rank and file to abide by the law, particularly as it concerns human rights. As long as impunity persists and top commanders remain free from prosecution in cases that observers on all sides agree are clear-cut and troubling, human rights promotion will fall flat. Legal reforms, training, and operational law will all suffer if impunity is not drastically reversed. Few soldiers raised in a society of violence and trained to use all means necessary to win a war will give credence to the human rights message when judicial authorities offer no real enforcement against wrongdoing. Impunity equates to permission of abuse on the battlefield.

More than any case in this book, Colombia presents a reality that U.S. efforts may be at a plateau, that they should continue to nurture the changes that they have influenced, but should not expect more significant progress unless the Colombian state makes great changes. In other words, the factor of democratic development and civil-military growth and consolidation has proven to be the most critical variable in improving human rights in Colombia. Indeed, the problems caused by democratic retrenchment far outstrip the gains made by human rights promotion efforts. If there is a policy prescription moving forward, then, it is for greater U.S. emphasis on, and more stringent requirements for, democratic change in Colombia. This message is not new, in fact it reverberates through multiple NGO studies cited in this chapter that call wholeheartedly for more U.S. focus on democracy building. What is perhaps different in the message here is that this book does not call to bolster democratic assistance at a cost to security assistance; rather it shows that security assistance has recently proven critical to what appears to be a strengthening war effort and a resulting decline in paramilitary abuses. The best approach, then, would be to maintain security assistance while placing greater emphasis on the congressional criteria already in place regarding impunity and collusion. This book demonstrates that consolidating security does not come by cutting critical military aid, but by maintaining security funding—along with U.S. human rights promotion efforts—and bolstering U.S. insistence on combating impunity and collusion.

Counterterrorism and Human Rights Abuses Require the Same Prescription

In spite of the major challenges posed by Colombian democratic short-falls, the country's recent impressive overall reductions in human rights abuses make clear that human rights and security can go hand-in-hand. Military assistance must not only be accompanied by human rights promotion, but the ultimate factor critical to progress on both fronts is what President Bush has publicly promoted as the key to defeating terrorism; the spread of democracy. Simply put, this case has shown that the change that would best improve human rights in Colombia is a stronger commitment to basic democratic norms, the same democratic norms that the United States is championing as key to beating terror.[120]

The Colombia case, however, drives home the point that promotion of democracy in name alone is not enough to consolidate human rights standards. Further, publicly touting democracy's cause while walking back democratic norms and human rights in the name of defeating terrorism erects an almost insurmountable wall to the promotion of human rights in the military. A war on terror in Colombia that ratchets back the most basic standards of democracy is in essence breaking down the very institutions and norms the state is seeking to defend.

One need look no further than Colombia's history of first propping up and supporting paramilitaries to the current struggle with paramilitary abuses and military-paramilitary collusion to conclude that the war on terror is treading on dangerous ground when it includes programs such as hometown soldiers or networks of civilian informants. I have argued that the virtue of these programs as short-term war-fighting tactics is not in question, what is in question is their long-term impact and whether human rights will suffer. Certainly 40 years ago the Colombian government thought it was bolstering security and winning a war by arming self-defense groups, and almost certainly the defenders of those policies would have also argued that security outweighed the risks to human rights. Without doubt, they were wrong, and in fact, even the benefits to security have been outstripped and reversed over time. The end cannot justify the means when the means undermines the very end one strives to achieve.

Finally, the Colombia case holds a critical lesson for the United States in showing an often overlooked positive relationship between human rights and war; namely that successful war can contribute to improving human rights. The thesis to this book assumed that human rights promotion and awareness could contribute to success in the war on terror, what we see in Colombia represents the opposite side of the same coin; successful war can be an asset to human rights. Perhaps it should not be a surprise. In hindsight, the war on terrorism can be a just war; a war against "terror" itself is a war on human rights abuses, a war against the slaying and indiscriminant targeting of the innocent. No human rights abuse is worse or fits the definition used in this book better than terrorism itself. So the message then is that one may be able to measure success on the battlefield by calculating success in human rights.[121] While this is unquestionably troubling to those concerned with the spread of war, the point here is not to justify war, rather, the argument here is that when in war with terrorists as the enemy, as in Colombia, the reduction of human rights abuses is a signal that the terrorists are on the run. In other words, to win a war, champion human rights.

Perhaps the greatest lesson in Colombia for the U.S. counterterrorism strategy is yet to come. If the Colombian government is able to prevail in its war in the foreseeable future, what will years of human rights abuses in the name of security signal for Washington? One U.S. military official noted that central to the human rights reality in Colombia is that at the end of the day, regardless of who wins the war and when, "Colombians have to live with each other, they have to come to terms with their own people."[122] In a sense, he cast the term "winning hearts and minds" in a whole new light. For the United States traditionally winning hearts and minds was about winning on the battlefield, about nudging the ideological divide to your side by respecting the enemy's basic human rights. In Colombia's war on terror, winning hearts and minds extends far beyond the end of the war, and like their Latin America neighbors, signals that Colombia will be dealing with its human rights abuses for decades after this war has ended. What is the lesson for Washington? While there may be no human rights without liberty, liberty is a difficult proposition in a country, whatever country, where human rights is placed second to security, rather than made a part of it.

5

Venezuela: Human Rights Awareness Falling by the Wayside

Venezuela's increasingly poor relationship with the United States and the country's flagging democracy are key factors influencing the deteriorating military human rights record and are likely to foment further decay in military awareness and respect for human rights. United States–Venezuela military relations have dipped to an all-time low amid Venezuelan President Hugo Chavez's systematic dismantling and militarization of democratic institutions. With the deterioration of bilateral relations has come near elimination of U.S. human rights training and awareness for Venezuelan armed forces. Human rights violations by the Venezuelan military, while still relatively low, have become more prominent, and some red flags signal that more abuses are likely. The military is increasingly paying short shrift to human rights awareness, particularly in the capital and the border with Colombia where the security environments are often volatile. A worsening of the situation in the capital or along the border could serve as a catalyst for significant military human rights problems.

This chapter is geared toward showing how diminishing influence of the United States and democratic decay are contributing to a retrenchment of Venezuelan armed forces' respect for human rights. The first section is a scene setter that will introduce the reader to the changing, and often turbulent, political environment in Venezuela and the international criticism that President Chavez has attracted. The second section will detail the military's recent abuse record in Venezuela and a troubling shift in military attitudes toward human rights. The third section three will highlight the cooling of U.S.–Venezuelan relations as a key factor influencing the negative human rights trend, focusing on military-to-military ties and the breakdown of what was a good military human rights-related relationship. The fourth section will focus on the decay of democracy in Venezuela, positing that the retrenchment of several civil and political rights has set a negative tone for human rights in general, and the militarization of the government and society has helped cultivate an environment of military impunity. The conclusion will focus on fleshing out the links among the above trends, emphasizing the importance of the Venezuelan case for evaluating the impact of U.S. military human rights promotion.

SCENE SETTER: VENEZUELA'S DEMOCRATIC DISTORTIONS DRAW FIRE

In her trip to South America in May 2005, U.S. Secretary of State Condoleeza Rice stated about Venezuela, "It is not enough for a government to be elected democratically if it does not govern democratically."[1] This comment encapsulates the problem in Venezuela in which President Chavez—a twice-failed coup leader in the 1990s—has now simultaneously become perhaps both a beneficiary and an abuser of democratic processes in Latin America. Chavez can boast the strongest mandate among presidents in the region. He won election to the presidency in 1998 with 56 percent of the vote, the largest majority ever recorded in the country's then 40-year-old democracy. Chavez topped this performance in 2000 by winning 60 percent of the vote and reelection to a 6-year term under a new constitution. He subsequently survived a coup that removed him from power for 48 hours in 2002, and then emerged victorious from a referendum on his presidency in 2004. He now firmly holds the presidency, enjoys a coalition-based absolute majority in the 165-seat unicameral National Assembly, and won his latest reelection bid in December 2006. In essence, he has won four electoral contests and survived an assault on his presidency during the last 6 years, an unparalleled display of executive democratic strength in the region.

Chavez has been anything but a champion of democracy, however. The president has used his electoral strength to ratchet back some basic foundations of democracy, drawing the ire of human rights groups, democratic watchdogs, and the United States. Chavez has increasingly found himself at odds with Washington and international NGOs over a variety of democracy-related issues, especially abuse of executive power, violation of separation of powers, increasing militarization of the federal government, and military human rights abuses committed during anti-Chavez protests. Chavez's public embracing of socialism, open friendship with Cuban President Fidel Castro, and the promotion of an anti-American, populist "Bolivarian Revolution"— albeit so far rather unsuccessful in rallying Latin America's leaders—have added to the cooling in U.S.–Venezuelan ties. Media allegations that Chavez is supporting insurgent groups in Colombia and Chavez's announcement in early 2005 of several controversial security-related policies, including purchase of 100,000 AK-47 Russian machine guns and creation of a 1.5–2 million civilian militia, have deepened fissures with Washington.[2] Democratic watchdog groups and human rights NGOs have joined the call for Chavez to stop his manipulation of democratic institutions, particularly the judicial branch and the national media. Indeed, a unique characteristic of the Venezuela case is that it has recently drawn almost equal criticism from NGOs and Washington, a trend that is rare in Latin America where the United States often finds itself on opposite sides of debates with human rights groups.[3]

Chavez's indiscretions have also stoked opposition at home, making for a turbulent tenure in office. A poorly organized coalition of center-right opposition groups, including some current and former military members, has tried on various occasions to challenge Chavez's authority. Active-duty officers in 2002 formed a shadow armed forces command, fomented public protest, and forced Chavez from office for 48 hours, only to fall victim to condemnation by the Organization of American States (OAS)—albeit with implicit endorsement of the coup from Washington—the resurgence of pro-Chavez military forces, and reinstallation of Chavez as president.[4] In late 2002 and early 2003, the opposition nearly crippled the economy of Venezuela with a national strike that lasted 2 months and virtually shut down the state-owned oil industry. An OAS-brokered agreement in 2003 led to a recall referendum on the Chavez presidency. Charges of corruption, fraud, and manipulation by both sides plagued the referendum process, which finally resulted in Chavez's victory in August 2004 when he won 59 percent of the vote in a contest deemed largely free and fair by international observers.[5]

The combination of flagging respect for democracy, retrenchment of civil and political rights, an increasingly high profile of the military in society and government, and the military's record of increasing abuses is a ripe setting for evaluating whether U.S. commitment to military human rights has an impact, if the status of bilateral relations matter, and whether other internal factors influence the military's respect for human rights. Last, Venezuela's approach toward military policy and human rights may hold some lessons for the U.S. war on terrorism and possible implications for military human rights standards.

WORRISOME MILITARY HUMAN RIGHTS PERFORMANCE

A negative shift in the Venezuelan military's attitude toward human rights and the growing insecurity on the border with Colombia and in the capital have spurred an increase in abuses and risk, fomenting further problems or a human rights crisis down the road. Indeed, the military's apparent aloofness toward human rights, combined with security problems on the border and in the capital, could serve as better barometers of future events than the recent abuses themselves. As one UN official in Venezuela has noted, the military is relatively less aggressive than the forces of many Latin American nations, but it has begun an evolution toward a more negative, aggressive tenor, and the question now is how much faster will this evolution move forward?[6]

Slow Upward Trend in Abuses

Military abuses in Venezuela have slowly increased under Chavez, adding to the armed forces' progressively poor human rights record over the past 15-plus years. While many observers, military and civilian alike, label the Venezuelan military as a traditionally less violent force—relative to others in Latin America, such as the Colombian or Chilean militaries—the armed forces' human rights record has been tainted by its role in policing domestic crises. The military aggressively quelled violence during the 1989 uprising against government energy price increases that left some 250–300 civilians dead.[7] The military today is still grappling with abuse charges from this event, now known by Venezuelans as the *Caracazo*. In 1992 military intervention in a detention center led to 60 deaths. Civic action deployments to help deal with the aftermath of mudslides in 1999 led to several human rights abuse charges against the military.

While these events colored the military's recent history, the current trend of ongoing and persistent abuses, in particular, has drawn the ire of human rights groups. The head of a respected Venezuelan human rights NGO, Red de Apoyo, reported that since 2000, abuses have steadily risen as a result of the military taking on policing roles.[8] U.S. Embassy sources, including Red de Apoyo, have reported hundreds of abuses since 2000.[9] Red de Apoyo indicates that independently reported violations committed by the National Guard and the Army now surpass those of the national police, which historically had been a worse violator than the military. The military in 2004, for example, accounted for more than 25 percent of the almost 100 abuses reported to the NGO that year, far outstripping municipal and national police forces. Further, State notes that "while civilian authorities generally maintained control over security forces, members of the security forces committed numerous and serious abuses."[10]

The National Guard, in particular, has fallen under the public spotlight for its role in policing various anti-Chavez demonstrations in the capital that have left several dead and hundreds injured. Human Rights Watch on multiple occasions has strongly condemned the Guard's increasing use of excessive force and violence against demonstrators.[11] In 2003, the most violent year in the capital where the National Guard was the primary security force, the local NGO Committee for the Families of the Victims of February

1989 (COFAVIC) recorded 300 wounded by gunfire in political violence and 57 killed.[12] During the political violence in February and March of 2004, again with the Guard assuming primary security duty in the capital, NGOs recorded 16 deaths and 193 injured.[13] By 2005, everyday National Guard policing in the capital had become synonymous with abuses.

The Army has suffered its own increase in charges of abuse, particularly against farmers and refugees on the Colombian border. Red de Apoyo, the UNCHR, and a Venezuelan military officer all point to the border region as the greatest source of growing violence, abuses, and possible future human rights crises.[14] While the exact number of refugees is difficult to track, Venezuelan and U.S. reports indicate that the Venezuelan government during 2004 naturalized or granted residency to at least 300,000 Colombians on the border, and a vast majority of the violations reported to Red de Apoyo during 2004 were committed on the border.[15] The UN High Commission on Refugees (UNHCR) reports that human rights violations on the border still are not severe, but that the ingredients for a human rights or humanitarian crisis are brewing with abuses on the rise, large numbers of Colombians applying for naturalization, the Venezuelan military bolstering its border presence, and diplomatic tiffs with Colombia over whether Chavez is allowing insurgents safe haven in the area.[16] Moreover, the UNHCR indicates that Army application of human rights standards on the border is inconsistent at best.[17]

Negative Attitudes Portend Future Problems

While abuses rise in number and become a more regular occurrence, signs of institutional military disregard for human rights awareness amid increasing insecurity are of greater worry to human rights activists and military personnel. U.S. military officers commend the National Guard for its ability generally to apply the proper use of force, and to maintain respect for human rights in difficult situations, but, along with numerous local NGOs and human rights observers, note that the force as a whole has shown signs of retreating from established human rights standards.[18] The Army, traditionally a force with few human rights abuses and a strong partner of human rights groups and the United States, has also shown a recent penchant for disregarding human rights.

As security in the capital has worsened, particularly since 2002 when a series of large-scale protests began, the National Guard has established a worsening record of paying short shrift to human rights, sending a signal that the force does not perceive a problem and that it does not need to dedicate resources and energy to the cause. Officials from local NGOs and the U.S. Embassy note that the National Guard has a robust human rights office, but several officials, including a Venezuelan military officer, indicate that the office has little expertise and does not follow its own standards and rules. The same military officer notes that commanders have recently refused to support officer requests for increased U.S. military human rights training to help the National Guard avoid abuses in the face of additional policing duties in the capital. The officer indicated that training within the National Guard's human rights office is grossly inadequate to ensure that the force will avoid future abuses if called on to quell significant violence or demonstrations in the capital. Even in the face of what appears to have been clear abuses by National Guard officers, the force has virtually disregarded the problem. State Department reporting and U.S. military officials, for example, indicate that the Guard has recently promoted officers while the individuals were under investigation for abuses.[19]

This lackadaisical military approach is shared by the Army and has been particularly noticeable on the border with Colombia. NGOs, the UN, and U.S. military officials have indicated that a central problem in the struggle for Army human rights awareness on the border has been President Chavez's penchant for total control, which has included purging the force of U.S. influence and the creation of a more insular force geared toward shielding the military from outside criticism.[20] The UNHCR, for example, notes that Chavez has intentionally bred animosity among his border units, an attempt to ensure against any type of collaboration or collusion that could undermine his authority.[21] The president frequently rotates commanders, according to multiple sources in Venezuela, in an effort to maintain his control and limit the sharing and movement of information.[22]

With this insularity and constant command change has come a flagging interest in human rights training and awareness, and lacking attention to abuses. The UN, for example, reports that the Army since late 2001 has been much less willing to attend human rights-related training organized by the UN and given by the Red Cross.[23] Red de Apoyo and the UN note that the constant movement of commanders and officers makes human rights training and evaluation difficult, if not useless, since it would be intermittent at best.[24] Moreover, numerous experts in Venezuela indicated that the Ministry of Defense has taken little notice of the problem and that its human rights office is a poorly staffed façade without the training or authority to enforce human rights standards on the border or elsewhere.[25]

FLAGGING UNITED STATES–VENEZUELA MILITARY RELATIONS

The troubling human rights trend appears to be linked to the significant cooling of U.S.–Venezuelan relations and a corresponding decline in military-to-military ties. The current historic low point in United States–Venezuela relations has been characterized by the Chavez and Bush administration officials exchanging barbs on a weekly and sometimes daily basis. Chavez has openly fostered anti-Americanism, positioning himself as an icon of anti-United States movements around Latin America. Washington, meanwhile, has made it a priority publicly to lobby regional leaders to condemn Chavez's human rights abuses and antidemocratic actions. The dip in relations has also meant a decrease in Venezuelan armed forces exposure to U.S. military human rights promotion, further reducing prospects for the military's adherence to human rights standards.

The relationship has cooled to such a point that some fear it could deteriorate into political and even military brinkmanship. The relationship reached its low point in February 2005 with a diplomatic flap between Colombia and Venezuela after Colombian officials crossed the Venezuelan border to arrest an insurgent leader, an action that led to a temporary recall of ambassadors and for which Chavez blamed Washington.[26] Chavez's subsequent public claims that Washington had been planning his assassination brought the diplomatic rift to a peak. At the November 2005 Summit of the Americas in Argentina, both presidents again faced off. The Bush administration tried to sideline Chavez by pushing for a regional free-trade zone, an effort that failed. Chavez grabbed the majority of press coverage by speaking to anti-United States demonstrations and attempting to shift the focus of the Summit from democracy-building to fighting U.S.-led capitalism and trade.

This tense bilateral political environment appears to have nudged both countries' militaries to step back from what was once one of the closest military relationships in the region. My numerous interviews and a trip to Venezuela made clear that Chavez's anti-United States posture has been the primary driver of the decline in military ties. The rise of Chavez supporters in the military command has also led to diminished interest in collaborating with U.S. rank and file. The decay of the relationship has been accompanied by significant decreases in U.S. funding and training for the Venezuelan military—often at Chavez's behest—and a corresponding drop in bilateral military contacts.

U.S. Military Assistance on the Decline

The most obvious measure of decreased U.S. influence with the Venezuelan military is the dramatic drop in recent years in U.S. assistance for the country's armed forces, including funds for training, exercises, and equipment. In 1998, prior to Chavez's inauguration, Venezuela received more than $7 million in U.S. military assistance, the sixth highest recipient in the hemisphere.[27] By 2005, U.S. military assistance to Venezuela was scheduled at just above $3.5 million, representing a 50 percent drop in security-related funding over 7 years.[28] Venezuela's level of U.S. military funding now stands on par with small Caribbean countries such as Haiti, the Bahamas, and the Dominican Republic.[29] There has also been a significant drop in U.S. training of Venezuelan military personnel, which has fallen from more than 1,200 personnel trained in 1998 (fourth highest among all Latin American and Caribbean nations), to just over 250 in 2003, among the lowest of all countries in the region.[30]

While the numbers tell an empirical story of flagging military ties, the less observable but perhaps more important shift has been the decline in the normal give and take that characterizes close armed forces relationships, including officer-to-officer contact and Venezuelan exposure to U.S. professionalism. In 2004, for example, Venezuela directed the U.S. Mil-Group—responsible for managing military assistance programs with Venezuela—to close its offices on the Army base in Caracas.[31] The U.S. Mil-Group moved its offices to a smaller site in the U.S. Embassy and has since cut its staff and planning for U.S. assistance to Venezuela based on the already marked decline in funding and training. In April 2005, Venezuela capped this decline in military relations with an abrupt termination of a 35-year exchange program between the two countries' armed forces and an order for one U.S. student and four U.S. instructors immediately to leave their posts in the Venezuelan military academies. Moreover, Chavez's announcement cast doubt on the possibility of future exchanges of any type: "All exchanges with US officers are suspended until who knows when. There will be no more combined operations, nothing like that."[32]

Military Human Rights Awareness Suffers

The deteriorating relationship has reduced, if not halted, officer exposure to what was one of the military's primary sources of human rights-related training and programs. At the most basic level, the significant drop in U.S. assistance for Venezuelan units has led to a decrease in Leahy vetting of military units for human rights abuses, thus removing a key source of leverage for Venezuelan military vigilance toward human rights. In other words, with retraction of the carrot, so went the stick for encouraging a strong human rights performance.[33]

The more profound impact has come with the resulting drop in Venezuelan exposure to human rights-related training. All courses that Venezuelans receive from U.S. military counterparts include an element of human rights promotion; thus, the number of Venezuelan personnel exposed to human rights awareness has dropped along with the overall decline in U.S. training. More specifically, this decrease in training has meant a decline in the number of Venezuelan officers trained and certified in human rights at the Western Hemisphere Institute for Security Cooperation (WHINSEC) for the sole purpose of returning to their country to promote and monitor human rights awareness. Unsurprisingly, the director of the Human Rights Program at WHINSEC cited Venezuela as a country that had seen its earlier marked progress on the human rights front diminish.

A Venezuelan military officer with direct knowledge of the armed forces' human rights efforts noted that the number of officers receiving training in the United States, specifically on human rights, has dropped sharply in just the past 3 years. The officer noted that the cooling of bilateral re-lations was the primary reason for the decline in targeted human rights training of Venezuelan officials. As noted in the discussion surrounding the National Guard's human rights posture, senior officers rejected specific re-quests for more Venezuelan officers to receive U.S. human rights training.[34] Further, UN and NGO officials note that the presence of United States–trained officials in high-risk zones, such as the border, has sharply declined. According to Red de Apoyo, even when Venezuelan officers receive U.S. human rights training, the Chavez regime appoints them to regions or ar-eas other than the border, where they are unlikely to apply what they have learned.

The cooling relationship has also blunted Venezuela's participation in larger targeted programs aimed at bolstering the human rights performance of militaries in the region. Interviews with several U.S. military and civilian officials involved in promoting human rights in the region revealed a signif-icant drop in regular contact with Venezuelan military counterparts, often because U.S. officials see their Venezuelan counterparts as unapproachable, or because U.S. officials have concluded that there is little room for the suc-cess of military human rights programs with a government that is unfriendly toward Washington.[35] The sentiment at U.S. Southern Command (SOUTH-COM) appears to be that it is difficult enough to promote military awareness of human rights among friendly nations. With Venezuela, U.S. officials sense an increasing potential for President Chavez to distort and mischaracterize the Command's Human Rights Initiative (HRI)—geared toward forging con-sensus on military human rights standards around the region and attended by officials of nearly every Latin American country—potentially undermin-ing its utility.[36] HRI participants and SOUTHCOM officials alike uniformly express doubt and despair over what has been Venezuela's slow but marked distancing from human rights–related programs.

Since 2002, for example, Venezuela has been largely absent from the nu-merous SOUTHCOM-sponsored human rights seminars.[37] Moreover, the previously strong relationship between the SOUTHCOM Judge Advocate General (JAG) and its Venezuelan counterpart has collapsed. The JAG rela-tionship had led to the establishment of the region's first-ever oral advocacy court-martial system—a model for the humane treatment of armed forces personnel—and has now disintegrated.[38] Numerous JAG exchanges and seminars that were ongoing as late as 2001 seemed to have ceased by late 2004. Indeed, no U.S. or Venezuelan official interviewed seemed to have had any recent exposure to, or knowledge of, the previously strong United States–Venezuela JAG ties.[39]

DEMOCRATIC DECAY SIGNALING MILITARY IMPUNITY

The deterioration of Venezuelan democracy has compounded the nega-tive impact of flagging bilateral military ties and has set a bad precedent for how the government values human rights broadly, spurred a breakdown in the rule of law, and signaled impunity for armed forces personnel loyal to the president. Chavez has scaled back basic civil and political rights while systematically chipping away at the autonomy and transparency of institutions that are vital to democratic growth and consolidation. Human Rights Watch has listed the deterioration of everyday civil rights as the root cause of decay in Venezuelan rule of law and respect for personal integrity.[40] Further, through his militarization of the government, the president has granted the armed forces a preeminent status in society, breeding a lax military attitude toward human rights obligations.

Civil Liberties Under Siege

Venezuela under Chavez has received its worst scores on the widely respected Freedom House rating scale, which measures political and civil rights, since that program's inception in 1972. Since 1999, Venezuela's political rights and civil liberties have received ratings of four and five on a scale in which seven is the worst possible score. During Chavez's tenure, the country has maintained a consistently worse combined average score than at any time over the last 30-plus years.[41] This shoddy record is the result of Venezuela's backsliding on a list of civil and political rights, which has set a negative tone for human rights awareness in general.[42]

Judicial Independence Constrained

While judicial corruption and ineffectiveness plagued the judicial system before Chavez's rise to power, the president has exacerbated these problems with his unscrupulous politicization of the courts. Chavez has significantly reined in the independence of the Venezuelan judicial branch through coercion and court packing. Human Rights Watch has vigorously condemned Chavez's manipulation of the judiciary, which included expansion of the Supreme Court in 2004 from twenty to thirty-two members and introduction of a provision that allows for relatively easy removal of justices with only a simple majority vote in the unicameral legislature.[43] The new law allowed Chavez's congressional coalition to appoint the twelve new judges by a simple majority vote in 2004, as opposed to the previously required two-thirds vote that ensured greater support across the political spectrum. In essence, the new law gave Chavez and his governing coalition the ability to maintain a politically friendly Court.

The law served to further politicize an already-problematic judicial branch that has recently summarily fired judges for handing down rulings in favor of Chavez opponents and provides no judicial tenure to judges, a standard mechanism for allowing independence from the other branches of government.[44] Exemplifying the political influences in the judiciary was the 2003 decision by the administrative judicial body, known as the Commission of the Functioning and Restructuring of the Justice System, to dismiss three federal judges and shut down the country's second highest court after it had ruled in favor of local-level challenges to Chavez security policies.[45]

Freedom of the Press, Free Speech Threatened

Chavez's relatively good record of respecting freedom of the press and free speech early in his tenure has deteriorated to the point where examples of restrained speech and media are now vast. Chavez has shown a penchant for censorship, government control, and intimidation of journalists. At the center of the president's attack on the media is the Law of Social Responsibility in Radio and Television, passed by Congress and signed by Chavez in late 2004. The law restricts broadcast of specific content and is billed as an effort to protect children from crude language, sexual content, and violence.

In fact, the law appears to be a veiled attempt to control and punish opposition to the president under the guise of reining in Venezuela's often-promiscuous media. For example, the legislation requires television and radio stations to air government educational, informative, or public safety broadcasts, preempting scheduled programming for up to 60 minutes per week. The law restricts broadcasts that include violence of any kind, including disasters, political conflicts, and criminal events to the hours of 11:00 P.M. to 5:00 A.M. The law established an eleven-member Directorate, seven of which are government appointees including the Directorate President hand-picked by Chavez, to enforce the new regulations. The body has the ability to fine a station up to 1 percent of its income if it airs content that the Directorate unilaterally deems an affront to the integral education of children or adolescents. The body can also punish broadcasters for anything it deems as inciting a lack of respect for government authorities. Human Rights Watch has charged that the legislation's "vaguely worded restrictions and heavy penalties are a recipe for self-censorship by the press and arbitrariness by government authorities."[46]

Chavez has also abused his already-excessive authority to inhibit media freedom under the 2000 Organic Telecommunications Law. After declaring a "year of the war against the media" in his 2003 state of the nation address, Chavez began persistently threatening to use his authority under the Telecommunications Law to unilaterally suspend any broadcast when he deemed it in the national interest to do so. State Department sources claim that the government has increasingly abused the Telecommunications Law requirement that all broadcasters preempt scheduled programming and transmit government messages (cadenas) in their entirety. Cadenas reportedly increased from 73 hours in 2002 to 162 hours in 2003, and to 280 hours in 2004.[47]

Chavez's onslaught against free press and speech has also included allowing only government radio and television stations at the presidential palace. Amnesty International and the State Department have documented numerous accounts of government or Chavez-backed militias intimidating journalists.[48] Further, the federal government in March 2005 implemented amendments to the country's criminal code, expanding the scope of existing protections that outlaw insults or disrespect against the president, vice president, government ministers, state governors, and members of the Supreme Court. The Code now expands the criminal offense to include insults or disrespect against national legislators, members of the National Electoral Council, the attorney general, the public prosecutor, the human rights ombudsman, the treasury inspector, and members of the high military command, all of which are dominated by Chavez loyalists.

Freedom to Associate and Gather Limited

While opposition groups have continued to have considerable freedom to gather, Chavez has aggressively sought to dissuade individuals from association with such groups. The opposition to Chavez has successfully organized numerous large-scale protests—often numbering in the hundreds of thousands—over the past several years with little or no restriction. The government, however, has actively sought out opposition members for reprisal. In 2002, Chavez decreed the establishment of eight federally controlled security zones in the capital, usurping municipal security and authority to permit demonstrations, a move critics claimed limited their freedom to gather.[49] In 2003 and 2004, Chavez ordered the blacklisting of those that had signed the petition calling for a referendum on his presidency. The Venezuelan press and U.S. Department of State reporting indicates that the government denied students internships, relieved military officials from duty, and denied passports to petition signatories.[50]

The author experienced the fear of association first hand. Several opposition members agreed to meet with U.S. officials and me only in specific public venues that they deemed safe. Active-duty and retired military officers noted their worries of being followed by, and retribution from, Chavez-backers. One officer requested to remain anonymous in this book and a second refused to meet with me to discuss human rights issues.

Government Militarization on the Rise

Perhaps the most troubling sign of democratic decay in Venezuela is the military takeover of civilian roles and institutions. As noted in the Introduction to this book, academicians have reached a virtual consensus that lack of civilian control of the military and significant military involvement in civilian institutions are key ingredients for engendering military impunity and spurring human rights abuses.

Relative to the rest of Latin America and the Caribbean, which have experienced a new spike in democratic instability since 2000—Argentina, Bolivia, Ecuador, Peru, and Haiti have seen one or more presidents fall from power during the last 5 years—Venezuela has the worst record of broad military encroachment on power. Indeed, the one silver lining that has emerged out of the most recent cases of instability in the region has been the relative obedience of military forces to civilians, and in most cases, the complete lack of military involvement in the removal of presidents.[51] In Venezuela, meanwhile, Chavez has systematically inserted the military into almost every realm of government and civilian life, and even those military officers that oppose him have disregarded civilian control, as witnessed by their 2002 coup attempt.

Several Venezuelan human rights activists and the UNHCR indicate that a key obstacle to democratic growth and the strengthening of human rights in particular has been Chavez's almost indiscriminant militarization of the government.[52] Numerous active and retired military officials hold high-level government positions outside the armed forces. Six of Chavez's twenty-one Cabinet ministers are retired military. Active-duty military officers head three major state-owned corporations.[53] The president himself has disregarded the principle of civilian control by delivering public addresses in military uniform.

The president's penchant for militarization has also carried over to civil-society more broadly through the creation of armed militias and civilian reserves. Chavez's so called "Bolivarian Circles" have an official role of mobilizing self-help initiatives and government responses to local needs, but the media have widely charged that these groups serve as armed street gangs, Chavez foot soldiers, and paramilitary groups that enforce the president's will.[54]

Chavez's most blatant affront on civilian democracy came in his early 2005 announcement of plans for a new military doctrine that includes division of the country into reserve districts and the mobilization of 1.5–2 million civilian reservists who will receive military training and possibly arms, without formally enlisting. The plan essentially stands up massive local militias and calls on the public to receive resources and training from the military in the name of defending sovereignty. In an overt perversion of democracy, and perhaps typifying the general mood of the Chavez government, the commander in charge of standing up the militia publicly stated that Venezuelans must be aware that participatory democracy includes a civilian role in the country's security system.[55]

Not only does the planning for this militia fly in the face of democratic norms, it is a sign that Chavez cares little about the likely complications for human rights, including a major deficit of professionalism, lack of human rights training, and aggressive militia interaction with civilians, all likely to worsen an already troubling human rights record. The human rights program director at WHINSEC lists the five most common causes of abuses as a lack of training, leadership, supervision, clear and concise orders, and discipline.[56] A two million-strong civilian militia almost certainly serves as a glaring invitation to a deficit in all the above.

Finally, the militarization of the government and society has granted the armed forces certain immunity from the law, exemplified by the impunity officials enjoy in the corrupt, politicized, and inept judicial system. As noted above, Venezuelan judicial problems predated Chavez's rise to power, but a glaring shift under his rule, in additional to politicization and manipulation of the courts, has been toward the favorable treatment of security forces and a lack of punishment for those who commit human rights abuses. As Amnesty International states in its observation of demonstrations and violence in Caracas in early 2004:

> [T]here is a clear disparity in the urgency and resources made available to investigate and prosecute those suspected of participating in or encouraging the week of demonstrations, compared to official efforts to investigate and prosecute those members of the security forces or police allegedly responsible for or complicit in human rights violations. While the systematic ineffectiveness of the judicial system pre-dates the present administration—denying access to justice to large sections of the population—the increasing lack of impartiality in the functioning of key security and judicial institutions, such as the military . . . is further undermining the rule of law.[57]

The State Department has also noted judicial lenience toward the military in cases involving abuses. State notes that prosecutors selectively target opposition leaders while rarely bringing charges against perpetrators of unlawful killings. Even when the judiciary files charges against security forces for human rights abuses, the cases typically linger in the courts with little or no forward movement, according to State.[58] State has further noted that few torture cases result in convictions, and investigations of security forces are intermittent at best. To paraphrase Amnesty International, the judiciary's unwillingness and inability to prosecute security forces for such abuses is a central feature of the country's recent history and a fundamental factor that weakens the rule of law.[59]

CONCLUSION: U.S. ENGAGEMENT CRITICAL, BUT VULNERABLE

The Venezuela case shows that a country that has an established military human rights relationship with the United States may see a decline in armed forces human rights performance if the relationship falters, particularly if accompanied by the decay of democracy. The long-term impact of U.S. military human rights awareness appears weak at best, and has been easily reversed by souring bilateral relations and the mere stoppage of persistent U.S. emphasis. Thus, while helping advance my argument that consistency of U.S. policy is a factor for success, the Venezuela case suggests that application of U.S. military human rights awareness and influence must be consistent and permanent.

Perhaps most important in this case is the overall deterioration of democracy and human rights in Venezuela. As suggested in my thesis, democratic development, specifically civil-military democratic consolidation and respect, would be critical to the success of U.S. military human rights awareness. In Venezuela, the lack of democratic development, and in this case democratic retrenchment, is proving a factor influencing military impunity and a lack of respect for human rights in general. President George W. Bush in his 2005 inaugural address opined that political rights must come before integrity of the person, in stating that "there can be no human rights without human liberty."[60] The Venezuelan case certainly suggests that lack of civil and political liberties can slowly encroach on other rights and foment an environment conducive to abuses of the person. Moreover, even if one credits Chavez with democratic credentials for having won elections, his militarization of society and the government appear to have lifted the armed forces to a place of prominence in which human rights problems are dealt with at the military's convenience rather than as a necessity.

If we measure Venezuela's democratic civil-military status against the criteria defined in Chapter 1, the country fails across the board. First, while large portions of the military do follow the president's orders without question, these forces are also enjoying an overt encroachment on civilian roles and authority, perverting the ideal of civilian control. Indeed, the president appears to grant military personnel favoritism over civilian public servants. In essence, civilian control is of little value if the civilian in charge is calling for military dominance of traditional nonmilitary institutions. The norm of civilian control calls for subordination of the armed forces, and is incompatible with the idea of a civilian controlling a military-run state, which Venezuela may well be slowly becoming. Finally, even those military officers who are not Chavez loyalists fail this test, having tried to oust the president as late as 2002.

Second, Venezuela has no framework of civilian supervision that meets the criteria detailed in the Introduction and employed by Mark Ruhl and Samuel Fitch. Rather, civilian control is dominated by the whims of a single person who does not even champion the norm. Chavez has perverted his civilian authority into a form of military subordination in name only. The only framework of civil-military supervision that appears to be emerging in

Venezuela—with increasing military control and authority over civilians—is essentially the opposite of what we have defined in the Introduction as consistent with the advancement of human rights.

Military submission to civilian judicial jurisdiction is almost a moot point because of the Venezuelan judicial branch's excessive politicization and loyalty to the president. Moreover, the preeminence of military power in the government and society appears to have lifted armed forces personnel above the law. With few if any prosecutions moving forward against human rights violators in the military, it is clear that Venezuela's democratic military development is severely lacking in enforcement. Indeed, several individuals told me that while the Venezuelan constitution is a strong document in terms of judicial authority and civilian jurisdiction over military abuses, in practice, the constitution serves little or no purpose to the Chavez government or military.[61]

The future for military human rights in Venezuela, therefore, is grim. With political tensions persisting in the capital and insecurity on the rise on the border with Colombia, abuses are likely to increase, particularly in the face of large-scale social, political, or military events in either area. Since the beginning of 2005, Venezuela has bolstered security forces on its border and has had several diplomatic flaps with Colombia that signal such an event is increasingly probable. Moreover, Venezuela may not even have control over the events that spark a humanitarian crisis, particularly if the Colombian war were to drive mass refugee movements across the border.

The U.S. military, meanwhile, has little recourse. With President Chavez systematically eliminating U.S. military influence from the rank and file and drawing down even the most long-standing cooperation agreements with DoD, the window of opportunity for inculcating better respect and awareness for human rights is closed for the moment. While I note the importance of persistence in the thesis, it is too much to expect repeated U.S. military programs to become foundations resilient to political change like that in Venezuela. U.S. military human rights promotion is only one of many factors that may contribute to greater human rights awareness, and cannot be expected to withstand a concerted government push in the opposite direction. Indeed, it is notable that in the Venezuela case, U.S. influence on military human rights behavior appeared particularly easy to block and reverse.

A Lesson for U.S. Counterterrorism Priorities

While this case fails to directly engage or address the counterterrorism–human rights relationship, a compelling lesson emerges from the details, namely that Washington should heed the connection between military mission creep and deterioration of human rights practices in the armed forces. Indeed, a troubling reality for the United States is the possibility that human rights observers and other Latin American nations will detect a hypocritical message from the United States, on the one hand condemning Venezuelan military encroachment of democracy, militarization of society, and human rights abuses, and on the other hand promoting counterterrorism-related military policing in more friendly countries around the region.[62]

For example, Chavez's most egregious plans to violate civil-military norms in forming a militia can be found in Colombia, where the government has called upon "citizen soldiers" to defend against insurgents, all with U.S. backing. While an arguably effective defensive military strategy, the tactic mirrors Chavez's actions and almost certainly poses similar problems of spurring human rights abuses, by breaking down civil-military separation and employing poorly trained civilians in national security. In the Venezuela case I caught myself prepared to argue that during the past close U.S.–Venezuelan military relationship, it would have been highly unlikely to see a militia promoted by Caracas, only to be repudiated by my own findings of U.S. encouragement of similar plans coming out of Bogota. Moreover, Venezuelan employment of its military in policing roles is increasingly common and encouraged by the United States throughout the region, where instability often overwhelms police capacity.[63]

In essence, the United States can observe in Venezuela the negative impact of counterterrorism policies that Washington backs in other countries around the region. Not only does the lesson of military mission creep create a credibility problem for the United States, it poses a conflict between foreign policy priorities. The Bush Doctrine clearly calls for fighting terrorism through the spread of democracy and freedom. The Venezuela case forces us to ask where the United States will come out when the military tactics for fighting terrorism run counter to, and often break down democracy.

If a country was to adopt military policing and civilian vigilance identical to that in Venezuela but in the name of fighting terrorism, and these polices proved effective while also significantly damaging democratic norms, would the United States favor the reduction of terror at a cost to democracy? More importantly, if military practices defeat terrorism at the cost of also harming democracy, has terrorism been permanently stifled, or will the lack of a strong democracy foment its reemergence? Lastly, if military policies run counter to democracy in the name of fighting terrorism, are we again seeing promotion of democracy reduced to mere rhetoric, similar to the façade of democracy that the United States often backed in Latin America during the cold war, or is the commitment to democracy paramount to the point that Washington will oppose any military policies that substantially threaten democracy and human rights?

6

At a Critical Juncture: Military Human Rights Promotion in the Counterterrorism Age

U.S. military human rights promotion today finds itself at a crossroads between achieving prominence as a critical element of the war on terrorism and losing significant ground to a policy approach that promotes a narrow definition of security. Chapter 2 of this book argues that the United States must reject the notion of a zero-sum tradeoff between promoting security and defending human rights, that it is in fact possible for the United States to assist a country with security while also insisting on—and actually promoting—improvements in its human rights record. In other words, security and human rights are codependent, not mutually exclusive. Unfortunately, the trend toward a more prominent role for human rights in foreign and security policy appears under threat now that we have moved from an era of relative peace to one of war. The war on terrorism and its various implications for civil and political rights and the integrity of the person pose a challenge to a critical assumption of this book that U.S. military human rights promotion can and will prove effective, and play a positive role in an overall counterterrorism strategy.

The human rights problem emerging from counterterrorism policy is not a surprise to most readers who have watched the many debates about treatment of prisoners in Iraq and Guantanamo. What is recognized now is deeper exploration of the relationship between U.S. counterterrorism policy and U.S. military human rights promotion on the ground. This chapter will assess the increasing tension between counterterrorism policy and military practitioners' mandate of promoting human rights. The Colombia case study reminds the reader that the effectiveness or necessity of Colombian security polices was not the critical question addressed by this book, rather, it was how security policies, regardless of their effectiveness, affected human rights promotion. The objective of this chapter is similar; it will discuss various aspects of the U.S. war on terror in terms of their impact on U.S. military human rights promotion, regardless of their tactical short-term effectiveness. This chapter will show that a central complication of counterterrorism policy is that it undermines U.S. goals in other critical areas, such as military human rights awareness. Moreover, some policies that appear effective at bolstering security in the short term are likely to undermine long-term security goals that have democratic growth as a key objective, particularly if the policies pay short shrift to human rights promotion. This chapter is not geared toward championing human rights at the expense of security, for the true challenge is finding the critical balance between security and human rights, a balance that U.S. policy in the region found over the past three-plus decades, and should seek to maintain during the counterterrorism age.

This chapter will assess human rights promotion in the context of post-9/11 counterterrorism policy and argue that human rights promotion can benefit U.S. counterterrorism policy. The following four sections will draw on some case study findings from the body of this book, while also bringing in new relevant information gained from extensive travel and research in a majority of Latin American countries. The first section will briefly review the literature that has helped set the parameters of the debate surrounding counterterrorism and human rights. The second section will highlight three key counterterrorism-related events that have affected, and promise to continue to challenge, the legitimacy and strength of U.S. military human rights promotion efforts in Latin America. The third section will detail three opposing trends, i.e., trends that signal the endurance of human rights promotion in the region. The conclusion will briefly detail key findings with emphasis on why and how human rights promotion can and should be a central factor in the U.S. war on terror, particularly in Latin America.

HUMAN RIGHTS REEMERGES AS A TOP POLICY DEBATE

This book's case study conclusions signal that the war on terror is again pushing Washington into a position of choosing between security and human rights, a challenge that hearkens to cold war-era tradeoffs. Indeed, the war on terror has sparked a proliferation of scholarly work detailing how and why Washington's counterterrorism approach has chipped away at the attention to and respect for human rights and the United States' ability to serve as a key proponent of human rights around the world. A sampling of relevant works, representative of several approaches to the issue, reveals a broad consensus that human rights has suffered during the war on terrorism, while debate rages over the extent of the damage to human rights and the level of U.S. culpability.

Jack Donnelly has argued that human rights has seen largely unintentional retrenchment during the war on terrorism. He has noted that the Bush administration has not consciously and overtly downgraded the place of human rights in foreign policy, but that "the overriding emphasis on combating terrorism has shifted (always limited) attention and resources from human rights. [T]he space in US foreign policy for human rights and democracy has been significantly reduced—not by design, but no less surely, and with unfortunate consequences for the international struggle to realize human rights."[1] In essence, Donnelly is recognizing a real retrenchment of human rights, but not one that is either intentional or irreversible.

Like Donnelly, Kathryn Sikkink has concluded that while counterterrorism will pose a difficult challenge to human rights, human rights will not suffer total retrenchment, and further, is likely to win out in the end. She eloquently notes:

> Some observers believe that the human rights era may be over; others fear that the war on terrorism is also going to be a war on democracy. There is no doubt that human rights policy is receiving the most severe questioning since its inception in the 1970s. Antiterrorism appears likely to replace anticommunism as the new guiding force of US foreign policy. And yet, exactly because the United States was never the main initiator or promoter of global human rights policy—and because human rights norms are embedded in regional and international institutions and in the foreign policies of diverse states around the world, and are promoted by a wide range of groups in global and domestic society—human rights policy is far more resilient than some pundits suggest.[2]

Kenneth Roth is far more pessimistic than Sikkink and places more blame on Washington than Donnelly for deliberate acts that have walked back human rights. He argues that the Bush administration has compromised the long U.S. engagement on human rights in a variety of ways, including intentionally allowing lax human rights standards for states like Pakistan and Indonesia that are willing to assist in the war on terror; refusing to be bound by the standards it insists others be bound by—such as the Geneva Conventions; and opposing enforcement of international human rights law from the International Criminal Court (ICC).[3] Unlike Donnelly, Roth sees Washington as intentionally limiting the space for human rights in foreign policy, stating that the Bush administration "refuses to be bound by human rights standards . . . rejects legal constraints . . . seems to want an international order that places no limits on its own actions."[4]

Tom Farer and David Forsythe have examined the impact of counterterrorism on human rights from a more theoretical perspective. Farer uses the war on terror to exemplify the current predominance of what he calls "neo-conservative" approaches to U.S. foreign policy. Farer charges that at the center of neoconservative security strategy is a sort of crusade for democracy as the primary vehicle for combating terrorism. He notes that no matter how moral or noble this crusade, it puts at risk some human rights—primarily integrity of the person, as defined in this book—that cannot be abrogated under any circumstance.[5] Farer, a self-coined "liberal hawk" notes his support for military intervention in cases of gross inhumanity, but argues that the war on terror must be balanced, weighing predictable collateral damage against the costs of human inaction. While leaving room for military action, his overall message is one of warning: "A crusade for democracy, even full-blown liberal democracy, overlaps but is not synonymous with a crusade for human rights." Simply put, Farer argues that integrity of the person trumps those democratic civil and political rights listed as a primary concern by "neoconservatives."[6]

Forsythe's thesis, similar to Farer's in tone and approach, looks at human rights through an ideational lens, through which a mix of approaches to foreign policy explains the current depletion of human rights on the foreign policy hierarchy. He casts the Bush administration as ultimately "unilateralist" and "ultra-nationalist" and paints the administration's emphasis on democracy and democratic growth as the primary vehicle to defeating terrorism as noble in principle, but in practice a largely rhetorical element justifying American "exceptionalism." Like Kenneth Roth, he blames Washington for ratcheting back human rights through a sort of hypocrisy, promoting democracy where it fits and ignoring authoritarian rule where convenient. Forsythe concludes:

> The rhetoric from Washington has not changed, and the administration still sees itself as the global leader for enlarging the democratic community. But in reality, the emphasis on a war against terrorism as the defining characteristics of the administration means that US officials cannot help but be ineffective in influencing political reform in allies and would-be partners in the short term. Foreign leaders know very well that the real Bush emphasis is on cooperation in the war on terrorism, not on democratic change that might undermine the power of the very leaders that are offering various types of concrete support to the US.[7]

Outside academe, various authors have taken a more tactical policy-specific look at the impact of counterterrorism on human rights. Haugaard, Garcia, and Anderson provide a blow-by-blow assessment of U.S. counterterrorism policy and its negative impact on human rights in Latin America, particularly Washington's stance on the ICC and congressional efforts to reduce human rights requirements attached to foreign assistance. The authors reach a similar conclusion to those above that 11 September "affected human rights, both by reinforcing the Bush [a]dministration's instinct to view human rights as of secondary importance, and by eroding the United States' moral authority to critique other governments' human rights practices."[8] They argue further that the war on terror has had particular resonance in Latin America where human rights abuses have been linked with fighting terrorism for decades.[9] The authors are particularly critical of Washington's policy toward the ICC and the events at the Abu Ghraib prison. For example, they note that Abu Ghraib "had a predictable and disturbing impact on the United States' ability to champion human rights abroad, including in Latin America."[10] They argue that the U.S. effort to sidestep the ICC "undercuts US credibility in calling for Latin American security forces to face prosecution for human rights abuses—which continues to be one of the most important human rights issues in Latin America."[11]

Despite widespread concern over the impact of 9/11 on U.S. promotion of human rights, the extent human rights has suffered and the intentions of the Bush administration remain subjects of intense debate. Further, the debate is largely limited to stand-back assessment of policy impact and the theoretical underpinnings of foreign policy approaches and their relationship to human rights generally. This book can illuminate these issues by assessing what is happening on the ground, evaluating the impact of counterterrorism on human rights broadly, as well as the specific relationship between the war on terror and human rights promotion. The case studies in this book and the fieldwork as a whole allow for a deeper look at working-level factors in the war on terror that help and hinder military human rights promotion in Latin America, and a more general conclusion about the survivability of human rights as part of U.S. security policy and strategy.

THREE COUNTERTERRORISM SETBACKS FOR HUMAN RIGHTS PROMOTION

Promoting human rights in Latin American militaries is already exceedingly difficult, especially as forces grapple with democratic shortfalls and lagging civil-military standards, as shown in all three cases in this book. Unfortunately, U.S. Department of Defense (DoD) personnel, whether charged solely with promoting human rights or simply making the issue a central part of training for Latin American armed forces, now face the greater challenge of defending their efforts against an increasingly tarnished U.S. human rights record. The war on terrorism has inserted a new dynamic in the human rights promotion arena, the dynamic of defending, justifying, explaining, or apologizing for U.S. human rights practices in fighting terrorism. The preeminent challenge for human rights promoters is to explain to Latin American officers why they should do something—respect human rights during war—which the United States often shuns.

The U.S. human rights record since September 11, 2001 has been of particular interest to Latin American countries for several reasons. On the one hand, many officials around the region are following the fight against terrorism that most countries in the region feel they fought during their own internal conflicts over the past several decades. Indeed, while typically seen as struggles against communism or leftist insurgents, the internal conflicts in most countries around the region since the 1960s included insurgent use of terror, something militaries typically used as justification for aggressive internal security measures and human rights abuses. In Argentina and Chile in particular, the militaries are infamous for labeling their 1970s-era struggles against revolutionaries as battles against terrorists.[12] More recently, the Peruvian government during most of the 1990s engaged in what it saw as a struggle against terrorism as much as against an ideology. In Colombia today the war is taking on a counterterrorism tenor that is overshadowing counternarcotics or ideological aspects of the conflict. Regardless of how outside observers see these characterizations, the Latin American military perception is that they have been engaged in wars on terror and now the United States is experiencing similar pains that such wars portend.[13] This sentiment is greatest when it comes to human rights; the United States is experiencing the trials of balancing human rights with counterterrorism, something Latin American governments dealt with over the past three decades, often drawing Washington's ire.

This attention to the U.S. war on terror and its impact on human rights is amplified for those Latin American officials charged with instilling human rights in the armed forces and who are looking to the United States for guidance. The U.S. war on terror has resonated to such an extent that its impact on human rights is now a top bilateral issue between various governments and the United States. Moreover, the author has found Latin American distaste for what is perceived as a clear contradiction between U.S. human rights promotion and the low priority of human rights in the U.S. war on terror. The author does not wish here to denigrate U.S. human rights promotion efforts; rather the goal is simply to point out that DoD human rights operators increasingly face an uphill battle. In fact, it is with interviews of dozens of U.S. military officials around Latin America and the United States that the author is able to offer an assessment of key challenges to human rights promotion. Interviews and field research reveal that military human rights promotion faces its greatest challenge in convincing host nations that in light of events in Abu Ghraib, Guantanamo, and Washington's approach to the ICC, the U.S. promotion of human rights in Latin America and elsewhere is not simply hypocrisy.

Abu Ghraib, A Critical Setback, A Motivating Event

The abuses at the Abu Ghraib prison in Iraq represent a sort of loss of innocence and credibility for U.S. military officials working to promote human rights in Latin America. The research for this book began more than 6 months before the Abu Ghraib abuses hit the international press, and even then the author was encountering numerous U.S. military personnel who were warning that the war on terrorism would present a critical obstacle to human rights promotion in Latin America.[14] These officials were not in a position to know if any wrongdoing was happening after the initial invasion of Iraq in March 2003, but they were already sensing a shift in the legal paradigm concerning human rights, and for them the writing on the wall seemed clear: the war on terror would setback U.S. military human rights promotion in Latin America.

While there was early concern, it was also clear that these human rights operators in the field already had a positive mindset. One Judge Advocate officer noted that the counterterrorism issue almost certainly would muddle the human rights arena, but he noted adamantly that counterterrorism should not bring a repeat of the 1950s–1980s' disregard for human rights and that he sincerely hoped the United States had learned a lesson from this era.[15] Unfortunately, the Abu Ghraib events proved highly detrimental to U.S. efforts in human rights promotion and the lessons of the 1950s–1980s immediately rose to the forefront as Latin American military personnel from around the region turned to their U.S. counterparts and asked why and how institutional abuses were taking place in U.S. military prisons. As one U.S. human rights advocate—well-respected by the U.S. military—noted, Abu Ghraib damaged his own belief and ability to argue that the U.S. military has never been trained to torture.[16]

When Abu Ghraib broke, Latin American military officials across the region began questioning the legitimacy of U.S. efforts to promote human rights. Various U.S. military officials interviewed by the author indicated that the Abu Ghraib events were the most significant setback to U.S. human rights promotion in Latin America to date.[17] First, the resonance of the abuses in Iraq appears to have been universal among Latin American military personnel. U.S. military officers in all eight South American countries the author visited after the Abu Ghraib events mentioned that Abu Ghraib had spurred their Latin American counterparts to comment on Washington's own approach to human rights and whether it fit what U.S. military officials were trying to encourage in their respective countries. Indeed, the author found real evidence of concern that Abu Ghraib had an immediate detrimental impact on U.S. military human rights promotion efforts. For example, U.S. Southern Command (SOUTHCOM) officials listed Abu Ghraib as a "black eye."[18] A senior U.S. diplomat noted that some observers in Latin America now say that because of Abu Ghraib, the United States can no longer claim a high ground in promoting human rights.[19]

Perhaps as striking as the widespread negative impact of Abu Ghraib is the positive and forward leaning attitude of U.S. military officials on how to take advantage of the negative events at the prison for positive gain in the struggle to promote human rights. Key U.S. personnel in charge of shaping and implementing U.S. military human rights promotion efforts noted in earnest that the most important impact of Abu Ghraib should be its utility as a teaching tool and a critical lesson learned.[20] The U.S. military already widely uses the Vietnam My Lai massacre as a central case study for showing Latin American officials that the U.S. trainers do not see themselves as exceptional or immune to abuses, rather, the United States is a country that has committed abuses that U.S. and Latin American officials can use as lessons learned.[21] Several U.S. military officials have already adopted the same mindset and approach toward the Abu Ghraib abuses, looking to use it in the classroom and in the field as a key example of military behavior gone awry and of subsequent reasonable government treatment of such problems.[22]

SOUTHCOM officials note that the Command would present Abu Ghraib as a learning experience rather than burying the issue in disgrace.[23] Western Hemisphere Institute for Security Cooperation (WHINSEC) instructors—at the same institution that has endured more than a decade of accusations that it intentionally trains Latin Americans to engage in abuses— emphasized that the single positive impact of Abu Ghraib is that it will show that human rights abuses are detrimental to war.[24] Two U.S. military in-structors commented that the distraction of Abu Ghraib from the war effort alone was enough to make one understand that you must "get it right" when it comes to human rights, or your military efforts will suffer.[25] A third instructor and well-known defender of U.S. military policy in Latin America noted that he feels that the United States should go further in condemning senior military officers responsible for allowing Abu Ghraib abuses and had written to President Bush indicating his feelings about the negative impact of Abu Ghraib on the U.S. military.[26] Multiple U.S. mil-itary officers around the region noted that the Abu Ghraib case should be used as a key example of what not to do in battle, and one officer indicated that he had already used Abu Ghraib as a learning experience by taking several Latin American counterparts to the United States where they viewed congressional proceedings moving forward on the Abu Ghraib case.[27]

Guantanamo Discounting Civil Liberties

While Abu Ghraib served both as a setback and motivator for U.S. mili-tary human rights promotion, the legal approach to treatment of prisoners at Guantanamo has emerged as a policy contradiction to U.S. military human rights promotion efforts that emphasize civil rights and responsible civilian judicial behavior. U.S. classification of prisoners as "enemy combatants" who are not protected by the Geneva Conventions is a policy that under-mines other SOUTHCOM objectives, such as human rights promotion, and sends a message that civilian control of the military is detrimental to human rights.

Many in the media and human rights community have recently focused on physical treatment of prisoners at Guantanamo, but a more significant impact on Latin American military officials has been the legal treatment of prisoners. This book has revealed that a leading, if not the central obstacle, to full consolidation of human rights awareness in Latin American militaries is impunity and ineffective judicial behavior and practices. Further, this book has shown that where civil rights suffer, such as in Colombia and Venezuela, there is a higher risk and propensity of military human rights abuses. The U.S. decision to hold prisoners as enemy combatants, as opposed to prisoners of war or another category defined by the Geneva Conventions, has sent a message to the region that civil rights and judicial professionalism is of secondary concern to security. Perhaps security is the ultimate goal and concern of the U.S. administration, but at a minimum, Washington must recognize the negative impact on human rights promotion efforts in Latin America, regardless of the security justification for such policies.

The Guantanamo case in particular resonates with Latin American military officials working with their U.S. counterparts to instill greater human rights standards and practices. First, the prisoners—held without internationally recognized rights to legal defense—are in Latin America's backyard, thus the level of attention in the region is particularly high.[28] The issue is particularly problematic for U.S. human rights promotion efforts in Latin America when the officials receiving U.S. training on international humanitarian law are left with few answers as to why the United States is undermining these very international norms just miles away. Second, Guantanamo falls under the responsibility of SOUTHCOM, the same Command championing human rights around the region, pushing for memorandums of action on human rights standards, and requiring the U.S. military's most rigorous human rights training attached to military assistance. In essence, the operators at SOUTHCOM charged with bolstering human rights are having the rug pulled from beneath them by their own command, which is carrying out policies that are 180 degrees opposite of SOUTHCOM human rights teachings.

SOUTHCOM leadership should not bear the brunt of criticism for promoting contradictory policies. The treatment of prisoners outside the Geneva Conventions is a policy imposed on the military by civilians. One of the great ironies that have emerged during the counterterrorism era is that military officials who know, respect, and believe in human rights standards for both moral and strategic reasons are seeing decades of progress reversed by their civilian superiors. One long-time human rights advocate commented that the United States is ironically showcasing a weakness of civilian control—a norm that Washington has tirelessly worked to promote in Latin America as central to military professionalism and respect for human rights.[29]

SOUTHCOM Judge Advocate General (JAG) officers are open about their resentment of the low civilian standards for prisoner treatment. JAG officers, for example, openly argue that the United States was mistaken in not declaring the so-called "enemy combatants" as civilians captured in combat under the Geneva Conventions.[30] One DoD JAG officer noted to the author that the Department of Justice would define treatment of prisoners that the military would then have to carry out and which would draw criticism from Latin American officials.[31] While this book was being written, three U.S. Air Force JAG officers had requested transfers from their positions at Guantanamo because they felt personally unable to carry out what they labeled "rigged" military commission hearings of prisoners.[32] Perhaps exemplifying the disconnect between civilian policy and military standards is Secretary of Defense Rumsfeld's public correction of a U.S. Army General who gave a tour of Guantanamo to the Secretary and media in 2002. When the General suggested to the press that the Guantanamo prisoners are treated according to the Geneva Conventions, Rumsfeld went out of his way to note to the General and the audience that the Geneva Conventions do not apply.[33]

Article 98, Breeding Resentment and Weakening U.S. Influence

The Article 98 issue—an effort by Washington to acquire agreements from foreign governments to not extradite U.S. military personnel to the ICC—has stoked perhaps the strongest resentment toward Washington from across Latin America.[34] The combination of trying to gain immunity for

Table 6.1. U.S. Article 98 Posture in Latin America[35]

Has not signed an Article 98 agreement, aid suspended	Barbados, Bolivia, Brazil, Costa Rica, Dominica, Ecuador, Paraguay, Peru, St. Vincent and the Grenadines, Trinidad and Tobago, Uruguay, Venezuela
Signed Article 98 agreements, aid unaffected	Antigua and Barbuda, Belize, Colombia, Honduras, Panama
Has not ratified Rome Statute, aid unaffected	Bahamas, Chile, Dominican Republic, El Salvador, Grenada, Guatemala, Guyana, Haiti, Jamaica, Mexico, Nicaragua, St. Kitts and Nevis, St. Lucia, Suriname
Major non-NATO Ally not subject to jurisdiction of the American Service-Members' Protection Act, aid unaffected	Argentina

possible U.S. human rights abusers, disavowal of an established and United States-signed international humanitarian treaty, and suspension of military assistance for those refusing to grant U.S. exceptions has been detrimental to U.S. military human rights promotion efforts in multiple realms. At the core of U.S. requests for Article 98 agreements is an inference of U.S. exception from the very human rights and international humanitarian standards U.S. military personnel are working to encourage. This exceptionalism has caused bilateral relations with Washington to cool with a number of governments around the region. Further, suspensions of military assistance have sent a message inconsistent with the norm of military respect and deference for civilian political affairs. Finally, by harming bilateral relationships, the policy of penalizing militaries actually detracts from U.S. leverage to encourage human rights.

Across the region, numerous U.S. officials reported to the author that the ongoing push for Article 98 agreements is a central source of bilateral friction between Washington and Latin American governments.[36] Many of the same officials noted that Latin American officials almost uniformly voice their regret that Washington has gone to lengths to distance itself from the ICC.[37] In particular, Latin American officials stress that the message they are hearing is one of American exceptionalism—whether this is what Washington intends or not.[38] The Article 98 issue, for example, has spurred bilateral fissures across the Southern Cone where countries typically maintain close military-to-military ties to Washington. In Brazil and Chile, the governments have been firm in their support for the ICC, even in the face of cuts in tens of millions of dollars in military assistance.[39] Paraguay and Uruguay, relatively small and presumably pliable, given the prospective loss of significant assistance, have also rejected U.S. Article 98 pressure. In Argentina—the region's only major non-NATO ally and thus exempt from the any Article 98-related assistance cuts—the government has still gone out of its way to voice opposition to U.S. pressure on the issue.

Where Latin American officials have appeared more willing to consider Article 98 agreements, the message to the military has been one that degrades judicial authority and undermines human rights promotion. In the Bolivia case, we can see first hand how the Article 98 issue sent mixed messages to the armed forces and the government as a whole on the military human rights issue. As noted in Chapter 3, at the same time the government was grappling with a landmark bill geared toward ensuring civilian jurisdiction over military human rights abuses, the U.S. Article 98 agreement was moving through the Bolivian Congress, undermining an effort to instill military respect for, and subordination to, civilian entities. In Colombia, one of the few Latin American countries to agree to an Article 98 exception, the message to the military is clear; if the United States is immune to international humanitarian standards, Colombia has grounds and cover for denying Geneva Convention application to its internal conflict.

Pressure on the Article 98 issue from Washington also has many Latin American officials wondering why the United States is imposing penalties on armed forces for a policy that is negotiated and decided by civilians. Again, the policy undermines a central aspect of U.S. military human rights promotion: the subordination of military officials to civilians and removal of military influence from civilian affairs, something the United States has worked for decades to encourage. As U.S. officials engage their civilian counterparts on the issue, Latin American military personnel either feel helpless to influence the issue or that they must look for a way to nudge their civilian colleagues in order to protect a primary source of military funding.

At best, military officials feel that U.S. efforts to encourage their removal from the political realm has now come to haunt them as they see funding slip from their hands. At worst, military officials feel that the circumstance and pressure from Washington are so unique that it justifies backdoor influence on civilians in an effort to protect their own prerogatives. Simply put, the perception by some Latin American officers is that they are suffering because their civilian counterparts do not agree with U.S. policy on a single issue. Peruvian officers, for example, feel Washington is telling the armed forces that the United States will punish them for something their civilian authorities reject, while simultaneously telling the military to refrain from interfering in politics, according to a U.S. officer.[40] One civilian DoD official reported that Latin American military officers are complaining that they now have to suffer cuts in funding because they have no influence over civilians, largely because they have followed the U.S. lead in respecting civilian control.[41]

Finally, the Article 98 approach seems to be a poor strategy that complicates U.S. foreign relations and has an immediate and direct negative impact on human rights promotion. Indeed, this policy has perhaps the most observable, tangible impact of all issues discussed in this chapter because of the real decrease in military-to-military relations, contact, and influence resulting from cuts in U.S. funding. By penalizing numerous countries around the region, the United States effectively undercuts its own military assistance policy, which is meant almost entirely to assert influence and promote U.S. ideals, and which has human rights at its core. U.S. military assistance, as noted by Nina Serafino and cited in Chapter 1, is typically justified by Washington as a vehicle for spreading U.S. ideals and influence; it is not simply a policy of need-based aid. Further, every dollar that was destined for training or equipping Latin American forces and is now suspended under Article 98 restrictions represents a real decrease in Leahy mandated human rights vetting and SOUTHCOM mandated human rights training. In simple terms, a reduction in U.S. military assistance directly equates to a reduction in human rights awareness. As this book has shown, human rights is now integral to U.S. security policy toward Latin America, and if bilateral ties are weakened, human rights promotion suffers. One need only contrast the Bolivia and Colombia cases with the Venezuela case to see that the two former saw significant human rights benefits from a close bilateral relationship with Washington, while the latter lost focus on human rights as U.S. influence on Caracas waned.

Military officials appear to agree that Article 98 is bad policy. SOUTHCOM Commander Craddock in his 2005 posture statement blasted the policy of suspending military assistance because it opens the door for third country influence in the region and limits critical U.S. military access to Latin American counterparts.[42] SOUTHCOM's congressional relations office reported to the author that Article 98 would diminish U.S. influence by reducing the number of Latin American personnel trained by the United States and by depleting overall military-to-military relations.[43]

Further, even in countries like Bolivia and Peru, where military relations have remained strong in the face of Article 98-related funding cuts, the impact of the policy on human rights promotion is likely to be negative. In these cases, funding and assistance is shifting from State Department foreign assistance to DoD military assistance programs that, as several human rights groups have noted, tend to have less rigorous human rights requirements. A group of NGOs reports that military assistance funded through DoD has seen dramatic increases since 2002 while State programs have increased only marginally.[44] While Leahy vetting also applies to DoD security assistance, U.S. officials in the field complained that the shift of funds had confused the process, and that it had become unclear what constituted appropriate vetting for DoD programs versus State.[45] Moreover, shifting funds sidesteps some 30 years of legislative record and precedent in applying rigorous oversight and attention to State-funded programs, so human rights standards that have developed as a part of standard U.S. security policy are at risk of retrenchment, unless Congress quickly recognizes the funding trend and applies equal human rights focus to DoD programs.

THREE SIGNS OF ENDURING HUMAN RIGHTS PROMOTION

While much U.S. policy has had a negative impact on U.S. military human rights promotion, several factors signal that human rights can overcome the obstacles and remain a critical part of U.S. policy. Donnelly and Sikkink have argued that human rights has not seen a complete retrenchment; this section corroborates that assertion in showing that there exists productive resistance to a full walking back of human rights in foreign policy, particularly military human rights promotion.[46] Field research revealed resilience among U.S. military human rights advocates who see human rights not just as a policy assignment, but as a critical element of winning wars. The reality on the ground is that U.S. military personnel—at least those working on Latin America—genuinely view winning hearts and minds as a strategic objective and take the challenge seriously. Indeed, this section will show that military personnel are a key source of hope for survival of the human rights-centered policy approach that this book has detailed and assessed as productive.

Three trends suggest that human rights promotion will successfully overcome the setbacks described above. First, the human rights promotion efforts are ongoing and increasing amid the uncertainly cultivated by the war on terrorism, suggesting that regardless of mixed messages and policy contradictions, SOUTHCOM has mandated human rights as a continuing priority. Part of what emerged out of field research for this book is the reality that warfighters and human rights activists agree more than they disagree, something made apparent by the ongoing military struggle for human rights promotion. Second, past counterterrorism-related abuses in the region weigh heavy on Latin American policymakers who are likely to prove resilient to pressure, and—at least with some more progressive governments, such as those in Brazil and Chile—more open to a human rights-centered war on terror. As noted in the concluding section to the Colombia case study, several countries, particularly in the Southern Cone, push back on U.S. efforts to blur the lines between military and civilian roles, helping foster the message and position of human rights activists and military practitioners alike. Finally, current Latin American problem areas, such as the three case studies in this book, are likely to resonate with leaders around the region as key lessons learned and foster greater acceptance of military human rights promotion.

Military Working to Maintain Human Rights Promotion

Perhaps the least obvious but most critical factor favoring the endurance of U.S. military human rights promotion in the counterterrorism era is that the efforts have continued and arguably increased over the past several years. Indeed, they have persisted amid civilian efforts to impose on the armed forces policies that subvert human rights—as detailed above. While civilians look for avenues to ratchet back civil rights, find loopholes in international humanitarian law, and push for U.S. human rights exceptions around Latin America, military personnel are on the ground working to ensure that human rights standards grow strong and that Latin American militaries see beyond the morass of counterterrorism toward the ultimate goal of winning the battle for hearts and minds.

A SOUTHCOM official suggested to the author that the research for this book would reveal an understanding, knowledge, and desire for human rights promotion among military personnel that often outstrips that of their civilian counterparts.[47] The problem is exemplified by the Article 98 and Guantanamo policies, civilian imposed mandates that military officials appear to resent. In the end, the explanation for the surprising and unexpected fact that armed forces personnel are more tuned in to human rights than their civilian colleagues is that military personnel have a strategic objective as the top priority, and they know that victory will prove elusive if human rights is given short shrift. Civilians often appear to see security in a single dimension—military defeat of the enemy—rather than a holistic view that includes winning the approval of a population and respect and loyalty of fence-sitting onlookers.

Further, a sign of the stamina of military human rights promotion in the counterterrorism era is the fact that there exists a broad consensus across military and civilian officials of all stripes that human rights is critical to counterterrorism. Despite current high-level civilian adoption of policies that violate human rights standards, the vast majority of individuals interviewed by the author—from academics and human rights activists to U.S. and foreign civilian and military officials—indicated that human rights promotion could only help and could never hurt military operations. This consensus across military and civilian circles was perhaps the least expected and most encouraging finding of the research the author conducted for this book. Of dozens of individuals interviewed, only a handful suggested that human rights awareness carries some risk to military operations, but only when soldiers misunderstand standards and application of humane treatment in combat and fail to act against a clear threat to security for fear of violating human rights standards. Even these individuals, however, noted that a true understanding of human rights standards and appropriate use of proportional force could only facilitate, not inhibit military operations, such as counterterrorism.[48] Indeed, the overarching trend that emerged from the author's field research signaled a sentiment that human rights would not harm military operations, and that awareness must be a part of military strategy and operations to guarantee success, assertions that are particularly notable amid a war on terrorism that has moved human rights to the backburner. As one U.S. official noted, human rights "is the answer" to effective, holistic military operations and strategy.[49]

The Cost of Past Counterterrorism Mistakes

While one cannot preclude complete backsliding of U.S. human rights policy in the region, the lessons learned by governments around Latin America will likely prove an enduring obstacle to retrenchment of human rights standards in the name of counterterrorism. Several countries around the region, most prominently Argentina, Brazil, Chile, Paraguay, and Uruguay saw human rights abuses occur in the name of counterterrorism in their own internal conflicts. The word "counterterrorism" today is a sort of taboo for military personnel, and the idea of adopting military counterterrorism roles is, for the most part, a nonstarter. With these governments serving as critical examples for the region and representing the bulk of South America's population, it seems unlikely that a full about-face will emerge on the human rights front, even if U.S. counterterrorism policies continue to move in the same direction.

As Hugh Byrne of the Latin American Working Group argues, human rights abuses in the name of counterterrorism have been among the greatest lingering problems for governments across the region.[50] Chile, for example, has effectively moved toward strong democratic growth and employs one of the region's most transparent and stable market economies. Unfortunately, while the authoritarian regime of the 1970s and 1980s under Augusto Pinochet can claim to have put the country on the right track economically, it left a scourge of abuses that serve as a major obstacle to finalizing the country's democratic consolidation. Even during 2004–2005, civilians and the military were steeped in the reconciliation process for abuses that are some 30 years old. Indeed, Argentina, Brazil, Paraguay, and Uruguay have all in the past year watched old abuses rise to the fore of domestic politics, hamstringing governments that would benefit from greater focus on good governance and institutional growth, but that are hindered by their inability to achieve accountability for human rights abuses committed in the name of counterterrorism.

The point here is not to delve into the debate about effective approaches to reconciliation, rather it is to point out the plague that human rights abuses have imposed on these governments and to note that the lessons and scars from this era run deep. The message is that U.S. efforts to encourage new counterterrorism roles and missions in Latin American that are more conducive to abuses, such as domestic policing and military intelligence collection, will ring hollow for many. It is highly unlikely that human rights awareness will see full retrenchment or that Latin American countries will adopt policies that run counter to decades of human rights promotion when those countries are still enduring the pains of abuses that stem from similar security postures in the past.

U.S. officials in several countries noted resistance from their Latin American counterparts on employing the military in counterterrorism efforts. In Chile, U.S. officials noted that their counterparts, both military and civilian, are solidly committed to zero tolerance for internal military roles in anything labeled counterterrorism.[51] In Argentina, military and civilian officials espoused a similar sentiment based almost solely on a desire to avoid past human rights mistakes, according to several U.S. officials.[52] Even in Brazil, where the military has increasingly engaged in domestic policing, the military has shied from taking on a full counterterrorism role. While this may resonate with some readers as bad news for U.S. security policy, the long-term effect should be greater democratic strength, rather than lingering regret over human rights abuses that—as displayed in the Southern Cone—is an ongoing civil-military problem and a hindrance to democracy. Moreover, it signals the attraction of a U.S. policy approach that genuinely champions democracy and human rights as critical to security.

Current Cases Hold Lessons for Counterterrorism

While the lessons of the past still resonate, ongoing lessons, particularly in problem countries such as Bolivia, Colombia, and Venezuela, are almost certain to influence governments around the region to carefully weigh counterterrorism policies and their impact on human rights. Colombia, in particular, is likely to be the focus of Latin American militaries over the next several years, as the war there heats up and the Colombian government increasingly sells its security efforts as counterterrorism. What all three cases hold in common is substantial evidence that military mission creeping toward internal or nontraditional roles hold only negative implications for human rights. While armed forces around the region see the United States shifting from a posture of discouraging internal military policing roles toward encouraging such efforts in the name of counterterrorism, the region's militaries need only look to Bolivia, Colombia, and Venezuela to see that even modern-day internal military efforts only portend trouble on the human rights front.

Bolivia's military abuse problems stemming from domestic security responsibilities garnered regional attention and served to reemphasize what the bulk of armed forces already knew—that they are not trained, equipped, or designed to take on internal policing. Even capable and professional forces will look at the Bolivia case as a warning that beyond the real abuses stemming from an internal security role, militaries are likely to attract vast opposition, rhetoric, and pressure from NGO networks committed to the human rights issue, a problem most military officers are likely to go to lengths to avoid.

In Colombia, even with the military successes in bolstering security around the country while using means that draw into question their commitment to human rights, the amount of international and regional criticism that nontraditional military efforts have attracted are likely to be a key lesson that Latin American armed forces take from the case. Further, the Colombia case sends a clear message that even in cases of internal conflict, in which the military has an internationally recognized role of combating insurgency, the only real progress in war has been accompanied by significant measurable improvements in the overall human rights picture. Further, sentiment that governments must maintain militias to do their dirty work in internal wars are almost entirely discredited by Colombia's remarkable reductions in paramilitary abuses and the parallel progress of government war efforts. As noted in the Colombia chapter, President Uribe's efforts to curtail civil rights in the name of fighting terror set a bad example, but the successful war efforts—even with many of Uribe's security efforts not taking root because of legal rulings against them—along with a true improvement in the overall human rights record, sends the message that human rights and counterterrorism are complementary.

Perhaps most important for U.S. human rights promotion in the Colombia case is that it provides an opening for the U.S. military to point to its vast efforts in the country as a model for how to effectively address human rights concerns while fighting terrorism, rather than seeing the emergence of a new tradeoff between fighting terror and respecting human rights. Colombia is the best manifestation of the complex policy mix detailed in Chapter 2, in which the United States seeks to defend its security interests while promoting human rights, not abandoning security because a country has human rights problems, or ignoring human rights needs in the name of security. Colombia sends the message that the United States can help with more than one issue at a time and that human rights can be a part of counterterrorism policy, no matter how complex.

Finally, Venezuela is an important case that will provide Latin American militaries further reason to highlight the human rights problems inherent in United States-backed internal military roles and missions. Further, no government is more critical of Venezuelan President Chavez's disregard for military and civil-military norms than the United States, particularly his use of militias in the name of security and increasing abuses by the military in its policing role in the capital and on the Colombian border. Latin American militaries are likely to point to Washington's posture toward Venezuela and use it in their own defense against mission creep. In other words, U.S. efforts to promote military counterterrorism roles and missions that are conducive to human rights abuses fly in the face of U.S. positions condemning similar security measures in Venezuela. Washington may find it increasingly difficult to condone policies in countries around the region while it condemns them in Venezuela. U.S. policy toward Venezuela on the human rights issue is sound, and others will point to that strength when or if the United States tries to promote an opposite counterterrorism posture with more friendly governments.

CONCLUSION: COUNTERTERRORISM: TESTING THE HEARTS AND MINDS APPROACH

U.S. policymakers, international human rights advocates, and most of all the U.S. military deserves commendation for what has become a holistic U.S. approach toward security policies in the region and the centrality of human rights to overall U.S. policy objectives. This chapter serves as a warning to all actors that the very approach that this work lauds and shows as largely effective is facing its most critical test, a test that will see human rights either diminishing or emerging as a stronger element of the war on terror.

As noted above, scholars have detailed the detrimental effect of U.S. counterterrorism policies on human rights more broadly. This work has allowed us to take a closer look at specific policies and to ask which factors appear likely to help and hinder U.S. military human rights promotion. The author, as made clear in the first two chapters of this book, is both a human rights optimist and an advocate of a U.S. security policy approach that mixes sticks and carrots to promote human rights and security simultaneously. The case studies presented here have shown that in Latin America, there is no basis for insisting that security requires a retreat from human rights. Instead it is clear that counterterrorism policies that violate human rights are harming U.S. security interests. Human rights and security are intrinsically linked, and without one, you are unlikely to achieve the other.

I am not alone in this sentiment. Indeed, perhaps the most surprising and most valuable conclusion revealed by months of field research and interviews is the high level of common ground between human rights advocates and the military. Both groups have a genuine concern for human rights and security, and both groups see human rights and security as codependent, not contradictory. The scholarly record is equally adamant on this point. Kenneth Roth states that "Terrorism is antithetical to human rights. Since targeting civilians for violent attack is repugnant to human rights norms, those who believe in human rights have a direct interest in the success of the anti-terrorism effort."[53] Adam Isacson and Ingrid Vaicius have put forward a similar message in arguing that "security and human rights are inseparable and mutually reinforcing."[54] Kathryn Sikkink best encapsulates the intrinsic relationship: "As the immediate security threat subsides and a long-term antiterrorism policy has to be justified and sustained, leaders will need to stress not only what we fear (terrorism, authoritarianism, fundamentalism) but also what we believe and take pride in (freedom, human rights, and democracy)."[55]

Unfortunately, terrorists have thrown this paradigm into question as they tempt Washington to adopt policies that restrict human rights. Fortunately, the U.S. military remains committed to human rights promotion in Latin America, and it will be difficult to fully reverse accepted standards around the region. Moreover, past and current history provides hard-learned lessons on the human rights front that are likely to prove insurmountable to any counterterrorism effort that looks to undermine human rights. In the end, human rights promotion in Latin America should survive and prevail during what promises to be a long fight against terrorism. Even mistakes made in the war on terror, such as the abuses at Abu Ghraib, are likely to eventually resonate as lessons learned and serve as critical human rights case studies, as opposed to simply serving to complicate efforts to promote human rights in the region.

Finally, we should not lose focus of the enemy during this critical era. Terrorists are the enemy. U.S. officials must remember that human rights advocates are not the enemy and that they serve a critical role in applying pressure and reminding United States and Latin American forces that human rights is integral to security. Indeed, several U.S. military officials have noted that even when they are highly perturbed by NGOs and what appear to be slanted, skewed, and incorrect messages against military policy, these groups are important for maintaining the profile and importance of the human rights issue.[56]

The message of remembering the enemy is of equal importance for human rights activists. Those concerned primarily with human rights must remember that terrorists wish to kill the innocent and purposely commit the most atrocious abuses possible. NGOs must make a concerted effort to remind military personnel that they wish to be on the same side, notwithstanding their preeminent focus on human rights. Further, and perhaps most important, human rights activists need to do a better job of recognizing U.S. and Latin American military efforts and victories in promoting human rights. The author admits that he conducted much of his research with a bias that human rights activists would be antimilitary and antisecurity. The author was quickly and repeatedly disabused of this bias in his interviews with various U.S. and foreign human rights activists. Officials at numerous human rights organizations emphasized that they are not against "just war," that they support military efforts against terrorism, and that they back U.S. efforts to help Latin American governments bolster their own security. Unfortunately, most military personnel seem not to have heard that message. If the war on terror is to move forward with human rights at its center, the human rights community must make clear that the military and human rights activists share a common cause in the war on terror.

7

Conclusion

This book has shown that military human rights promotion is integral to U.S. security policy in Latin America, that it can have a positive impact, that the status of U.S. relations with a country is linked to the salience of such efforts, and that a country's level of democratic civil-military development is critical to the success of human rights awareness. Building on a growing body of human rights literature that highlights the permanence of human rights in U.S. foreign policy, this book has also argued that there is hope for strengthening and enduring military human rights promotion amid a U.S. war on terror that has walked back some human rights and has some observers questioning if human rights is seeing intentional, significant retrenchment. Most importantly, this book in its several case studies has revealed the resilient commitment of U.S. military officials to human rights promotion, which they see as central to effective U.S. security policy in Latin America. Even amid critical setbacks and obstacles posed by democratic retrenchment or underdevelopment in Latin America, U.S. military officials have stayed the course in promoting human rights. Not only have these officials sent the message that winning hearts and minds is more than Vietnam-era presidential rhetoric, they have revealed the preeminence of human rights in security policy and strategy during both war and peace.

This significant role of the U.S. military in promoting human rights around Latin America is unmatched by U.S. military efforts anywhere in the world. This book has documented an approach to human rights that could become a model for Department of Defense (DoD) strategy and behavior around the world. Perhaps the most important finding of this book is that the true heroes on the human rights front are U.S. military officials, a conclusion that is too often ignored by activists, missed by scholars, and would have been unthinkable only a decade ago. In an effort to summarize this heroism, the remainder of this chapter will review the key successes of U.S. military human rights promotion as revealed by the case studies, the factors critical to these successes, and finally, the obstacles that have blocked and promise to further stymie progress in military awareness.

INSTITUTIONAL AND CULTURAL SUCCESSES

This book has revealed several critical effects of U.S. human rights promotion, including standing up training programs, nudging governments to adopt regional human rights standards, and some arguably measurable reductions in abuses. Most evident, however, have been U.S. successes in helping promote institutional change and related movement toward shifting cultural views of military human rights.

In Bolivia, the United States has nudged the military to take a comprehensive approach toward human rights that is focused primarily on institutional changes, such as reforming human rights doctrine, monitoring, and enforcing. Further, the fact that the Bolivian military is working with civilian ministries to ensure implementation of these reforms bodes well for institutionalization and broad acceptance of the efforts. In other words, Bolivia's efforts are not just geared toward awareness, but toward placing certain norms at the center of how the armed forces operate.

In Colombia, the United States has played a critical role in transforming how the military deals with human rights. Beyond simply training and vetting, Colombia has followed the U.S. lead in establishing a legal corps and human rights school that are increasingly integral to military policy and strategy. Human rights is moving from simply a topic or training requirement toward an institutional element of military planning and war fighting. With legal advisors in the field, trained penal justice officials, and curriculums geared toward human rights, Colombia has begun to institutionalize human rights standards in the armed forces. Chapter 6 shows that U.S. JAG officials play a critical role in the United States in inculcating human rights and even pushing back on civilian polices that undermine human rights. The JAG in a sense is the institutional guardian of human rights in the U.S. military. Colombia has moved in this critical direction and is using U.S. military assistance to transform the armed forces, not just to inform them.

Perhaps as critical to the institutional impact are the signs that U.S. military human rights promotion is affecting Latin American military culture and thinking. The Bolivia case details the specific personal and genuine commitment of many military officials focusing on human rights. The U.S. ability to emphasize the importance of human rights in defending the armed forces as an institution appears to be sinking in. As the Bolivian armed forces see their prestige diminished by abuses and allegations of abuse, the attractiveness of human rights promotion increases. In other words, U.S. military human rights promotion has pragmatic benefits that the Bolivian military realizes can help it avoid public relations problems and legal proceedings. To put it bluntly, cultural change is as much about realizing that good human rights practices are good policy as it is about accepting that they are morally imperative. If the first step toward full appreciation of human rights is the realization of its policy and strategic benefits, Bolivia seems to be on the right track, thanks in large part to U.S. influence.

Colombia's adoption of human rights promotion has been more extensive and impressive, while also more complex and difficult to gauge. The cultural change in Colombia is similarly complex in that events signal some cultural shifts, while democratic civil-military problems, noted further below, make cultural change less observable in Colombia. If cultural change is taking root in Colombia, it is most prominent in the military's willingness and ability to see human rights as an issue that requires legal understanding and management. The increasing influence of legal advice on the battlefield signals an apparent shift in attitudes. Indeed, comments by the International Committee of the Red Cross, cited in Chapter 4, lauding Colombian military respect for, promotion, and understanding of international humanitarian law—even while Colombian civilians reject the application of international humanitarian law to categorizing or conducting the conflict—represent perhaps the most convincing sign that the armed forces are thinking in a progressive manner.[1]

Colombia's problematic mix of data—some showing military abuses on the rise while all data indicate a massive decline in paramilitary abuses—complicates the human rights picture in the country. On the one hand it appears human rights culture has retrenched, on the other hand the military's greatest human rights liability—collusion with human rights abusers—is arguably showing progress. It is certain, however, that the culture of human rights awareness has taken root to the point that this debate and problem is front and center in the Colombian military, something that was absent only a few years ago. Cultural change in the Colombian military is on the brink of genuine awareness and appreciation, and the U.S. armed forces are working to help Colombia move in the right direction.

U.S. LEVERAGE, A KEY FACTOR FOR SUCCESS

While military human rights promotion efforts have had some important institutional and cultural victories, the ultimate success of these programs rests largely on the U.S. ability to influence and relate to Latin American governments. The successes have come only through the mix of carrots and sticks detailed in Chapter 2, which includes human rights requirements, penalties, and inducements all working in concert to influence armed forces' human rights performance. Indeed, as opposed to the assumptions of much statistical work on U.S. security policy and human rights—that U.S. appreciation of human rights can only come in the form of denying abusing countries assistance—an assessment of U.S. policy toward Latin America today reveals that emphasis on human rights correlates directly and positively with strong U.S. bilateral and military-to-military relations.[2] Rather than evaluating U.S. willingness to cut assistance to a violating state, this book has shown through three case studies that U.S. interests in human rights suffer where Washington is disengaged and are bolstered where Washington is present and influential.

Certainly, part of U.S. influence in promoting human rights is linked directly to funding and assistance. Colombia and Bolivia, two top recipients of U.S. military assistance in the region, undoubtedly accept human rights promotion, in part, to keep assistance flowing.[3] In Colombia, no less, U.S. human rights certification is required for disbursement of a significant portion of security assistance. In Bolivia, a country that has seen Article 98 restrictions threaten to deplete military funding, human rights awareness is a certain avenue to encouraging other Article 98-exempt assistance. For the author, this sort of human rights clientelism is not only acceptable, it is critical. Forcing a start in human rights awareness is better than no start at all. If the funding leverage leads to institutional change, as shown here, human rights can gain a momentum of its own.

Funding influence, however, cannot stand alone. Much of the success in human rights promotion derives strength from close and ongoing military-to-military relations. While somewhat presumptuous to point to the strong U.S. military relations with Bolivia and Colombia as proof, the point garners credibility from the negative United States–Venezuela relationship and the simultaneous decline of Venezuelan military human rights standards. Venezuela is perhaps the best case study for proving the negative impact of declining U.S. influence and leverage. As recently as 1998, Caracas boasted one of the region's closest military relationships with Washington, a relationship that emphasized human rights and showed movement toward institutional change and military justice. Venezuela today stands out in the region as the one Latin American country going backward on the human rights awareness front. While military abuses are relatively low, they are also on the rise, and red flags signal that abuses may see an increase in the near future. At the same time, the U.S. relationship with Venezuela, both military-to-military and overall bilateral, is on the rocks. While relations with the United States are not an a priori requirement for human rights progress—certainly several countries in the region, including Argentina and Chile, have done well in human rights development with little U.S. influence—relations with the United States can be a key ingredient. In other words, military human rights efforts are better off with the United States, worse off without the United States, and in Venezuela's case apparently highly reliant on U.S. military encouragement and backing.

Not only are close military-to-military relations a key driver of successful military human rights promotion, they appear critical to the sustainability of such efforts. To an extent it is obvious to note that in order for U.S. human rights promotion to succeed it requires close military-to-military relations. Success over the long term, however, also requires sustained relations. Those efforts that Venezuela undertook with U.S. backing, even institutional in nature, appear to have been fully reversible and had little or no lasting impact. With the decline in relations, so too went the fruits of human rights promotion. For example, U.S. military personnel cannot point to any ongoing Venezuelan military judicial programs, initially established and backed with U.S. assistance. The message then is that not only is U.S. engagement critical for startup, it is needed for endurance of human rights efforts.[4] This chapter argues above that a clientelistic start of human rights programs is a good start that can gather momentum; the Venezuela case shows that this momentum requires continued U.S. support and marshaling.

DEMOCRATIC PROBLEMS A TOP OBSTACLE

U.S. military human rights promotion is hardly infallible. Failures on the human rights front in Latin America are likely, particularly in volatile situations such as those described in Bolivia and Colombia. Moreover, certainly if the United States can have its own military human rights crisis in Iraq, it is logical to bet that either instability in Bolivia or the war in Colombia will bring about major human rights violations. A human rights crisis or setback in Bolivia or Colombia, however, is not simply a failure of military human rights promotion, rather it signals the inability of U.S. military efforts to overcome democratic problems. While U.S. leverage and influence emerged from this work as a top driver of successful human rights promotion, lagging democratic civil-military relations proved to be the leading factor inhibiting human rights efforts.

Across the three case studies, employment of Mark Ruhl and Samuel Fitch's criteria for democratic civil military development revealed judicial problems as the most prominent obstacle to strong military human rights performance.[5] In Bolivia, the military's failure to acknowledge civilian jurisdiction over human rights cases hampers full appreciation of human rights norms. Colombia's ongoing struggles with impunity of military officials that violate human rights is at the center of the armed forces' inability to move past the human rights problem. Venezuela's impunity problem, coupled with presidential manipulation of the judiciary, hampers civilian judicial authority over military human rights abusers. NGO officials around the region and in the United States consistently told the author that military professionalism is a lesser concern than the lack of judicial enforcement against abusers.

This book vindicates this sentiment and shows not only that judicial ineffectiveness is a crucial problem in the countries covered here, but a key obstacle to U.S. military efforts that are trying to effect change.

Finally, if judicial problems are a key obstacle to human rights promotion, a lack of full military subordination to, and respect for, civilian authority and control were discouraging factors that appeared across the case studies. If military officers persist in denying the authority of the president, or if the president's authority is perverted and distorted, human rights promotion can only go so far. With insubordination or poor civilian control comes lacking incentive to respect the ordinary citizen.

The Bolivian military's insubordination toward former President Mesa, specifically against his backing of civilian judicial jurisdiction over military human rights cases, flies in the face of everything military human rights promotion champions. Colombian military disregard for President Uribe's orders to cease collusion with human rights abusing paramilitaries discredits ongoing military human rights efforts as well as the president's overall security strategy. Even with overall human rights abuses falling dramatically and security improving markedly, the Uribe administration remains vulnerable to criticism for military-paramilitary collusion that runs counter to his orders and undermines his authority. Again, the significant drop in paramilitary abuses is notable and arguably bolsters the idea that total collusion is down, but numerous observers, including U.S. government officials, agree that collusion casts continuing doubt on the Colombian military's sincerity in promoting human rights.[6]

Venezuela presents a bit of a different lesson, in which only a small group of military officials is insubordinate—albeit having tried in 2002 to overthrow President Chavez—and the bulk of the military follows the president's orders. Unfortunately for human rights promotion, Chavez has perverted his authority to a point where he represents a case of authoritarian rule. The author earlier cited U.S. Secretary of State Rice's observation that it is not enough to be elected democratically if one does not rule democratically.[7] This contention is nowhere stronger or correct than in civil-military relations. Chavez's arming of civilians, standing up of militias, isolating the military, and imposing draconian restrictions on civilian rights makes his civilian rule and its importance to military human rights moot. Military respect for civilian authority has little positive impact for human rights when the president is working to undermine the very human rights norms that democratic civilian authority is supposed to enhance.

THE ROAD FORWARD: CHANGE THROUGH RECOGNITION

Even if this assessment has effectively demonstrated the existence, centrality, and utility of U.S. military human rights promotion in U.S. security policy toward Latin America, it seems likely that these efforts will continue to be overshadowed by continuing abuses, NGO criticism and focus on the negative trends around the region, and U.S. counterterrorism policy. The author's underlying goal has been to give voice to a policy that is moral, effective, strategically imperative, and underappreciated. One may hope that the progressive military work taking place on the ground around the region will be better appreciated—and endorsed—by human rights activists, human rights scholars, and most of all, senior U.S. military officials.

There is one central reason for raising the profile of U.S. military human rights awareness and that is to bolster its effectiveness. This book has shown that human rights promotion has its limits, particularly when it bumps up against lagging democratic civil-military standards. Calling for greater military attention to the obstacles detailed above is simple enough. Only broad attention to U.S. military efforts, critique and evaluation of their utility, and recommendations for improvements can help strengthen existing programs and enhance their value for promoting change in the region.

SOUTHCOM appears to be doing its part to raise the profile of military human rights promotion through publication of its programs, roundtables with human rights experts, and even contracting academic studies on aspects of the Command's human rights efforts.[8] The human rights community should now step up to the plate. Many human rights activists in the United States and Latin America that the author interviewed had either never heard of SOUTHCOM's efforts, or knew little about them.[9] While activists do not owe the U.S. military recognition, the author's experience in persistently encountering progressive SOUTHCOM efforts—for example, in Bolivia they are nearly impossible to avoid—suggests that human rights advocates of all stripes would do well to pay greater attention. While human rights activists must always search out and reveal violations and wrongdoing, their cause could benefit from their paying closer attention to what is helping on the human rights front. As of now, there are few if any detailed NGO assessments of U.S. efforts to promote human rights, particularly in the armed forces. Indeed, the author found not a single human rights NGO publication that offers a discussion or assessment of SOUTHCOM's extensive human rights efforts.

Finally, perhaps the greatest onus for raising the profile of these efforts and encouraging their improvement rests with civilian DoD authorities and other U.S. military commands. SOUTHCOM's efforts should serve as a model for U.S. military assistance and relations around the world. Interestingly, the Secretary of Defense has received from SOUTHCOM a request to commit DoD to the same rigorous human rights standards that the Command promotes around the region. Not surprisingly, the Command has not heard a response.[10] The time is ripe for the United States to more effectively champion human rights both in Latin America and around the world. Following the events at Abu Ghraib and the ongoing debate surrounding

Guantanamo, DoD would benefit from stepping up its commitment to human rights by making the SOUTHCOM model a DoD-wide mandate.

With civilian officials already trying to nudge the armed forces to carry out policies that run against decades of U.S. military human rights standards, there is little basis for optimism that the above recommendation will gain footing in the near term. There is hope, however, for military human rights to become an even more central aspect of U.S. military policy at home, in Latin America, and in the world. That hope resides in the U.S. military officials that have demonstrated an irreversible commitment to human rights promotion.

Travel to eight countries and dozens of interviews revealed to the author that something in the human rights arena really is changing. Though the level of conviction one encounters is impossible to quantify and difficult to convey, it is nevertheless the case that U.S. military human rights promoters have deeply engaged the struggle for hearts and minds, becoming the best hope for human rights to finally claim a permanent place in the armed forces of Latin America. The good news is that military human rights has the ability to gain ground, even in the midst of the age of counterterrorism. The irony is that warfighters may be turning out to be human rights' greatest proponents.

Notes

1: INTRODUCTION

1. See Department of Defense, U.S. Southern Command, *US SOUTHCOM's Theater Strategy*, www.southcom.mil/pa/Facts/Strategy.htm; Department of Defense, Western Hemisphere Institute for Security Cooperation, *Democracy and Human Rights at WHINSEC*, www.benning.army.mil/whinsec; Department of Defense, U.S. Southern Command, *SC Regulation 1–20: Human Rights Policy and Procedures* (Miami, April 8, 2002).

2. While WHINSEC is not formally under SOUTHCOM command, all training of Latin American officials at the Institute is coordinated and facilitated by SOUTHCOM.

3. Dozens of interviews revealed more in common between human rights groups and the armed forces than either side realizes. Civilians at SOUTHCOM are probably the most cognizant of this fact and have listed this problem as a key impediment that would have to be overcome to effectively improve military respect for human rights in the region. NGOs are able to pinpoint some commonalities, but these sentiments are often drowned out by their tenor, or conversely, an unwillingness to listen on the part of military officials.

4. I argue that it is counterintuitive to assume that funding or military assistance to countries with poor human rights records is a bad idea. Indeed, the funding and military assistance could be seen as a critical element in changing a particular country's approach to human rights.

5. Steven Poe, Suzanne Pilatovsky, Brian Miller, and Ayo Ogundele, "Human Rights and US Foreign Aid Revisited: The Latin American Region," *Human Rights Quarterly* 16, no. 3 (1994): 539.

6. Lars Schoultz, *Human Rights and United States Policy toward Latin America* (Princeton, NJ: Princeton University Press, 1981); Latin American Working Group Education Fund, Center for International Policy, Washington Office on Latin America, *Paint by Numbers: Trends in US Military Programs with Latin America & Challenges to Oversight* (Washington, DC: Author, August 2003); Latin American Working Group Education Fund, Center for International Policy, Washington Office on Latin America, *Blurring the Lines: Trends in US Military Programs with Latin America* (Washington, DC: Author, October 2004); Lisa Haugaard, Sean Garcia, Philip Schmidt, and Mavis Anderson, *September's Shadow: Post-9/11 US-Latin American Relations* (Washington, DC: Latin American Working Group Education Fund, September 2004); Center for International Policy, *Just the Facts 2001–2002: A Quick Tour of US Defense and Security Relations with Latin America and the Caribbean* (Washington, DC: Author, October 2001).

7. See Chapter 2 for a more in-depth discussion of the tradeoff problem in foreign policy and human rights.

8. K. Pritchard, "Comparative Human Rights: Promise and Practice," in D.L. Cingranelli, ed., *Human Rights: Theory and Measurement* (Hong Kong: Macmillan, 1988); C. W. Henderson, "Conditions Affecting the Use of Political Repression," *Journal of Conflict Resolution* 35, no. 1 (1991): 120–142; D.L. Cingranelli and D.L. Richards, "Respect for Human Rights After the End of the Cold War," *Journal of Peace Research* 36 no. 5 (1999): 511–534.

9. The White House, *The National Security Strategy of the United States of America* (Washington, DC, September 2002).

10. Haugaard et al., *September's Shadow.*

11. Please see my reasoning in the "Refocusing the Debate" section below for a more subjective look at the issue and for moving away from attempts to empirically measure progress in the field.

12. Numerous studies that assess military-related human rights issues have relied on the U.S. State Department category definition of *integrity of the person* as the appropriate definition for scholarly work. See Michael Stohl, David Carleton, and Steven Johnson, "Human Rights and US Foreign Assistance from Nixon to Carter," *Journal of Peace Research* 21, no. 3 (1984): 215–226; David L. Cingranelli and Thomas E. Pasquarello, "Human Rights Practices and the Distribution of US Foreign Aid to Latin American Countries," *American Journal of Political Science* 29, no. 3 (1985): 539–563.

13. Mark J. Ruhl, "Curbing Central America's Militaries," *Journal of Democracy* 15, no. 3 (July 2004): 137–151.

14. While these countries are correct in arguing that they have moved beyond the problem of gross military human rights abuses, it is a mistake for them to exclude themselves from regional human rights promotion efforts that would bolster the professionalization of their armed forces and to which they could add valuable context. U.S. practitioners have engaged these countries, but appear to have encountered less welcoming environments. U.S. SOUTHCOM Human Rights Division official Leana Bresnahan, interview by author, July 2004, Miami; U.S. SOUTHCOM Human Rights Initiative Seminar Participant Dr. Victor Uribe, interview by author, July 2004, Miami; Western Hemisphere Institute for Security Cooperation Human Rights Instructor Major Antonio Raimondo, interview by author, November 2004.

15. Latin American Working Group Education Fund, *Blurring the Lines.* Also, Center for International Policy, *Just the Facts* at www.ciponline.org/facts. Author rounded all numbers to the nearest tenth. Funding levels can also be found in the State Department Congressional Presentations for Foreign Operations, and the Department of Defense and State Department Foreign Military Training and DoD Engagement Activities of Interest at www.state.gov. CIP's publication of *Just the Facts*, however, is the only single source for combined security assistance funding and provides assistance levels broken down in more detail than is readily available in State documents. Some government officials have also indicated that the CIP data set is the most comprehensive available, U.S. SOUTHCOM Congressional Affairs Official Christopher Crowley, interview by author, July 2004; Deputy Political Counselor, U.S. Embassy Mexico City, Kevin O'Reilly, interview by author, July 2003.

16. This work will strive to provide historical context without becoming steeped in arguments regarding U.S. involvement in past abuses. The book will not focus on historical human rights crimes and will move past the drawn out debates in an effort to evaluate current U.S. military practices in the human rights area and countries' acceptance of U.S. efforts.

17. While some literature preceded that of Schoultz, including Odell 1974, Pearson 1976, McKinlay and Little 1977, Schoultz's work is recognized by subsequent academicians as the first comprehensive attempt at evaluating human rights and U.S. foreign and military policy toward Latin America.

18. Schoultz, *Human Rights and United States Policy toward Latin America*, 242, 246.

19. Ibid., 247

20. Stohl, Carleton, and Johnson, "Human Rights and US Foreign Assistance from Nixon to Carter"; Cingranelli and Pasquarello, "Human Rights Practices and the Distribution of US Foreign Aid to Latin American Countries"; David Carleton and Michael Stohl, "The Role of Human Rights in US Foreign Assistance Policy: A critique and Reappraisal," *American Journal of Political Science* 31, no. 4 (1987): 1002–1018; James McCormick and Neil Mitchell, "Is US Aid Really Linked to Human Rights in Latin America?" *American Journal of Political Science* 32, no. 1 (1988): 231–239; Poe, Pilatovsky, Miller, and Ogundele, "Human Rights and US Foreign Aid Revisited: The Latin American Region," 539–558; Robert P. Watson and Sean McCluskie, "Human Rights Considerations and US Foreign Policy: The Latin American Experience," *The Social Science Journal* 34, no. 2 (1997): 249–258; Steven C. Poe, "Human Rights and Economic Aid Allocation under Ronald Reagan and Jimmy Carter," *American Journal of Political Science* 36, no. 1 (1992): 147–167; Shannon Lindsey Blanton, "Promoting Human Rights and Democracy in the Developing World: US Rhetoric versus US Arms Exports," *American Journal of Political Science* 44, no. 1 (2000): 123–131.

21. The bulk of SOA Watch arguments and the group's history and mission can be found at www.soawatch.org.

22. CIP's objectives can be found at www.ciponline.org. Adam Isacson, interview by author, October 2004. CIP publications suggest that CIP would prefer assistance to be geared toward nonmilitary institutional development. See Latin American Working Group Education Fund, *Blurring the Lines.*

23. CIP, WOLA, and LAWG.

24. Amnesty International USA, *Unmatched Power, Unmet Principles: The Human Rights Dimensions of US Training of Foreign Military and Police Forces* (New York: Amnesty International USA, 2002).

25. Russell W. Ramsey and Antonio Raimondo, "Human Rights Instruction at the US Army School of the Americas," *Human Rights Review* 2, no. 3 (2001): 92–116. The author does not see studies about a particular issue or agency by individuals who work in the field or at the agency as naturally biased. Rather each piece should be evaluated on its substance. The point here is that the one relatively balanced assessment of WHINSEC comes from individuals that work at the institution, so the field suffers from a dearth of outside assessments.

26. Jeffrey F. Addicott and Guy B. Roberts, "Building Democracies with Southern Command's Legal Engagement Strategy," *Parameters* (Spring 2001): 72–84.

27. Max G. Manwaring, ed., *Security and Civil-Military Relations in the New World Disorder: The Use of Armed Forces in the Americas* (Carlisle, PA: Strategic Studies Institute, U.S. Army War College, 1999).

28. Ibid., 43, by Donald E. Schulz.

29. Lars Schoultz, William C. Smith, and Augusto Varas, eds., *Security, Democracy, and Development in US-Latin American Relations* (Miami, FL: North-South Center Press, 1994).

30. Ibid., 59.

31. Ramsey deserves credit for an unmatched contribution to the field of Latin American studies as a whole. His reviews of literature on Latin America make up what is the most comprehensive review of literature on all topics in Latin America. Please see Russell W. Ramsey, *Strategic Reading on Latin America*, 3rd ed. (Bloomington, IN: First Books, 2001). Russell W. Ramsey, *Essays on Latin American Security: The Collected Writings of a Scholar-Implementer* (Bloomington, IN: First Books, 2003).

32. Argentina and Chile now have laws prohibiting military counterterrorism roles because of the associated past abuses.

33. Alfred Stepan, *Rethinking Military Politics: Brazil and the Southern Cone* (Princeton, NJ: Princeton University Press, 1988).

34. J. Samuel Fitch, *Armed Forces and Democracy in Latin America* (Baltimore, MD: Johns Hopkins University Press, 1998).

35. Ruhl, "Curbing Central America's Militaries."

36. As cited in Ramsey, *Strategic Reading*. Donald Schulz, *The Role of the Armed Forces in the Americas: Civil-Military Relations for the 21st Century* (Carlisle Barracks, PA: US Army War College, Strategic Studies Institute, 1998).

37. Frederick M. Nunn, *The Time of the Generals: Latin American Professional Militarism in World Perspective* (Lincoln: University of Nebraska Press, 1992). -

38. Paul W. Zagorski, *Democracy vs. National Security: Civil-Military Relations in Latin America* (Boulder, CO: Lynne Rienner Publishers, 1992).

39. Wendy Hunter, "State and Soldier in Latin America," *USIP* (1999).

40. David Pion-Berlin, ed., *Civil-Military Relations in Latin America: New Analytic Perspectives*, (Chapel Hill: University of North Carolina Press, 2001).

41. Jorge I. Dominguez, ed., *International Security and Democracy: Latin America and the Caribbean in the Post Cold War Era* (Pittsburgh, PA: University of Pittsburgh Press, 1998). Also cited in Ramsey, *Strategic Reading*.

42. Schoultz, Smith, Varas, eds., *Security, Democracy, and Development in US-Latin American Relations.*

43. Manwaring, ed., *Security and Civil-Military Relations in the New World Disorder.*

44. Schulz, *The Role of the Armed Forces in the Americas.*

45. David Pion-Berlin and Craig Arceneaux, "Decision-Makers of Decision-Takers? Military Missions and Civilian Control in Democratic South America," *Armed Forces & Society* 26, no. 3 (2000): 413–436.

46. Latin American Working Group Education Fund, *Blurring the Lines.*

47. General James Hill, United States Army Commander, *United States Southern Command Testimony before House Armed Services Committee*, United States House of Representatives (March 24, 2004), cited in, Latin American Working Group Education Fund, *Blurring the Lines.* General James Hill, United States Army Commander, *Speech to Florida International University* online at *www.southcom.mil.*

48. Latin American Working Group Education Fund, *Blurring the Lines.*

49. Russell Ramsey, a respected Latin America scholar and instructor at WHINSEC, argues that the *Blurring the Lines* authors confuse militarization with military-to-military diplomacy. He agrees that mixing defense with policing, institutionally, is a mistake. Russell Ramsey, interview by author, November 2004.

50. Haugaard, et al., *September's Shadow.*

51. Much of the literature also asks whether human rights affect U.S. economic aid decisions. The more directly relevant question, and more pertinent to this work, however, is whether U.S. military assistance is effected.

52. Schoultz, *Human Rights and United States Policy toward Latin America.*

53. Cingranelli and Pasquarello, "Human Rights Practices and the Distribution of US Foreign Aid to Latin American Countries." While Schoultz was among the first to try to measure U.S. policymaking in regard to human rights, Cingranelli and Paquarello's piece appears to have been the piece that spurred the debate forward because of its controversial finding, that there was a correlation between human rights trends and U.S. assistance, and its limited methodology. Moreover, Carleton, Stohl, and Johnson published a similar piece reaching opposite conclusions almost one year prior to Cingranelli and Pasquarello who claimed that their study was the first to measure human rights abuses during more than a single point in time. This claim, while not technically correct due to the publication of the Carleton, Stohl, and Johnson piece, appears to have been the result of the slow academic review process, since Cingranelli and Pasquarello did submit their first manuscript prior to the Carleton et al. publication.

54. Carleton and Stohl, "The Role of Human Rights in US Assistance Policy"; Poe, "Human Rights and Economic Aid Allocation under Ronald Reagan and Jimmy Carter"; Poe, Pilatovsky, Miller, and Ogundele, "Human Rights and US Foreign Aid Revisited: The Latin American Region."

55. Blanton, "Promoting Human Rights and Democracy in the Developing World."

56. Carleton and Stohl, "The Role of Human Rights in US Assistance Policy," 1008. Poe, Pilatovsky, Miller, Ogundele, "Human Rights and US Foreign Aid Revisited: The Latin American Region," 540.

57. Cingranelli and Pasquarello, "Human Rights Practices and the Distribution of US Foreign Aid to Latin American Countries"; Blanton, "Promoting Human Rights and Democracy in the Developing World."

58. Carleton, Stohl, and Johnson, "Human Rights and US Foreign Assistance from Nixon to Carter"; Carleton and Stohl, "The Role of Human Rights in US Assistance Policy"; McCormick and Mitchell, "Is US Aid Really Linked to Human Rights in Latin America?"; Watson and McCluskie, "Human Rights Considerations and US Foreign Policy."

59. Poe et al., "Human Rights and US Foreign Aid Revisited: The Latin American Region"; Poe, "Human Rights and Economic Aid Allocation under Ronald Reagan and Jimmy Carter."

60. Stephen B. Cohen, "Conditioning US Security Assistance on Human Rights Practices," *American Journal of International Law* 76, no. 2 (1982): 278–279.

61. Here, and in the rest of this section, I am referring to all works cited in footnote 21. Each study, regardless of its findings on correlation of U.S. assistance and human rights records, failed to properly consider the complex makeup of aid packages.

62. Cingranelli and Pasquarello, "Human Rights Practices and the Distribution of US Foreign Aid to Latin American Countries"; Poe, "Human Rights and Economic Aid Allocation under Ronald Reagan and Jimmy Carter."

63. For the purposes of this work, the author is referring to military assistance only. If one includes economic assistance, which the statistical subfield does, the debate is even more flawed. Assessment of U.S. State Department Foreign Assistance publications reveal notably large amounts of aid geared toward democratic development and often human rights promotion. This aid is not given to the countries considered stalwarts of human rights awareness; rather, it is awarded with the objective of promoting change and greater awareness of democratic norms, such as human rights. The debate should concentrate on whether this focused assistance is effective, rather than if it correlates to abuse trends, something this assessment attempts to achieve.

64. Serafino, in Schoultz, Smith, and Varas, eds., *Security, Democracy, and Development in US-Latin American Relations*, 68.

65. Department of State, *Foreign Military Training: Joint Report to Congress, Fiscal Years 2003 and 2004* (Washington, DC, June 2004).

66. Department of Defense, *US SOUTHCOM Vision*, at www.southcom.mil/pa/Facts/Vision.htm.

67. See Chapter 2 for a more comprehensive discussion of why the United States began undermining human rights in Latin America and how and why U.S. policy has changed. Some supporters of military training and assistance during the 1970s made similar arguments. These arguments have been effectively rebuked by Stephen B. Cohen in his article, "Conditioning US Security Assistance on Human Rights." My assertions, however, are based on a changed reality of DoD's policy. DoD's policy in the 1970s, and U.S. Southern Command in particular, did not include human rights awareness as a primary strategic objective. Moreover, the record of the 1970s rightly proved that U.S. military relations either assisted or at a minimum influenced significant abuse of human rights, a problem that is not predominant today. Second, the argument put forward in the 1970s in favor of assistance assumed that

providing some materiel, particularly spare parts, would induce human rights aware-ness. Again, Cohen effectively rebukes this almost nonsensical causal relationship. The facts today, however, are different, and include a complex mix of carrots and sticks, combined with human rights promotion efforts geared toward bolstering awareness in foreign militaries. Cohen, "Conditioning US Security Assistance on Human Rights Practices," 274.

68. A large majority of military and civilian officials noted in interviews that the pressure applied by experts outside the government has been, and continues to be, a key driver of U.S. military human rights promotion efforts. A central irony of the military human rights issue is that those fighting for change in U.S. approaches to human rights often are slow to recognize real policy change that is the result of their own efforts. This irony plays out as a key problem in the Bolivia and Colombia case studies and is touched on in the concluding chapter.

2: THE EVOLUTION OF U.S. MILITARY HUMAN RIGHTS PROMOTION IN LATIN AMERICA

1. Samuel Flagg Bemis, *A Diplomatic History of the United States* (New York: Holt, Reinhart, and Winston, 1965), 198–202; Martin Sicker, *The Geopolitics of Security in the Americas* (Westport, CT: Praeger, 2002), 13.

2. Bemis, *A Diplomatic History of the United States*, 208; Sicker, *The Geopolitics of Security in the Americas*, 22; Richard McCall, "From Monroe to Reagan: An Overview of US–Latin American Relations," in Richard Newfarmer, ed., *From Gunboats to Diplomacy: New US Policies for Latin America* (Baltimore, MD: Johns Hopkins University Press, 1984), 18.

3. Bemis, *A Diplomatic History of the United States*, 208.

4. Ibid.

5. McCall, "From Monroe to Reagan: An Overview of US–Latin American Relations," 20.

6. Foreign Relations of the United States (1905) 333–335, cited in Sicker, *The Geopolitics of Security in the Americas*, 61–62.

7. McCall, "From Monroe to Reagan: An Overview of US–Latin American Relations," 22.

8. Ibid., 26.

9. Ibid., 25.

10. Ibid.

11. Bemis, *A Diplomatic History of the United States,* 769.

12. Russell Ramsey and Antonio Raimondo argue that human rights promotion by the U.S. military has existed for decades. The current form of targeted human rights promotion through required training, and specific programs geared toward implementation and evaluation of human rights standards, however, is unarguably new. Ramsey is correct in his repeated assertion that military diplomacy has and can be a positive aspect of foreign policy. Indeed, it is this very notion that, in part, the assertions of this work rest. Ramsey and Raimondo, "Human Rights Instruction at the US Army School of the Americas," *Human Rights Review* 2, no. 3 (2001); Interview with Ramsey, November 2004.

13. David P. Forsythe, "US Foreign Policy and Human Rights," *Journal of Human Rights* 1, no. 4 (2002): 501.

14. Kathryn Sikkink, *Mixed Signals: US Human Rights Policy and Latin America* (Ithaca, NY: Cornell University Press, 2004), 208.

15. Stephen B. Cohen, "Conditioning US Security Assistance on Human Rights Practices," *American Journal of International Law* 76, no. 2 (1982): 272.

16. Jack Donnelly, *International Human Rights* (Boulder, CO: Westview Press, 1998), 87, 89.

17. Ibid., 87.

18. All Interviews listed in Bibliography.

19. Cohen, "Conditioning US Security Assistance on Human Rights Practices," 274. Cohen also notes that Washington made exceptions for provision of safety-related items, such as rescue equipment. This exception was in the name of protecting basic rights and needs, but not as a source of leverage, and thus is not as pertinent to my argument of a new middle ground.

20. Lars Schoultz, *Human Rights and United States Policy toward Latin America* (Princeton, NJ: Princeton University Press, 1981), 249.

21. The author recognizes that identifying a middle ground between suspending assistance and offering unconditional assistance would be a difficult, case by case task. Without doubt, enemies of the United States would rarely if ever receive military assistance as a means to promote human rights. Further, a middle ground approach to providing military assistance with an objective—at least in part—of improving human rights would have to come with significant oversight and evaluation, or risk states using U.S. assistance as a source of furthering their own oppressive policies. In the counterterrorism age, for example, there are numerous cases of regimes attempting to classify their enemies as terrorists simply to qualify for U.S. assistance. Chapter 4 holds up U.S. military policy and assistance to Colombia as a model of a functioning middle ground; U.S. military assistance there is significant, but rooted in achievable goals toward improving human rights, all with U.S. oversight and the help of U.S. military human rights promoters.

22. Practitioners and scholars still disagree about whether U.S. sanctioning of Latin American authoritarian regimes was a good policy in the face of a growing communist threat in the region during the 1970s and 1980s. Indeed, the author in his several years working in Washington has come across numerous officials who argue that the economic policies of the military dictator Pinochet in Chile are the root cause of the country's stability and strength today.

23. Schoultz, *Human Rights and United States Policy toward Latin America*. Cohen, "Conditioning US Security Assistance on Human Rights Practices"; David P Forsythe, "Congress and Human Rights in US Foreign Policy: The Fate of General Legislation," *Human Rights Quarterly* 9, no. 3 (1987): 382–404.

24. Schoultz, *Human Rights and United States Policy toward Latin America*, 370–375.

25. Donnelly, *International Human Rights*, 91–103.

26. Schoultz, *Human Rights and United States Policy toward Latin America*, 370–373. In his comprehensive review of U.S. foreign policy and human rights, Schoultz identifies the human rights awareness of the 1970s with five events: (1) the unpopularity of Vietnam, (2) the Nixon Watergate scandal leading to the rise of a

predominantly Democratic Party-controlled Congress, (3) the 1973 coup in Chile, (4) Carter's rise to power as a human rights proponent, (5) the lack of a credible threat to U.S. security in Latin America. Schoultz also refers to three structural changes as critical: (1) increased influence of interest groups, (2) a resurgence of congressional interest in humanitarian, and as a consequence United States–Latin America issues, (3) the development of a human rights bureaucracy within the executive branch.

27. While I define human rights in the introduction principally as integrity of the person, I state it explicitly here because, as Donnelly notes, most U.S. administrations during the cold war saw the promotion of human rights in a different light, primarily with emphasis on civil and political rights. Cold war administrations would justify the overthrow of a Marxist government, even if elected democratically, as the promotion of civil and political human rights. In their view, the political and civil rights violations by communist regimes presented a more preeminent danger to world and national security than did the violations against the integrity of the person carried out by noncommunist regimes. Unfortunately, this view excused the fact that authoritarian governments, such as that which took power in Chile, also clearly violated civil and political rights. Donnelly, *International Human Rights*, 87–88.

28. Ramsey and Raimondo also note that the attention paid to human rights issues in Latin America is disproportionate to the number of abuses and amount of assistance to the region. This is particularly the case when contrasted to the attention paid to other problematic regions, namely Africa and Asia. Ramsey and Raimondo, "Human Rights Instruction at the US Army School of the Americas," 103, 116 n. 23.

29. While U.S. government involvement in the Chilean coup is well known and documented, the full extent and facts should be better understood with the pending publication of Foreign Relations of the United States documents from that era. The Senate Select Committee on Intelligence in 1975 published what is largely irrefutable evidence that the U.S. government supported clandestine efforts against Salvador Allende. For a detailed account see Schoultz, *Human Rights and United States Policy toward Latin America*, 243–246.

30. U.S. Congress, *Foreign Assistance Act of 1961* (P.L. 87-195) Section 502(B), (1976), cited in Cohen, "Conditioning US Security Assistance on Human Rights Practices," 50. The details of congressional action on human rights-related legislation has been recounted in great detail by several authors, including Stephen B. Cohen, David P. Forsythe, and Lars Schoultz. The point in recounting some of the key events here is to give the reader an understanding of how the legislative actions formed the base of three decades of human rights-related events and the eventual change in military policy toward Latin America. Cohen offers the most comprehensive review of U.S. congressional efforts to curtail military assistance based on human rights abuses, and the majority of my data is attributed to his work. Forsythe and Schoultz offer similar but less comprehensive versions.

31. U.S. Congress, *Foreign Assistance Act of 1974*, §36, 88Stat. 1815 (1974).

32. Ibid. also cited in Cohen, "Conditioning US Security Assistance on Human Rights Practices," 251.

33. Cohen, "Conditioning US Security Assistance on Human Rights Practices," 252.

34. Ibid., 253.

35. Ibid., 261.

36. Ibid., 253, 261.

37. Ibid., 261–264. Now known as the Bureau of Democracy, Human Rights, and Labor, it has become a cornerstone of the Department and produces widely read and cited human rights reports covering the human rights performance of all countries.

38. U.S. Congress, *H. R. Rep. No. 95-1546,* 95th Cong., 1st sess. 16 (1977), cited in Cohen, "Conditioning US Security Assistance on Human Rights Practices," 254.

39. U.S. Congress, *Department of Defense Appropriations Act,* H.R. 2561 § 8098 (1999).

40. Cohen, "Conditioning US Security Assistance on Human Rights Practices," 254–255; Forsythe, "Congress and Human Rights in US Foreign Policy: The Fate of General Legislation," 383.

41. Schoultz, *Human Rights and United States Policy toward Latin America,* 372.

42. Mark Danner, *The Massacre at El Mozote* (New York: Vintage, 1993). Most information on the massacre cited here is from Danner's book.

43. The UN Security Council puts the number of massacred fare below 800, at around 200. The UN does note that the figure is higher if unidentified persons are included. At one point in its report, the UN claims that more than 500 people were massacred. See United Nations, *UN Security Council Annex, from Madness to Hope: The 12-year War in El Salvador: Report of the Commission on the Truth for El Salvador* (s/25500, 1993), 5–8.

44. United State General Accounting Office, *El Salvador: Military Assistance Has Helped Counter but not Overcome the Insurgency* (GAO/NSIAD-91-166, April 1991). The majority of the facts surrounding the El Salvador human rights abuses are now well known and, for the most part, can be found in this GAO publication, with the exception of the events at El Mazote.

45. The GAO also notes its hesitance to call the overall improved human rights record in El Salvador during the 1980s a complete success, largely due to the Jesuit murders. GAO, *El Salvador,* 32.

46. Ibid., 9.

47. Ibid.

48. United State General Accounting Office, *Central America: Impact of US Assistance in the 1980s,* Report to the Chairman, Committee on Foreign Relations, US Senate (GAO/NSIAD-89-170, July 1989), 11.

49. GAO, *El Salvador,* 27.

50. While human rights concerns played key a role in congressional actions, it appears that at least part of the carrot and stick approach was not human rights in general, but to keep the government from killing American citizens.

51. GAO, *El Salvador,* 27–28.

52. John Feeley, Deputy Political Counselor, U.S. Embassy Mexico City 2001–2003, interview by author, June 2003; Major Michael Knutson, Office of Secretary of Defense, interview by author, July 2003; Lt. Colonel Dennis Fiemeyer, Office of Secretary of Defense, interview by author, July 2003.

53. Many of these developments are well known by U.S. military and civilian personnel that have worked in the region. Many of the same details provided above can be found in GAO, *El Salvador*, 28–29.

54. UN Annex, sec. B, 1.

55. GAO, *El Salvador*, 31.

56. See next section, The 1990s, for a full description of the development and content of U.S. military human rights promotion.

57. United States Institute for Peace, *Special Report, US Human Rights Policy to Latin America* (January 23, 2001), 3.

58. The history and mission of SOA Watch can be found at the group's Web site, www.soaw.org.

59. Office of the Assistant Secretary of Defense/Public Affairs Office, *Fact Sheet Concerning Training Manuals Containing Materials Inconsistent with US Policy* (Washington, DC: The National Security Archive, 1996).

60. Douglas Waller and Richard de Silva, "Running a 'School for Dictators,'" *Newsweek* 122, no. 6 (1993): 34–37.

61. The chairman of the WHINSEC Board of Visitors and the current WHINSEC human rights program director both note that nobody has been able to make a direct link between specific training and abuses committed. Indeed, the WHINSEC instructor notes that on many occasions, violators had taken nothing more than simple maintenance courses, completely unrelated to any types of abuse. The Board of Visitors Chairman, a renowned human rights advocate and lawyer, noted that no charges of a direct link between the School and abuses would ever stand up in Court. Both men acknowledged that human rights was perhaps too compartmentalized as a topic before the significant curriculum changes in the 1990s. Steven M. Schneebaum, Chairman WHINSEC Board of Visitors 2004, interview by author, November 2004; Raimondo, interview by author, November 2004.

62. The general sense the author gained through field research is that early human rights sessions—because they resulted from outside pressure and were traditionally left out of military training—were initially seen as checking-the-box exercises by many U.S. and foreign officials. However, U.S. persistence in pushing human rights as a military training priority appears to have changed this sentiment for U.S. and Latin American officials, most of whom now list the mandatory sessions as key training and acknowledge the shift in attitude.

63. Lisa Haugaard, *Declassified Army and CIA Manuals Used in Latin America: An Analysis of Their Content* (Washington, DC: Latin America Working Group, 1997).

64. CNN, "US Protester Call for Closing School of the Americas," http://archives.cnn.com/2000/us/04/03/school.protest/ (4-3-2000).

65. U.S. Congress, *H.R. 5408, National Defense Authorization Act*, sec 911 (2000), also detailed at www.siponline.org/facts/soa.htm.

66. SOUTHCOM leadership in particular was mentioned as key in several interviews: George Vickers, SOUTHCOM Human Rights Initiative Participant, interview by author, July 2004; Leana Bresnahan, SOUTHCOM Human Rights Coordinator, interview by author, July 2004; Jose Miguel Vivanco, Human Rights Watch Executive Director Americas Division, interview by author, February

2005; and Colonel Supervielle, SOUTHCOM JAG, interview by author, July 2003.

67. Interview, Bresnahan. Alexander T. Roney, "US Southern Command's Human Rights Program," *Dialogo*, www.dialogo-americas.com.

68. Ibid.; U.S. Southern Command, *SC Form 165* (January 2001). Copy provided to author by SOUTHCOM JAG.

69. Roney, "US Southern Command's Human Rights Program," 2. Interview, Supervielle.

70. Roney, "US Southern Command's Human Rights Program," 3.

71. Interview, Bresnahan.

72. Roney, "US Southern Command's Human Rights Program," 4.

73. Interview, Bresnahan.

74. SOUTHCOM, *Consensus Document* (2002). Provided to author by SOUTHCOM Human Rights Division staff.

75. While Vickers did not promote himself as the advocate most responsible for kickstarting the Initiative in 1998, Roney identifies Vickers as the central figure. Bresnahan also noted Vickers influence during the 1998 roundtable and the subsequent reinitiation of Initiative seminars.

76. The NGO is the Centro para la Capacitacion en Derechos Humanos (CEDADH).

77. Current U.S. policy toward Saudi Arabia and Pakistan are good examples of policy that is still geared toward emphasizing security cooperation with little or no focus on human rights. While this is the case, I argue that it need not be, and that promotion of human rights through the U.S. military is an appropriate and effective avenue for trying to balance security and human rights concerns.

78. This sentiment was particularly notable in Colombia as well as with the Office of the Secretary of Defense staff. Interview, Knutson, Fiemeyer; Lt. Colonel Bruce Gillooly, US Army Counterterrorism Program, Bogota, Colombia, interview by author, September 2004.

79. See Samuel P. Huntington, *The Soldier and the State: The Theory and Politics of Civil-Military Relations* (Cambridge, MA: Harvard University Press, 1957). Huntington not only proposes that the military and civilian society are largely separate, he advocates an autonomous military as a more effective security institution. Thomas E. Ricks recently revived the debate over whether there is a civil-military divide in the United States. See Thomas E. Ricks, *Making the Corps* (New York: Scribner, 1997). For a selection of articles surrounding the debate see Peter D. Feaver and Richard H. Kohn, eds., *Soldiers and Civilians: The Civil-Military Gap and American National Security* (Cambridge, MA: MIT Press, 2001).

80. See Morris Janowitz, *The Professional Soldier: A Social and Political Portrait* (Glenco, IL: The Free Press, 1960). Other selected works in this school include Edward M. Coffman, "The Long Shadow of The Soldier and the State," *The Journal of Military History* 55, no. 1 (1991): 69–82; and John M. Gates, "The Alleged Isolation of US Army Officers in the Late 19th Century," *Parameters* 10 (Spring 1980): 33–37, 40–42, also cited in Coffman.

81. The civil-military divide almost certainly would affect human rights awareness in Latin American armed forces; Latin American countries have a dearth of

civilian expertise in the defense arena, suggesting that the gap is wider than in the United States and human rights awareness even more difficult to achieve.

3: BOLIVIA: HUMAN RIGHTS PROMOTION YIELDS MIXED RESULTS

1. Military human rights awareness efforts were robust upon writing this chapter and depended largely upon U.S. assistance. Signs of a possible cooling United States–Bolivia relationship in 2006, however, signal that human rights promotion could hit a stumbling block at any moment. Nonetheless, this chapter assesses the efforts on the ground and should serve as a good case study for the effectiveness of U.S. efforts in the military human rights area.

2. U.S. State Department, *Bolivia: Country Reports on Human Rights Practices* (February 2003).

3. The national police have primary responsibility for public security, but the president can call on the military in critical situations. Sanchez de Lozada did so in February and October of 2003.

4. *Bolivia Country Report.*

5. Presidencia de la Republica, Bolivia, *DECRETO SUPREMO* N. 27420 (March 2004).

6. Even the strongest critics of Bolivia's human rights record and the State Department's representation of the record before Congress recognize the constructive U.S. engagement with the Bolivian military on the human rights problem. See Washington Office on Latin America and Andean Information Network, *Flawed State Department Report on Human Rights in Bolivia*, Memorandum to Foreign Policy Aids (July 9, 2004).

7. Bresnahan, SOUTHCOM Human Rights Coordinator, interview by author, July 2004; *Bolivia Country Report.*

8. It is common that the State Political-Military Officer in the Embassy will help promote U.S. military interests and efforts in a host country. The foreign national's assistance in Bolivia is not a typical element of mil-to-mil relations. While the arrangement with the foreign national is well known by SOUTHCOM and the individual has served a critical role, it is not something SOUTHCOM can count on in other embassies. Indeed, SOUTHCOM may find other host countries more difficult to push along on the HRI in the absence of such a foreign national championing the cause.

9. Interviews around the region with civilian and military officials consistently revealed a preponderance for stove piping of civil-military issues within individual ministries. Indeed, a common theme in South America is a dearth of civilian military expertise. The Bolivian cooperation between the defense and justice ministries in itself is a sign of serious interaction and cooperation that is lacking in nearly every country in the region.

10. See section in this chapter on lagging civil-military institutional development where the author emphasizes NGO critique of military justice and the military for its lack of respect for civilian authority, both which run counter to effective human rights practices.

11. Latin American Working Group Education Fund, Center for International Policy, Washington Office on Latin America, *Blurring the Lines: Trends in US*

Military Programs with Latin America (Washington, DC: Author, October 2004); Center for International Policy, *Just the Facts 2001–2002: A Quick Tour of US Defense and Security Relations with Latin America and the Caribbean* (Washington, DC: Author, October 2001). It is noteworthy that every Bolivian military official that receives U.S. military training, whether funded by the State Department or Department of Defense, is vetted for previous human rights abuse. All U.S. military training given to Bolivian officials, and other military officials from around the region, includes segments on human rights.

12. See box titled "United States Sending Mixed Messages on Human Rights and Justice" on U.S. mixed messages in this chapter.

13. One U.S. NGO official whose office coauthored *Blurring the Lines* also opined that the Article 98 policies would further push funding from State to DoD. Bolivia's prominence as a U.S. recipient now, 2 years after Article 98 restrictions, bolsters this argument. Joy Olson, Executive Director Washington Office on Latin America, interview by author, November 2004.

14. Peter Harding, Human Rights Officer U.S. Embassy La Paz, interview by author, September 2004; Patricia Viscarra, Foreign Service National U.S. Embassy La Paz, interview by author, September 2004.

15. Foreign Broadcast Information Service, "Highlights: Bolivia Press" (February 8, 2005).

16. WOLA and State, *Human Rights Reports*.

17. Interview, Harding; Anonymous, U.S. Embassy La Paz, interview by author, September 2004.

18. Ibid.; State, *Human Rights Reports*. The author encountered some discussion of when and whether organized nongovernment groups or individuals looking to violently block government antidrug policies can be charged with human rights abuses. Human rights law, as detailed by the International Community of the Red Cross, applies only to government treatment of individuals. International Humanitarian Law (IHL), however, recognizes abuses by government or opposition groups during times of war or armed conflict. Human rights advocates certainly could argue that they have not championed the cause of violence by civilians or groups looking to violently oppose government economic and antidrug policies because Bolivia is not involved in a war and IHL does not apply. Even this argument, however, does not solve the problem that Bolivia is facing, which is a perception by Bolivian and U.S. officials that NGOs have a dual standard when it comes to human rights abuses. Even though the standard of human rights law does not apply to civilians, the acts in Bolivia against government officials are still prosecutable as gross violations of the law. Further, more high-profile NGO reporting of violence, torture, or murder by civilians or opposition groups would bolster the credence of NGO reporting and claims against the military. In the current setting, the NGOs appear to be taking sides, emphasizing human rights standards only when the government is guilty of abuses, rather than seeking to promote a true as environment of respect for human rights.

19. Interview, Anonymous.

20. Interview, Viscarra.

21. The author found U.S. Embassy officers quite emotional over this issue. While they often displayed sympathy for those that had filed legitimate human rights

abuse claims against the military, these sympathies seemed difficult to express in the face of public officials enduring torture in public. Indeed, one anonymous Embassy officer became visibly infuriated during our discussion, asking rhetorically how the military was supposed to take a public security role seriously when Bolivian law enforcement and society was letting pass the beating and murder of a public official on television.

22. Interviews, Anonymous, Harding. I use proportional force in quotes because this is a U.S. term that the Bolivian military does not yet fully employ or appreciate. The Bolivian fear in essence is about proportional force and the fear of facing a lethal enemy with only nonlethal defenses. Mesa stepped down from office in 2005, but without any significant human rights problems.

23. Foreign Broadcast Information Service, "Highlights: Bolivia Press" (February 8, 2005).

24. Interview, Harding; Lt. Colonel Timothy Hodge, DAO Army Attaché U.S. Embassy La Paz, interview by author, September 2004.

25. Department of State, Bureau of Political-Military Affairs. *American Service-Members' Protection Act* (Washington, DC, 2003).

26. Interview, Joy Olson.

27. Southern Command, *Posture Statement of General Blantz J. Craddock before the 109th Congress House Armed Services Committee* (March 9, 2005). For a broader discussion of the Article 98 issue and its impact on the war on terrorism, see Chapter 6.

28. Interviews, Harding, Viscarra. SOUTHCOM rules of engagement seminar, La Paz, attended by author, September 2004.

29. Several U.S. military and civilian officials and a respected Argentine human rights NGO expressed this concern regarding human rights training for unprofessional militaries. In Colombia, SOUTHCOM officials cited one case where soldiers took fire from a sniper in a church but did not return fire for fear of a human rights violation, a clear case of rule of engagement failure. Interview, Bresnahan; Lt. Col. Bruce Gillooly, U.S. Army Counterterrorism Program, Bogota, interview by author, September 2004; CELS Argentina, interview by author, December 2004.

30. Adam Isacson, Center for International Policy Program Director, interview by author, October 2004; Eric Olson, Amnesty International Advocacy Director for the Americas, interview by author, September 2004; Sacha Llorenti, Asamblea Permanente de Derechos Humanos de Bolivia President, interview by author, September 2004; Javier Ciurlizza Contreras, Instituto de Democracia y Derechos Humanos Executive Director, interview by author, September 2004; Interview, Joy Olson.

31. Interview, Eric Olson.

32. Interview, Joy Olson; Interview, Harding; Interview, Viscarra; Audalia Zurita, District Prosecutor La Paz, Bolivia, interview by author, September 2004.

33. Memorandum to Foreign Policy Aids. While U.S. Embassy officials are less adamant about the preponderance of evidence against members of the military, the State Department human rights report and interviews revealed a consensus that some soldiers did commit abuses. Interview, Harding; Interview, Anonymous.

34. *Bolivia Country Report.*

35. Memorandum to Foreign Policy Aids; Interview, Zurita.

36. Memorandum to Foreign Policy Aids; Interview, Viscarra.

37. Foreign Broadcast Information Service, "Highlights: Bolivia Press" (February 8, 2005).

38. J. Samuel Fitch, *Armed Forces and Democracy in Latin America* (Baltimore, MD: Johns Hopkins University Press, 1998).

39. Latin American Working Group Education Fund, Center for International Policy, Washington Office on Latin America, *Blurring the Lines*.

40. It is important to repeat here that civilian State officers and a civilian Bolivian officer in the U.S. Embassy have been key proponents of the SOUTHCOM HRI. The civilian engagement called for here, however, is for greater institutional collaboration, with the Department of Justice playing a greater role with its Bolivian counterparts similar to that of SOUTHCOM. The U.S. Agency for International Development also provides vast civilian assistance to Latin American governments across ministries. No civilian reform efforts in Bolivia, however, currently rival the HRI in scope or profile.

4: COLOMBIA: A COMPLEX MIX OF VICTORIES AND LESSONS FOR U.S. MILITARY HUMAN RIGHTS PROMOTION

1. Colombia is widely known for producing 90 percent of United States-consumed cocaine. While the Colombian government in the 1990s had success in bringing down large narcotics organizations, coca cultivation increased, small trafficking organizations filled in when the larger regimes fell, and paramilitary and guerrilla involvement keeps production strong. See Economist Intelligence Unit, *Country Profile Colombia 2004/2005 Main Report* (September 2004) and *Country Profile Colombia 2006/2007 Main Report* (September 2006).

2. For a concise history of the Colombian conflict see Inter-American Commission on Human Rights (IACHR), *Process of Demobilization in Colombia 2004* (Author), www.cidh.org/countryrep/Colombia04eng, Chapter 3.

3. Economist, *Colombia Country Profile;* Adam Isacson, *Peace or "Paramilitarization?" Why a Weak Peace Agreement with Colombian Paramilitary Groups May Be Worse Than No Agreement At All* (Washington, DC: Center for International Policy, July 2005).

4. U.S. State Department, *Colombia: Country Reports on Human Rights Practices* (February 2005), 20.

5. Comision Colombiana de Juristas (CCJ), *En contravia de las recomendaciones internacioneales: 'Seguridad democratica,' derechos humanos y derecho humanitariano en Colombia: agosto de 2002 a agosto de 2004* (Bogota: Author, 2004), 153–154.

6. Vicepresidencia de la Republica, Programa Presidencial de los Derechos Humanos y Derecho International Humanitariano, *Situacion de Derechos Humanos y Derecho Internacional Humanitario* (2003); Vicepresidencia de la Republica, Programa Presidencial de los Derechos Humanos y Derecho International Humanitariano, *Indicadores Comparados Sobre la Situacion de los Derechos Humanos en Colombia Noviembre de 2004* (2004); *Colombia Country Report*, 2.

7. *Colombia Country Report*, 20.

8. Demobilization data from U.S. Department of State, *Plan Colombia: Major Successes and New Challenges*, Roger Noriega, Assistant Secretary for Western

Hemisphere Affairs. Statement before the House International Relations Committee (May 11, 2005).

9. Ibid.

10. CCJ, *En contravia*, 153–154.

11. State, *Plan Colombia: Major Successes*.

12. Comision Colombiana de Juristsas, *Colombia: veinte razones para afirmar que la sitaucion de derechos humanos y derecho humanitario es muy grave y tiende a empeorar* (Bogota: Author, September 2004), 50.

13. CCJ, *En contravia*, 153.

14. Ibid., 154.

15. Programa Presidencial, *Sitaucion de derechos Humans*; Programa Presidencial, *Indicadores Comparados*, final table.

16. CCJ, *En contravia*, 36.

17. Programa Presidencial, *Sitaucion de derechos Humans*; Programa Presidencial, *Indicadores Comparados*, final table.

18. Ibid., 32.

19. CIP's Adam Isacson's latest work states that "Colombia is considered somewhat less dangerous than a year ago." He also acknowledges real reductions in murders, kidnappings, and acts of sabotage. Human Rights Watch officials in interviews were candid in their views that the peace talks with the paramilitaries combined with the military's offensive against guerrillas have led to real declines in abuses across the board. Jose Miguel Vivanco noted that for the first time, the FARC is under a military offensive. As noted below, however, both HRW officials doubted that current Uribe policies could sustain the positive movement on the human rights front. Jose Miguel Vivanco, Executive Director Human Rights Watch Americas Division, interview by author, February 2005; Maria McFarland, Human Rights Watch, Washington, DC, interview by author, January 2005.

20. See for example, State, *Plan Colombia: Major Successes*.

21. Programa Presidencial, *Sitaucion de derechos Humans*; Programa Presidencial, *Indicadores Comparados*, final table; *Colombia Country Report*, 12.

22. Interviews with Vivanco and McFarland.

23. As the author notes in this chapter, collusion has declined significantly following demobilization of more than 30,000 paramilitaries since 2004. Still, nearly every piece of literature that discusses human rights in Colombia deals with the problem of military-paramilitary collusion. For the most comprehensive assessment of the problem see Human Rights Watch, *The "Sixth Division" Military-Paramilitary Ties and US Policy in Colombia* (Washington, DC: Author, 2002). The most recent account of the military-paramilitary relationship is, Adam Isacson, *Peace or Paramilitarization*. A brief but good historical perspective is in IACHR, *Process of Demobilization*.

24. CCJ, *En contravia*, 153.

25. Ibid., 154.

26. Ibid.

27. *Colombia Country Report*, 1. The Colombian government's military attache in Washington told the author that the government does not publish such abuses because investigation of such allegations is ongoing. The attache suggested that the author could obtain government abuse numbers through formal written

request to his office, but the author never received said data. The attache seemed willing but unable to attain the data from officials in Bogota. The lack of such official information complicates the overall picture for the public and human rights community, and conversely for the Colombian military itself. Colombian Defense Attache, Washington, DC, phone conversations and written correspondence with author, June 2005. Written correspondence on file with author.

28. U.S. Department of State, *Memorandum of Justification Concerning Human Rights Conditions with Respect to Assistance for Colombian Armed Forces* (September 2004).

29. Ibid.

30. Ibid.

31. Interviews with Vivanco, McFarland; Craig Conway, Human Rights Officer U.S. Embassy, Bogota, interview by author, September 2004; Three anonymous U.S. government officials, interview by author, July 2003.

32. Interview with three anonymous. What was striking about these government officials' statements is that they were put forward as widely known and understood facts. The officials said that military-paramilitary collusion was commonplace, publicly known by all who follow Colombia, and unlikely to stop regardless of U.S. pressure or incentives. The officials noted the ease with which collusion continues and cited collusion as the critical military link to human rights abuses.

33. HRW, *Sixth Division*, 9–51.

34. State, *Memorandum of Justification*.

35. IACHR, *Process of Demobilization*, paragraph 36.

36. Ibid.

37. U.S. State Department, *58th UNGA: Third Committee Debate on Human Rights Issues* (December 17, 2003).

38. Foreign Broadcast Information Service, *Colombian Government Report Minimizes Army Role in Human Rights* (September 9, 2003).

39. Latin American Working Group Education Fund, Center for International Policy, Washington Office on Latin America, *Blurring the Lines: Trends in US Military Programs with Latin America* (Washington, DC: Author, October 2004), 11. Also see CIP's Colombia Program "US Aid to Colombia since 1997: Summary Tables," www.ciponline.org/colombia/aidtable.htmm (February 2005). Also see Table 1.1. in Chapter 1.

40. Ibid.

41. Ibid., 2.

42. Captain Michael Gomez and Sergeant Barry Grissom, U.S. Army 7th Special Forces, Espinal, Colombia, interview by author, September 2004; Captain Daza, Colombian National Police, Espinal, Colombia, interview by author, September 2004.

43. State, *Memorandum of Justification*.

44. For examples of how multiple NGOs are able to use the certification process as a window to air concerns see Amnesty International, Human Rights Watch, Washington Office on Latin America, *Colombia Human Rights Certification III, Briefing Paper* (Washington, DC: Author, February 2002); Human Rights Watch, *Colombia: Flawed Certification Squanders US Leverage—US Aid Released Despite Evidence of Colombia's Failure to Meet Conditions* (Author, January 23, 2003).

45. Colonel DeLeon, USAF JAG, U.S. Embassy Bogota, interview by author, September 2004; Lt. Col. Mark Gingras, Assistant JAG SOUTHCOM, interview by author, July 2003; SOUTHCOM JAG Plan Colombia Talking Points, provided to author (July 2003 and December 2005).

46. Ibid.

47. Ibid.

48. Interview with DeLeon.

49. U.S. State Department, *Military Penal Justice Corps School Seeks to Improve the Colombian Military Justice System* (April 10, 2003); Interview with Vivanco.

50. Ibid.

51. SOUTHCOM JAG Talking Points.

52. Ibid.

53. Ministerio de defensa Nacional, *Strengthening of the Human Rights and IHL Culture in the Colombian Police and Armed Forces*, http://aplpha.mindefensa.gov.co/index.php?page=181&id=903.

54. Fuerzas Militares de Colombia, Comando General, *Plan de integracion del derecho internacional de los derechos humanos y del derecho internacional aplicable en situaciones de conflicto armado las fuerzas militares* (March 2003) copy provided to author.

55. Ministerio de Defensa, *Strengthening of Human Rights*.

56. Interview, Gingras; Lt. Col. Maria Cordero, Commander SOUTHCOM Human Rights Division, interview by author, July 2003; Raimondo, interview by author, November 2004; O'Reilly, Deputy Political Counselor, U.S. Embassy Mexico City, interview by author, July 2003; Feeley, Deputy Political Counselor U.S. Embassy Mexico City 2001–2003, interview by author, June 2003.

57. Bresnahan, SOUTHCOM Human Rights Coordinator, interview by author, July 2004; Miles, Political Officer U.S. Embassy Buenos Aires, interview by author, December 2004.

58. Interviews, Cordero and Gingras.

59. Interviews with Pierre Ferrand and Mauricio Hernandez, International Committee of the Red Cross, Bogota, September 2004.

60. Latin American Working Group Education Fund, *Blurring the Lines*, 11; CIP, *Colombia Program*.

61. U.S. State Department, *Supporting Human Rights and Democracy: The US Record in Colombia 2004–2005* (February 2005); U.S. State Department, *Supporting Human Rights and Democracy: The US Record in Colombia 2003–2004* (February 2004); U.S. State Department, Embassy Human Rights Strategy (February 2003).

62. Ibid.

63. Ibid.

64. Ibid.

65. All data and statistics on USAID and DOJ efforts from Ibid.

66. Interviews, Fiemeyer, Knutson, DeLeon; Colonel W. Jay Schell, U.S. Mil-Group, U.S. Embassy Bogota, interview by author, September 2004; Colonel Simeon Trombitas, U.S. Mil-Group Commander, U.S. Embassy Bogota, interview by author, September 2004.

67. Interviews, Knutson, Fiemeyer, DeLeon, and Conway.

68. Interview, DeLeon; SOUTHCOM JAG Talking Points.

69. SOUTHCOM JAG Talking Points.

70. Interviews, Bresnahan and Trombitas.

71. Interview, Trombitas. This amounts to a serious criticism of SOUTHCOM. Based on the evidence in this work, the point is probably more appropriate in gauging the level of Colombian commitment, as opposed to entirely discrediting the impact of SOUTHCOM efforts.

72. *Colombia Country Report*, 18; Economist, *Country Profile Colombia*.

73. Economist, *Country Profile Colombia*.

74. Ibid.

75. *Colombia Country Report*, 19.

76. U.S. State Department, *Staffdel Meeting with Minister of Defense* (August 25, 2004).

77. U.S. State Department, *Colombia: Country Reports on Human Rights Practices* (February 2004), 11.

78. The State Department has largely praised Uribe's deployment of hometown soldiers in U.S. Department of State, *Uribe's Peasant Soldiers: Key to Extending Security throughout Colombia* (June 2003). For a recent critique of this policy see The Latin America Working Group Education Fund, *The Wrong Road: Colombia's National Security Policy* (Washington, DC: Author, July 2003), 11.

79. The Latin America Working Group Education Fund, *The Wrong Road*, 3; *Colombia Country Report*, 9, 12; Freedom House, *Freedom in the World: Colombia*, www.freedomhouse.ord/research/freeworld/2004/countryratings/colombia.htm.

80. Freedom House, *Colombia*.

81. United Nations High Commissioner for Human Rights, "Informe del Alto Comisionado de las Naciones Unidas para los Derechos Humanos sobre la situacion de los derechos humanos en Colombia," (UN Document E/CN.4/2003/13, February 2003), 33, cited in The Latin America Working Group Education Fund, *The Wrong Road*, 9.

82. The Latin America Working Group Education Fund, *The Wrong Road*, 9.

83. In Argentina and Chile the term counterterrorism seems to be nearly taboo for security forces. The armed forces in both countries will give no consideration to a counterterrorism role for fear of repeating their shared histories of abuse.

84. State, *Uribe's Peasant Soldiers. Colombia Country Report*, 29.

85. State, *Uribe's Peasant Soldiers*.

86. Ibid.; The Latin America Working Group Education Fund, *The Wrong Road*, 12.

87. Quoted in The Latin America Working Group Education Fund, *The Wrong Road*, 13.

88. Part IV Article 13 of Geneva Conventions Protocol II dealing with treatment of civilians in noninternational armed conflict states that the civilian population is protected against the dangers of war, unless the civilians take direct part in hostilities. Law of War Documentary Supplement, *Protocol Additional to the Geneva Conventions of 12 August 1949, and Relating to the Protection of Victims of Non-International Armed Conflicts (Protocol II), 8 June 1977* (Charlottesville, VA: The Judge Advocate General's Legal Center and School, 2004), 392. See box titled "Colombia's Geneva Protocol Conundrum" in this chapter.

89. The Latin America Working Group Education Fund, *The Wrong Road*, 12.

90. See footnote 88 on Protocol II of the Geneva Conventions.

91. Documentary Supplement, Protocol II, Part I Art. 1, 389.

92. Ibid.

93. *Colombia Country Report*, 1.

94. Documentary Supplement, Protocol II, Part I Art. 1, 392.

95. Ramsey, interview by author, November 2004.

96. See Chapter 5.

97. State, *Colombia Country Report*, 1, 3, and 9.

98. State, *Memorandum of Justification*.

99. Amnesty, *Human Rights Certification III*, 10.

100. Presidencia de la Republica, Ministerio de Defensa Nacional, *Politica de Defensa y Seguridad Democratica* (Bogota, 2003).

101. State, *Memorandum of Justification*.

102. Ibid.

103. Ibid.

104. Interview, McFarland.

105. All data and facts in this paragraph are from *Memorandum of Justification*. The author found it almost disconcerting that State would list this very data—cited here as proof of Colombia's poor judicial record—as part of its effort to certify Colombian compliance with congressional human rights requirements for foreign assistance.

106. Human Rights Watch, *A Wrong Turn: The Record of the Colombian Attorney General's Office* (Washington, DC: Author, November 2002).

107. Ibid., 6–13.

108. Ibid., 10.

109. Ibid., 9–12.

110. Ibid.

111. Ibid.

112. State, *Memorandum of Justification*.

113. Adam Isacson, *Re: Colombia's Peace Talks with Paramilitaries: Conditions for US Support* (Center for International Policy Memorandum to Colleagues and Legislative Staff, December 7, 2004), 11.

114. As the author notes in this chapter, the demobilization of more than 30,000 paramilitary forces has left the AUC essentially defunct. With its roots still intact, however, this argument of AUC reemergence cannot be dismissed out of hand. Isacson, *Peace or Paramilitarization*, 3; Human Rights Watch, *Colombia: Letting Paramilitaries Off The Hook, A Human Rights Watch Briefing Paper* (Washington, DC: Author, January 2005), 8; Jose Miguel Vivanco and Maria McFarland Sanchez-Moreno, "A Bad Plan in Colombia," *International Herald Tribune* (May 16, 2005).

115. Interview, Vivanco.

116. Isacson, *Peace or Paramilitarization*, 4.

117. Ibid., 2; HRW, *Letting Paramilitaries Off The Hook*, 11.

118. Ibid.; HRW, *Letting Paramilitaries Off The Hook*, 5.

119. U.S. Congressional Research Service, *Plan Colombia: A Progress Report*, by Connie Veillette (Order Code RL32774, February 17, 2005).

120. Whether the spread of democracy would reduce terror is debatable. The focus of this book does not permit a full debate of the issue, which would serve as a good future research topic building on this work. The point here is that if Washington is going to push democracy as the key prescription to terror, it should be able to promote human rights simultaneously, particularly in Colombia where democratic norms appear to be central to improving human rights.

121. The possible positive impact of war on human rights may depend on the human rights visions of opposing sides in a conflict. Who wins a war may decisively affect the human rights outcome. In a civil war or insurrection, the human rights values of the two sides are of critical importance. In some cases, victory by the insurrection can prove a disaster for human rights (the Bolshevik victory in Russia). In some cases, victory by the government is a disaster for human rights (China in Tienamen Square).

122. Interview, Trombitas.

5: VENEZUELA: HUMAN RIGHTS AWARENESS FALLING BY THE WAYSIDE

1. Foreign Broadcast Information Service, *Highlights: Brazil Magazine Review* (May 2, 2005).

2. For the latest on FARC support in Venezuela, see Thor Halvorssen, "The Arrest of FARC Terrorist Ricardo Granda Sheds New Light on Hugo Chavez's Ongoing Support of Terrorism," *The Weekly Standard* (January 26, 2005). For Chavez's policy announcements, see BBC, "Chavez Creates New Loyal Reserve" (April 4, 2005); Foreign Broadcast Information Service, "Highlights: Venezuela Political Press" (April 6, 2005); Foreign Broadcast Information Service, "Venezuelan Opposition Thinks Armed Reserves Will Replace FAN" (April 5, 2005); Foreign Broadcast Information Service, "Venezuelan Government Promoting New Defense System" (March 13, 2005); Foreign Broadcast Information Service, "Venezuela: Chavez Explains Defense Strategy in Nationwide Broadcasts" (March 23, 2005).

3. Human Rights Watch, *Rigging the Rule of Law: Judicial Independence under Siege in Venezuela* (Washington, DC: Author, June 2004); Human Rights Watch, *Venezuela: Media Law Undercuts Freedom of Expression* (Washington, DC: Author, November 24, 2004).

4. There is no evidence that the United States at any level supported the coup. Washington's failure to condemn the coup plotters, however, has allowed Chavez to bolster his claims that the United States was behind his temporary ouster.

5. Good summaries of Venezuela's recent history can be found in Economist Intelligence Unit, *Country Profile Venezuela 2004/2005 Main Report*; Freedom House, *Venezuela Country Rating*, www.freedomhouse.org/research/freeworld/2004/countryratings/venezuela.htm.

6. Maria Virginia Trimarco, Regional Representative, UN High Commission on Refugees, Caracas, interview by author, December 2004.

7. U.S. military officials and human rights activists agreed on labeling the Venezuelan force traditionally less aggressive. Colonel Terry DeRouchy, U.S. Mil-Group U.S. Embassy Caracas, interview by author, December 2004; Interview, Trimarco.

8. Alfredo Ruiz and anonymous assistant, Red de Apoyo, Caracas, interview by author, December 2004.

9. U.S. State Department, *Venezuela: Country Reports on Human Rights Practices* (February 2004); U.S. State Department, *Venezuela: Country Reports on Human Rights Practices* (February 2005).

10. *Venezuela Country Report* 2005.

11. Amnesty International, *Venezuela: Human Rights under Threat* (Washington, DC: Author, AI Index: AMR 53/005/2004, May 2004).

12. In Freedom House, *Venezuela.*

13. *Venezuela Country Report 2005.*

14. Interviews, Trimarco and Ruiz. Anonymous Venezuelan National Guard officer, Caracas, interview by author, December 2004.

15. Red de Apoyo, *Casos Atendido Por La Red de Apoyo, Periodo: Enero–Noviembre 2004.* Provided to author by Red de Apoyo; *Venezuela Country Report* 2005.

16. Interview, Trimarco.

17. Ibid.

18. Interview, DeRouchy; Lt. Colonel Humberto Rodriguez and Major Jorge Zequeira, U.S. Defense Attache Office U.S. Embassy Caracas, interview by author, December 2004.

19. *Venezuela Country Report 2005*; Interviews, Col. Rodriguez and Maj. Zequeira.

20. Interviews, Trimarco, DeRouchy, Col. Rodriguez, Zequeira, and Ruiz.

21. Interview, Trimarco.

22. Ibid.

23. Ibid.

24. Interviews, Trimarco and Ruiz.

25. Interviews, Trimarco, DeRouchy, Col. Rodriguez, Zequeira, and Ruiz; Alexandra Freitas, Consorcio Justicial, Caracas, interview by author, December 2004; Rocio San Miguel, former Venezuela War College Professor, Caracas, interview by author, December 2004; General Enrique Prieto Silva, Retired Venezuelan Army, Caracas, interview by author, December 2004; Admiral Rafael Huizi, Retried Venezuelan Navy, Caracas, interview by author, December 2004.

26. ANNCOL, "FARC Commander Kidnapped in Venezuela" (December 30, 2004).

27. Latin American Working Group Education Fund, Center for International Policy, Washington Office on Latin America, *Blurring the Lines* (Washington, DC: Author, October 2004), 11. The same data can be found at www.ciponline.org/facts. Primary sources include Foreign Military Training and DoD Engagement Activities reports to Congress. For the purposes of this book, the Center for International Policy, coauthor of *Blurring the Lines* and publisher of *Just the Facts*, should be considered the most reliable source of compiled training and funding numbers for the region. State Department and DoD officials on more than one occasion indicated that CIP is the most comprehensive source for such data. Chris Crowley and Lt. Colonel Robert Levinson, SOUTHCOM Legislative Affairs, Washington, DC, interview by author, July 2004; Kevin O'Reilly, Deputy Political Counselor, U.S. Embassy Mexico City, interview by author, July 2003.

28. Ibid.

29. Ibid.

30. Ibid.

31. Interview, DeRouchy. The fact that the Mil-Group had offices on a Venezuelan base is a sign of the previously close military-to-military relationship. The vast majority of U.S. Mil-Group offices are in their respective U.S. Embassies. Only the closest bilateral relationship would lead to U.S. military offices on the base of a host country.

32. Reuters, "Chavez ends Venezuela Military Cooperation with US" (April 24, 2005).

33. Several U.S. civilians and military officials noted that the human rights vetting, commonly known as Leahy vetting, since it is mandated by a foreign assistance amendment sponsored by U.S. Senator Leahy, is a significant lever for emphasizing human rights in Latin America. While several officials pointed to the rule as cumbersome, and often confusing, they agreed that the vetting rule was something that over the years has prompted foreign militaries to either push for greater human rights practices to gain access to U.S. assistance, or at a minimum put forward only "clean" candidates that had no abuse record. See Chapter 2 for further discussion of the Leahy Amendment. Lt. Col. Bruce Gillooly, U.S. Army Counterterrorism Program, Bogota, Colombia, interview by author, September 2004; Maj. Michael Knutson, Office of Secretary of Defense, interview by author, July 2003; Lt. Col. Dennis Fiemeyer, Office of Secretary of Defense, interview by author, July 2003; Lt. Colonel Maria Cordero, SOUTHCOM Human Rights Division Commander, interview by author, July 2003; Lt. Colonel Mark Gingras, SOUTHCOM Assistant JAG, interview by author, July 2003.

34. Interviews, Raimondo, anonymous Venezuelan officer, and Zequeira.

35. Interviews, Bresnahan, Raimondo; Victor Uribe, SOUTHCOM Human Rights Initiative Participant, interview by author, July 2004; George Vickers, SOUTHCOM Human Rights Initiative Participant, interview by author, July 2004.

36. Ibid.

37. Interviews, Cordero, Bresnahan, Gingras.

38. Addicott and Roberts, "Building Democracies with Southern Command's Legal Engagement Strategy," *Parameters* (Spring 2001).

39. Interviews, anonymous Venezuelan officer, DeRouchy, Zeguiria; Col. Supervielle, SOUTHCOM JAG, interview by author, July 2003; Lt. Colonel Humberto Rodriguez, U.S. Defense Attache Office Caracas, interview by author, December 2004.

40. Amnesty International, *Venezuela: Human Rights Agenda for the Current Crisis* (Washington, DC: Author, AI Index: AMR 53/001/2003).

41. Freedom House, *Freedom in the World Country Ratings: 1972 through 2003*, www.freedomhouse.org.

42. The U.S. State Department Country Report on Human Rights Practices is the best single source for recounting the numerous violations of civil liberties in Venezuela. In an attempt to bolster the sourcing of my claims, I supplement all State Department reporting with independent sources, particularly because the U.S. government has been at loggerheads with the Chavez administration. For the specific definitions of human rights used in this book see Chapter 1.

43. HRW, *Rigging the Rule of Law*.

44. Ibid.

45. Ibid., 15–16.

46. HRW, *Media Law Undercuts Freedom of Expression*.

47. *Venezuela Country Report 2004*, 9.

48. *Venezuela Country Report 2004*; HRW, *Media Law Undercuts Freedom of Expression*.

49. *Venezuela Country Report 2004* and *2005*.

50. *Venezuela Country Report 2004* and *2005*.

51. Ecuador is the one case listed above in which the military played a role in forcing the country's president from office in 2000. The same military, however, refrained from taking any political action during the most recent presidential ouster in April 2005. Military forces played a controversial security role during Bolivia's political instability, as detailed in Chapter 3. Former and deposed military forces involved themselves in wide-ranging unrest against the national police in Haiti, leading to the presidential resignation in 2004. Military forces were glaringly absent from the 2001–2002 instability in Argentina that saw five elected and interim presidencies in only a few weeks. The Peruvian military played no active role in the ouster of that country's president in 2001. In none of the countries listed has the military taken on as broad a political role as the armed forces in Venezuela.

52. Interviews, Trimarco, Freitas, and San Miguel.

53. *Venezuela Country Report 2004*.

54. Wall Street Journal, "Americas: At State, A Chavez Foe is Labeled a 'Terrorist'" (July 15, 2003); Wall Street Journal, "Americas: Read the Fine Print on the Chavez Charm Offensive" (June 4, 2003); Wall Street Journal, "Chavez's Cheatin' Heart" (August 6, 2004); Latin American Newsletters, LTD., "Chavez's Revolution has yet To Materialize" (October 23, 2003).

55. BBC, "Chavez Creates New Loyal Reserve" (April 4, 2005); Foreign Broadcast Information Service, "Highlights: Venezuela Political Press" (April 6, 2005); Foreign Broadcast Information Service, "Venezuelan Opposition Thinks Armed Reserves Will Replace FAN" (April 5, 2005); Foreign Broadcast Information Service, "Venezuelan Government Promoting New Defense System" (March 13, 2005); Foreign Broadcast Information Service, "Venezuela: Chavez Explains Defense Strategy in Nationwide Broadcasts" (March 23, 2005).

56. Interview, Raimondo.

57. Amnesty, *Human Rights under Threat*, 12.

58. *Venezuela Country Report 2005*, 2–4.

59. Amnesty, *Human Rights Agenda*, 2.

60. The White House, *President Sworn in to Second Term*, www.whitehouse.gov/news/releases/2005/01.html (Inauguration 2005).

61. Interviews, anonymous Venezuelan officer, Ruiz, and San Miguel.

62. See Introduction for a discussion of SOUTHCOM's promotion of such roles through its former Commander.

63. Numerous Latin American countries are again turning to their armed forces for police-type duties. Several Central American countries, including El Salvador, Nicaragua, and Guatemala all deploy their military forces to combat gangs. In Mexico, the military is the primary counternarcotics and counterterrorist force. Even in

the Southern Cone, where counterterrorism is taboo and linked with past abuses, militaries take on policing roles to control rural unrest, such as in Brazil and Paraguay.

6: AT A CRITICAL JUNCTURE: MILITARY HUMAN RIGHTS PROMOTION IN THE COUNTERTERRORISM AGE

1. Jack Donnelly, "International Human Rights: Unintended Consequences of the War on Terrorism," in Thomas G. Weiss, Margaret E. Crahan, and John Goering, eds., *War on Terrorism and Iraq: Human Rights, Unilateralism, and US Foreign Policy* (New York: Routledge, 2004), 98.

2. Sikkink, *Mixed Signals: US Human Rights Policy and Latin America* (Ithaca, NY: Cornell University Press, 2004), 21.

3. Kenneth Roth, "The Fight against Terrorism: The Bush Administration's Dangerous Neglect of Human Rights," in Weiss, Crahan, and Goering, eds., *War on Terrorism and Iraq*, 113–131.

4. Ibid., 113.

5. Tom Farer, "The Interplay of Domestic Politics, Human Rights, and US Foreign Policy," in Weiss, Crahan, and Goering, eds., *War on Terrorism and Iraq*, 48.

6. Ibid.

7. David P. Forsythe, "US Foreign Policy and Human Rights in an Era of Insecurity: The Bush Administration and Human Rights after September 11," in Weiss, Crahan, and Goering, eds., *War on Terrorism and Iraq*, 93.

8. Lisa Haugaard, Sean Garcia, Philip Schmidt, and Mavis Anderson, *September's Shadow: Post-9/11 US-Latin America Relations* (Washington, DC: Latin America Working Group, September 2004).

9. Ibid.

10. Ibid., 5

11. Ibid., 6

12. Author interviews in Argentina and Chile revealed a strong consensus among government officials, military and civilian, that the armed forces would not play any counterterrorism role because of the negative connotation and the lesson learned that it increases the propensity for human rights abuses.

13. Defining terrorism has itself become a politically charged issue in the region and in U.S.–Latin American relations. For example, various countries around the region, including Argentina, Brazil, and Chile refuse to define some security-related threats as "terrorism threats" because the governments fear stoking domestic conflicts over the past, when the militaries engaged in counterterrorism. Brazil has refused to identify insurgents in Colombia—they often cross the border into Brazil—as terrorists groups because it apparently fears that such classification promotes problems for the government in promoting the country and region as safe for business and travel.

14. Lt. Col. Mark Gingras, Assistant JAG SOUTHCOM, interview by author, July 2003, Miami; Lt. Col. Maria Cordero, Commander SOUTHCOM Human Rights Division, interview by author, July 2003, Miami; Col. Supervielle, SOUTH-COM JAG, interview by author, July 2003, Washington, DC. As this book entered the review process, the United States was grappling with investigations surrounding abuse allegations in Haditha, Iraq. Neither U.S. investigators nor human rights

groups had published final determinations of innocence or guilt on the part of U.S. forces.

15. Interview, Supervielle.

16. Steven M. Schneebaum, Chairman WHINSEC Board of Visitors 2004, interview by author, November 2004, Washington, DC.

17. Leana Bresnahan, SOUTHCOM Human Rights Coordinator, interview by author, July 2004; Colonel Miller, Commander SOUTHCOM Human Rights Division, interview by author, July 2004; Western Hemisphere Institute for Security Cooperation Human Rights Instructor Russell Ramsey, interview by author, November 2004; and Western Hemisphere Institute for Security Cooperation Human Rights Instructor Major Antonio Raimondo, interview by author, November 2004; Colonel Daniel Barretto, U.S. Mil-Group U.S. Embassy La Paz, interview by author, September 2004; Joseph Leuer, Instructor, Western Hemisphere Institute for Security Cooperation, interview by author, November 2004.

18. Interviews, Bresnahan and Miller.

19. Lino Gutierrez, U.S. Ambassador U.S. Embassy Buenos Aires, interview by author, December 2005.

20. This admission is arguably naïve. The United States continues to push policies that human rights promoters denounce as blatantly violating accepted international standards, and the military has been using "lessons learned" for more than three decades. To their credit, however, the U.S. military operators appear to be looking for a way to correct mistakes quickly, and to find a way through training to admit wrongdoing, rather than ignore it.

21. Interview, Raimondo.

22. Unfortunately for these military trainers, the civilian response has been weak and leaves working level military efforts to make amends for the past looking inadequate. Again, the military human rights promoters deserve credit for quickly admitting wrongdoing and looking for a way to make this admission clear. These efforts would be far more effective if senior civilian and defense officials made it immediately clear that anyone abusing prisoners would be immediately punished, even if it means firing Cabinet officials. In other words, the military working level efforts to right great wrongs are weakened by administration policies that signal that torture, in some circumstances, is warranted.

23. Interviews, Bresnahan and Miller.

24. Interviews, Leuer, Raimondo, and Ramsey.

25. Interviews, Leuer and Raimondo.

26. Interview, Ramsey.

27. Interview, Barretto; Lt. Colonel Sal Gomez, US Mil-Group U.S. Embassy Lima, interview by author, September 2004; Captain Ray Anderson and Lt. Colonel Kris Cuello, U.S. Defense Attache Office, U.S. Embassy Lima, interview by author, September 2004; Lt. Colonel Dan Alabre, U.S. Defense Attache Office, U.S. Embassy Santiago, interview by author, November 2004.

28. For legal rights of prisoners of war under the Geneva Conventions see Article 105 of Geneva Convention III Relative to the Treatment of Prisoners of War of August 12, 1949, Geneva, in U.S. JAG Documentary Supplement.

29. Margaret Crahan, Hunter College/SOUTHCOM Human Rights Advisor, interview by author, April 2005.

30. Author attendance at U.S. JAG Law of War course, Washington, DC (April 2005).

31. Interview, Gingras.

32. ABC South Australia, "Third Prosecutor Critical of Guantanamo Trials," http://abc.net.au/news/items/200508/1428749.htm?sa (August 3, 2005).

33. National Public Radio, "Rumsfeld in Guantanamo Bay," *Morning Edition* (January 28, 2002).

34. The executive branch is essentially trying to enforce the American Service-Members' Protection Act (ASPA), passed by Congress in 2002 and requiring suspension of specific military assistance to countries that have signed and ratified the Rome Treaty of 1998, which established the ICC and provides in its Article 98 for countries to extradite military officials from another country to the ICC in cases of human rights violations. President Clinton signed the Rome Treaty with some reservation and Congress never ratified it. For more on the Article 98 see the box titled "United States Sending Mixed Messages on Human Rights and Justice" in Chapter 3 of this book. Also see Department of State, Bureau of Political-Military Affairs, *American Service-Members' Protection Act* (Washington, DC, 2003).

35. In 2006 Washington issued Article 98 waivers to restore some training assistance for several Latin American countries. Latin American Working Group Education Fund, Center for International Policy, Washington Office on Latin America, *Below the Radar: US Military Programs with Latin America, 1997–2007* (Washington, DC: Author, March 2007), 15. Latin American Working Group Education Fund, Center for International Policy, Washington Office on Latin America, *Blurring the Lines: Trends in US Military Programs with Latin America* (Washington, DC: Author, October 2004), 6.

36. Interviews, Gomez, Leuer; Chris Crowley, SOUTHCOM Legislative Affairs, Washington, DC, interview by author, July 2004; Lt. Col. Robert Levinson, SOUTHCOM Legislative Affairs, Washington, DC, interview by author, July 2004; Lawrence Cohen, Political Officer U.S. Embassy Brasilia, interview by author, December 2005; Colonel William Dalson, U.S. Defense Attache Office, U.S. Embassy Buenos Aires, interview by author, December 2004; Commander Lowell McClintock, U.S. Mil-Group, U.S. Embassy Buenos Aires, interview by author, December 2004; Captain Bruno and Colonel Karol, U.S. Embassy Brasilia, interview by author, December 2004; Jeff Galvin, U.S. Embassy Political Officer, Santiago, interview by author, November 2005.

37. Ibid.

38. Ibid.

39. Interviews, Cohen and Galvin.

40. Interview, Gomez.

41. Interview, Leuer.

42. Southern Command, Posture Statement.

43. Interview, Crowley and Levinson.

44. Latin American Working Group Education Fund, *Blurring the Lines*, 8.

45. Lt. Col. Bruce Gillooly, U.S. Army Counterterrorism Program, Bogota, Colombia, interview by author, September 2004; Stan Brown, U.S. Narcotics Affairs Section U.S. Embassy Bogota, interview by author, September 2004.

46. Donnelly, "Unintended Consequences"; Sikkink, *Mixed Signals*.

47. Interview, Bresnahan.

48. Interviews, Bresnahan, DeLeon, Miller; Col. W. Jay Schell, U.S. Mil-Group, U.S. Embassy Bogota, interview by author, September 2004; Steve Berger, U.S. Mil-Group, U.S. Embassy Bogota, interview by author, September 2004.

49. Craig Conway, Human Rights Officer U.S. Embassy Bogota, interview by author, September 2004.

50. Hugh Byrne, *We Will Be Known by the Company We Keep: Lessons from US-Latin America Policy for the post-September 11th World* (Washington, DC: Latin America Working Group, 2002).

51. Interview, Alabre; Jeff Galvin, U.S. Embassy Political Officer, Santiago, interview by author, November 2004; Colonel Jorge Matos, U.S. Mil-Group, U.S. Embassy Bogota, interview by author, September 2004; Colonel Alex Trujillo, U.S. Defense Attache Office U.S. Embassy Bogota, interview by author, September 2004.

52. Interviews, Dalson, McClintock; Hugo Llorens, Deputy Chief of Missions, U.S. Embassy Buenos Aires, interview by author, December 2004; Richard Miles, Political Officer U.S. Embassy Buenos Aires, interview by author, December 2004; David Aarid, Political-Military Officer U.S. Embassy Buenos Aires, interview by author, December 2004.

53. Roth, "The Fight against Terrorism," 114.

54. Ingrid Vaicius and Adam Isacson, The "War on Drugs" Meets the "War on Terror": The United States' Military Involvement in Colombia Climbs to the Next Level (Washington, DC: Center for International Policy, February 2003), 18.

55. Sikkink, *Mixed Signals*, 21.

56. Interviews, Cordero, Gingras, Supervielle; Maj. Michael Knutson, Office of Secretary of Defense, interview by author, July 2003; Dr. Richard Downie. Director of Center for Hemispheric Defense Studies, interview by author, September 2004.

7: CONCLUSION

1. Interview, ICRC.

2. For a sampling of statistical works see Chapter 1. Carleton and Stohl, "The Role of Human Rights in US Assistance Policy: A Critique and Reappraisal," *American Journal of Political Science* 31, no. 4 (1987); Pilatovsky, Miller, Ogundele, "Human Rights and US Foreign Aid Revisited: The Latin American Region," *Human Rights Quarterly* 16, no. 3 (1994); Cingranelli and Pasquarello, "Human Rights Practices and the Distribution of US Foreign Aid to Latin American Countries," *American Journal of Political Science* 29, no. 3 (1985); Blanton, "Promoting Human Rights and Democracy in the Developing World: US Rhetoric versus US Arms Exports," *American Journal of Political Science* 44, no. 1 (2000). Carleton, Stohl, and Johnson, "Human Rights and US Foreign Assistance from Nixon to Carter," *Journal of Peace Research* 21, no. 3 (1984); McCormick and Mitchell, "Is US Aid Really Linked to Human Rights in Latin America?" *American Journal of Political Science* 32, no. 1 (1988); Watson and McCluskie, "Human Rights Considerations and US Foreign Policy: The Latin American Experience," *The Social Science Journal* 34, no. 2 (1997).

3. For funding levels see Table 1.1. in this book, or see Latin American Working Group Education Fund, Center for International Policy, Washington Office on

Latin America, *Blurring the Lines: Trends in US Military Programs with Latin America* (Washington DC: Author, October 2004).

4. The future of human rights in Venezuela will be critical for determining if my assertions here are perhaps too harsh. For example, if a human rights culture has taken root, regardless of whether the United States can take credit or not, it will presumably be harder for "bad" regimes to maintain power, and more likely that human rights will be quickly reinstitutionalized when the regimes are gone.

5. See Chapter 1 definition of democratic development. Fitch, *Armed Forces and Democracy in Latin America* (Baltimore, MD: Johns Hopkins University Press, 1998); Ruhl, "Curbing Central America's Militaries," *Journal of Democracy* 15, no. 3 (July 2004).

6. Three anonymous U.S. government officials, interview by author, July 2003; Craig Conway, Human Rights Officer U.S. Embassy Bogota, interview by author, September 2004.

7. FBIS, Brazil Magazine Review.

8. Leana Bresnahan, SOUTHCOM Human Rights Coordinator, interview by author, July 2004.

9. Gustavo Gallon, Director International Commission of Jurists, interview by author, December 2004; Isacson, Program Director Center for International Policy, interview by author, October 2004; Llorenti, President Asamblea Permanente de Derechos Humanos de Bolivia, interview by author, September 2004; MacFarland, Human Rights Watch, interview by author, January 2005; E. Olson, Advocacy Director Amnesty International for the Americas, interview by author, September 2004; J. Olson, Executive Director Washington Office on Latin America, interview by author, November 2004.

10. Interview, Bresnahan; Colonel Miller, Commander SOUTHCOM Human Rights Division, interview by author, July 2004.

Bibliography

Addicott, Jeffrey F. and Guy B. Roberts. "Building Democracies with Southern Command's Legal Engagement Strategy," *Parameters* 31 (Spring 2001), 72–84.

Amnesty International, Human Rights Watch, Washington Office on Latin America. *Colombia Human Rights Certification III, Briefing Paper*. Washington, DC: Author, February 2002.

Amnesty International. *Venezuela: Human Rights Agenda for the Current Crisis*. Washington, DC: Author, 2003. AI Index: AMR 53/001/2003.

———.*Venezuela: Human Rights Under Threat*. Washington, DC: Author, May 2004. AI Index: AMR 53/005/2004.

Amnesty International USA. *Unmatched Power, Unmet Principles: The Human Rights Dimensions of US Training of Foreign Military and Police Forces*. New York: Author, 2002.

Bemis, Samuel Flagg. *A Diplomatic History of the United States*. New York: Holt, Reinhart, and Winston, 1965.

Blanton, Shannon Lindsey. "Promoting Human Rights and Democracy in the Developing World: US Rhetoric versus US Arms Exports," *American Journal of Political Science* 44, no. 1 (2000), 123–131.

Bolivia, Presidencia de la Republica. *DECRETO SUPREMO* N. 27420. March 2004.

Byrne, Hugh. *We Will Be Known by the Company We Keep: Lessons from US-Latin America Policy for the post-September 11th World*. Washington, DC: Latin America Working Group, 2002.

Carleton, David and Michael Stohl. "The Role of Human Rights in US Foreign Assistance Policy: A Critique and Reappraisal," *American Journal of Political Science* 31, no. 4 (1987), 1002–1018.

Center for International Policy. *Just the Facts 2001–2002: A Quick Tour of US Defense and Security Relations with Latin America and the Caribbean.* Washington, DC: Author, October 2001.

Cingranelli, D.L., ed. *Human Rights: Theory and Measurement.* Hong Kong: Macmillan, 1988.

Cingranelli, D. L. and D. L. Richards. "Respect for Human Rights after the End of the Cold War," *Journal of Peace Research* 36, no. 5 (1999), 511–534.

Cingranelli, David L. and Thomas E. Pasquarello. "Human Rights Practices and the Distribution of US Foreign Aid to Latin American Countries," *American Journal of Political Science* 29, no. 3 (1985), 539–563.

Coffman, Edward M. "The Long Shadow of the Soldier and the State," *The Journal of Military History* 55, no. 1 (1991), 69–82.

Cohen, Stephen B. "Conditioning US Security Assistance on Human Rights Practices," *American Journal of International Law* 76, no. 2 (1982), 246–279.

Colombia, Fuerzas Militares de Colombia, Comando General. *Plan de integracion del derecho internacional de los derechos humanos y del derecho internacional aplicable en situaciones de conflicto armado las fuerzas militares.* March 2003.

Colombia, Ministerio de Defensa Nacional. *Politica de Defensa y Seguridad Democratica.* 2003.

———. *Strengthening of the Human Rights and IHL Culture in the Colombian Police and Armed Forces.* 2005.

Colombia, Vicepresidencia de la Republica, Programa Presidencial de los Derechos Humanos y Derecho International Humanitariano. *Indicadores Comparados Sobre la Situacion de los Derechos Humanos en Colombia Noviembre de 2004.* 2004.

———.*Situacion de Derechos Humanos y Derecho Internacional Humanitario.* 2003.

Comision Colombiana de Juristsas. *Colombia: veinte razones para afirmar que la sitaucion de derechos humanos y derecho humanitario es muy grave y tiende a empeorar.* Bogota: Author, September 2004.

———. *En contravia de las recomendaciones internacionales: "Seguridad democratica," derechos humanos y derecho humanitariano en Colombia: agosto de 2002 a agosto de 2004.* Bogota: Author, 2004.

Danner, Mark. *The Massacre at El Mozote.* New York: Vintage, 1993.

Dominguez, Jorge I. ed. *International Security and Democracy: Latin America and the Caribbean in the Post Cold War Era.* Pittsburgh, PA: University of Pittsburgh Press, 1998.

Donnelly, Jack. *International Human Rights.* Boulder, CO: Westview Press, 1998.

———. "International Human Rights: Unintended Consequences of the War on terrorism," in Thomas G. Weiss, Margaret E. Crahan, and John Goering, eds., *War on Terrorism and Iraq: Human Rights, Unilateralism, and US Foreign Policy.* New York: Routledge, 2004.

Economist Intelligence Unit. *Country Profile Colombia 2004/2005 Main Report.* Author, September 2004.

———. *Country Profile Colombia 2006/2007 Main Report.* Author, September 2004.

———. *Country Profile Venezuela 2004/2005 Main Report*. Author, September 2004.

Farer, Tom. "The Interplay of Domestic Politics, Human Rights, and US Foreign Policy," in Thomas G. Weiss, Margaret E. Crahan, and John Goering, eds., *War on Terrorism and Iraq: Human Rights, Unilateralism, and US Foreign Policy*. New York: Routledge, 2004.

Feaver, Peter D. and Richard H. Kohn, eds. *Soldiers and Civilians: The Civil- Military Gap and American National Security*. Cambridge, MA: MIT Press, 2001.

Fitch, J. Samuel. *Armed Forces and Democracy in Latin America*. Baltimore, MD: Johns Hopkins University Press, 1998.

Forsythe, David P. "Congress and Human Rights in US Foreign Policy: The Fate of General Legislation," *Human Rights Quarterly* 9, no. 3 (1987), 382–404.

———."US Foreign Policy and Human Rights," *Journal of Human Rights* 1, no. 4 (2002), 501–521.

———. "US Foreign Policy and Human Rights in an Era of Insecurity: The Bush Administration and Human Rights after September 11," in Thomas G. Weiss, Margaret E. Crahan, and John Goering, eds., *War on Terrorism and Iraq: Human Rights, Unilateralism, and US Foreign Policy*. New York: Routledge, 2004.

Freedom House. *Freedom in the World Country Ratings: 1972 through 2003*. Author, 2004.

Gates, John M. "The Alleged Isolation of US Army Officers in the Late 19th Century," *Parameters* 10 (Spring 1980), 32–45.

Halvorssen, Thor. "The Arrest of FARC Terrorist Ricardo Granda Sheds New Light on Hugo Chavez's Ongoing Support of Terrorism," *The Weekly Standard* (January 26, 2005).

Haugaard, Lisa. *Declassified Army and CIA Manuals Used in Latin America: An Analysis of Their Content*. Washington, DC: Latin America Working Group, 1997.

Haugaard, Lisa, Sean Garcia, Philip Schmidt, and Mavis Anderson. *September's Shadow: Post-9/11 US-Latin American Relations*. Washington, DC: Latin American Working Group Education Fund, September 2004.

Henderson, C. W. "Conditions Affecting the Use of Political Repression," *Journal of Conflict Resolution* 35, no. 1 (1991), 120–142.

———. *A Wrong Turn: The Record of the Colombian Attorney General's Office*. Washington, DC: Author, November 2002.

Human Rights Watch. *Colombia: Flawed Certification Squanders US Leverage—US Aid Released Despite Evidence of Colombia's Failure to Meet Conditions*. Washington, DC: Author, January 2003.

———. *Colombia: Letting Paramilitaries off the Hook, A Human Rights Watch Briefing Paper*. Washington, DC: Author, January 2005.

———. *Rigging the Rule of Law: Judicial Independence under Siege in Venezuela*. Washington, DC: Author, June 2004.

———. *The "Sixth Division" Military-Paramilitary Ties and US Policy in Colombia*. Washington, DC: Author, 2002.

———. *Venezuela: Media Law Undercuts Freedom of Expression*. Washington, DC: Author, November 2004.

Huntington, Samuel P. *The Soldier and the State: The Theory and Politics of Civil-Military Relations*. Cambridge, MA: Harvard University Press, 1957.

Inter-American Commission on Human Rights. *Process of Demobilization in Colombia*. 2004.

Isacson, Adam. *Peace or "Paramilitarization?" Why a Weak Peace Agreement with Colombian Paramilitary Groups May Be Worse Than No Agreement At All*. Washington, DC: Center for International Policy, July 2005.

———. *Re: Colombia's Peace Talks with Paramilitaries: Conditions for US Support, Memorandum to Colleagues and Legislative Staff*. Washington, DC: Center for International Policy, December 7, 2004.

Janowitz, Morris. *The Professional Soldier: A Social and Political Portrait*. Glenco, IL: The Free Press, 1960.

Latin American Working Group Education Fund, Center for International Policy, Washington Office on Latin America. *Below the Radar: US Military Programs with Latin America, 1997–2007*. Washington, DC: Author, March 2007.

———. *Blurring the Lines: Trends in US Military Programs with Latin America*. Washington, DC: Author, October 2004.

———. *Paint by Numbers: Trends in US Military Programs with Latin America & Challenges to Oversight*. Washington, DC: Author, August 2003.

Manwaring Max G., ed. *Security and Civil-Military Relations in the New World Disorder: The Use of Armed Forces in the Americas*. Carlisle, PA: Strategic Studies Institute, U.S. Army War College, 1999.

McCall, Richard. "From Monroe to Reagan: An Overview of US-Latin American Relations," in Richard Newfarmer, ed., *From Gunboats to Diplomacy: New US Policies for Latin America*. Baltimore, MA: Johns Hopkins University Press, 1984.

McCormick, James and Neil Mitchell. "Is US Aid Really Linked to Human Rights in Latin America?" *American Journal of Political Science* 32, no. 1 (1988), 231–239.

Nunn, Frederick M. *The Time of the Generals: Latin American Professional Militarism in World Perspective*. Lincoln: University of Nebraska Press, 1992.

Office of the Assistant Secretary of Defense/Public Affairs Office. *Fact Sheet Concerning Training Manuals Containing Materials Inconsistent with US Policy*. Washington, DC: The National Security Archive, 1996.

Pion-Berlin, David ed. *Civil-Military Relations in Latin America: New Analytic Perspectives*. Chapel Hill: University of North Carolina Press, 2001.

Pion-Berlin, David and Craig Arceneaux, "Decision-Makers of Decision-Takers? Military Missions and Civilian Control in Democratic South America," *Armed Forces & Society* 26, no. 3 (2000), 413–436.

Poe, Steven C. "Human Rights and Economic Aid Allocation under Ronald Reagan and Jimmy Carter," *American Journal of Political Science* 36, no. 1 (1992), 147–167.

Poe, Steven, Suzanne Pilatovsky, Brian Miller, and Ayo Ogundele. "Human Rights and US Foreign Aid Revisited: The Latin American Region," *Human Rights Quarterly* 16, no. 3 (1994), 539–558.

Ramsey, Russell W. *Essays on Latin American Security: The Collected Writings of a Scholar-Implementer.* Bloomington, IN: First Books, 2003.

———. *Strategic Reading on Latin America*, 3rd ed. Bloomington, IN: First Books, 2001.

Ramsey, Russell W. and Antonio Raimondo. "Human Rights Instruction at the US Army School of the Americas," *Human Rights Review* 2, no. 3 (2001), 92–116.

Red de Apoyo. *Casos Atendido Por La Red de Apoyo, Periodo: Enero–Noviembre 2004.* Caracas: Author, 2004.

Ricks, Thomas E. *Making the Corps.* New York: Scribner, 1997.

Roney, Alexander T. "US Southern Command's Human Rights Program," *Dialogo.* www.dialogo-americas.com.

Roth, Kenneth. "The Fight against Terrorism: The Bush Administration's Dangerous Neglect of Human Rights," in Thomas G. Weiss, Margaret E. Crahan, and John Goering, eds., *War on Terrorism and Iraq: Human Rights, Unilateralism, and US Foreign Policy.* New York: Routledge, 2004.

Ruhl, Mark J. "Curbing Central America's Militaries," *Journal of Democracy* 15, no. 3 (July 2004), 137–151.

Schoultz, Lars. *Human Rights and United States Policy toward Latin America.* Princeton, NJ: Princeton University Press, 1981.

Schoultz, Lars, William C. Smith, and Augusto Varas, eds. *Security, Democracy, and Development in US-Latin American Relations.* Miami, FL: North-South Center Press, 1994.

Schulz, Donald. *The Role of the Armed Forces in the Americas: Civil-Military Relations for the 21st Century.* Carlisle Barracks, PA: US Army War College, Strategic Studies Institute, 1998.

Sicker, Martin. *The Geopolitics of Security in the Americas.* Westport: Praeger, 2002.

Sikkink, Kathryn. *Mixed Signals: US Human Rights Policy and Latin America.* Ithaca, NY: Cornell University Press, 2004.

Stepan, Alfred. *Rethinking Military Politics: Brazil and the Southern Cone.* Princeton, NJ: Princeton University Press, 1988.

Stohl, Michael, David Carleton, and Steven Johnson. "Human Rights and US Foreign Assistance from Nixon to Carter," *Journal of Peace Research* 21, no. 3 (1984), 215–226.

The Latin America Working Group Education Fund. *The Wrong Road: Colombia's National Security Policy.* Washington, DC: Author, July 2003.

The White House. *President Sworn in to Second Term*, 2005. www.whitehouse.gov/news/releases/2005/01.html.

———. *The National Security Strategy of the United States of America.* Washington, DC, September 2002.

United Nations, High Commissioner for Human Rights. *Informe del Alto Comisionado de las Naciones Unidas para los Derechos Humanos sobre la situacion de los derechos humanos en Colombia.* February 2003, UN Document E/CN.4/2003/13.

United Nations. *UN Security Council Annex, from Madness to Hope: The 12-year War in El Salvador: Report of the Commission on the Truth for El Salvador.* 1993, s/25500.

United States Institute for Peace. *Special Report, US Human Rights Policy to Latin America*. January 2001.

U.S. Army. *Law of War Documentary Supplement*. Charlottesville, 2004.

U.S. Congress. *Department of Defense Appropriations Act*. H.R. 2561 §8098, 1999.

———. *Foreign Assistance Act of 1961*. §502(B), 1976.

———. *Foreign Assistance Act of 1974*. §36, 88 Stat. 1815, 1974.

———. *H. R. Rep. No. 95-1546*, 95th Cong. 1st sess. 16, 1977.

———. *H.R. 5408, National Defense Authorization Act*, §911, 2000.

U.S. Congressional Research Service. *Plan Colombia: A Progress Report*, by Connie Veillette. Order Code RL32774. February 17, 2005.

U.S. Department of Defense, US Southern Command. *Consensus Document*. 2002.

———. *Posture Statement of General Blantz J. Craddock before the 109th Congress House Armed Services Committee*. March 9, 2005.

———. *SC Regulation 1–20: Human Rights Policy and Procedures*. April 8, 2002.

———. *US SOUTHCOM's Theater Strategy*. 2003.

U.S. Department of Defense, Western Hemisphere Institute for Security Cooperation. *Democracy and Human Rights at WHINSEC*. 2005. www.benning.army.mil/whinsec.

U.S. General Accounting Office. *Central America: Impact of US Assistance in the 1980s*. Report to the Chairman, Committee on Foreign Relations, US Senate. July 1989, GAO/NSIAD-89-170.

———. *Drug Control: US Nonmilitary Assistance to Colombia Is Beginning to Show Intended Results, but Programs Are Not Readily Sustainable*, Report to the Honorable Charles E. Grassley, Chairman, Caucus on International Narcotics Control, US Senate. July 2004.

———. *El Salvador: Military Assistance Has Helped Counter but not Overcome the Insurgency*. April 1991, GAO/NSIAD-91-166.

U.S. State Department, Bureau of Political-Military Affairs. *American Service- Members' Protection Act*. 2003.

U.S. State Department. *Bolivia: Country Reports on Human Rights Practices*. February 2003.

———. *Colombia: Country Reports on Human Rights Practices*. February 2004.

———. *Colombia: Country Reports on Human Rights Practices*. February 2005.

———. *Embassy Human Rights Strategy*. Colombia, February 2003.

———. *58th UNGA: Third Committee Debate on Human Rights Issues*. December 17, 2003.

———. *Memorandum of Justification Concerning Human Rights Conditions with Respect to Assistance for Colombian Armed Forces*. September 2004.

———. *Military Penal Justice Corps School Seeks To Improve the Colombian Military Justice System*. Colombia, April 10, 2003.

———. *Plan Colombia: Major Successes and New Challenges, Roger Noriega, Assistant Secretary for Western Hemisphere Affairs Statement before the House International Relations Committee*. May 11, 2005.

———. *Staffdel Meeting with Minister of Defense*. Colombia, August 25, 2004.

———. *Supporting Human Rights and Democracy: The US Record in Colombia 2003–2004*. February 2004.

———. *Supporting Human Rights and Democracy: The US Record in Colombia 2004–2005*. February 2005.

———. *Uribe's Peasant Soldiers: Key to Extending Security throughout Colombia*. Colombia, June 2003.

———. *Venezuela: Country Reports on Human Rights Practices*. February 2004.

———. *Venezuela: Country Reports on Human Rights Practices*. February 2005.

Vaicius, Ingrid and Adam Isacson. *The "War on Drugs" meets the "War on Terror": The United States' Military Involvement in Colombia Climbs to the Next Level*. Washington, DC: Center for International Policy, February 2003.

Vivanco, Jose Miguel, and Maria McFarland Sanchez-Moreno. "A Bad Plan in Colombia." *International Herald Tribune* (May 16, 2005).

Waller, Douglas and Richard de Silva. "Running a 'School for Dictators,'" *Newsweek* 122, no. 6 (1993), 34–37.

Washington Office on Latin America and Andean Information Network. *Flawed State Department Report on Human Rights in Bolivia: Memorandum to Foreign Policy Aids*. Washington, DC: Author, July 9, 2004.

Watson, Robert P. and Sean McCluskie. "Human Rights Considerations and US Foreign Policy: The Latin American Experience," *The Social Science Journal* 34, no. 2 (1997), 249–258.

Zagorski, Paul W. *Democracy vs. National Security: Civil-Military Relations in Latin America*. Boulder, CO: Lynne Rienner Publishers, 1992.

INTERVIEWS

All interviews took place in person and responses were hand-written by author.

Aarid, David. Political-Military Officer U.S. Embassy Buenos Aires. Interview by author, December 2004, Buenos Aires.

Alabre, Lt. Col. Dan. U.S. Defense Attache Office, U.S. Embassy Santiago. Interview by author, November 2004, Santiago.

Anderson, Capt. Ray. U.S. Defense Attache Office, U.S. Embassy Lima. Interview by author, September 2004, Lima.

Anonymous Venezuelan National Guard Officer. Caracas. Interview by author, December 2004, Caracas.

Anonymous. U.S. Embassy La Paz. Interview by author, September 2004, La Paz.

Barretto, Col. Daniel. U.S. Mil-Group, U.S. Embassy La Paz. Interview by author, September 2004, La Paz.

Berger, Steve. U.S. Mil-Group, U.S. Embassy Bogota. Interview by author, September 2004, Bogota.

Bresnahan, Leana. SOUTHCOM Human Rights Coordinator. Interview by author, July 2004, Miami.

Brown, Stan. U.S. Narcotics Affairs Section U.S. Embassy Bogota. Interview by author, September 2004, Bogota.

Bruno, Capt. U.S. Embassy Brasilia. Interview by author, December 2004, Brasilia.

CELS Argentina. Interview by author, December 2004, Buenos Aires.

Ciurlizza Contreras, Javier. Executive, Director Instituto de Democraciay Derechos Humanos. Interview by author, September 2004, Lima.

Cohen, Lawrence. Political Officer U.S. Embassy Brasilia. Interview by author, December 2004, Brasilia.

Conway, Craig. Human Rights Officer U.S. Embassy Bogota. Interview by author, September 2004, Bogota.

Cordero, Lt. Col. Maria. Commander SOUTHCOM Human Rights Division. Interview by author, July 2003, Miami.

Crahan, Margaret. Human Rights Advisor Hunter College/SOUTHCOM. Interview by author, April 2005, New York.

Crowley, Chris. SOUTHCOM Legislative Affairs, Washington, DC. Interview by author, July 2004, Washington, DC.

Cuello, Lt. Col Kris. U.S. Defense Attache Office, U.S. Embassy Lima. Interview by author, September 2004, Lima.

Dalson, Col. William. U.S. Defense Attache Office, U.S. Embassy Buenos Aires. Interview by author, December 2004, Buenos Aires.

Daza, Cpt. Colombian National Police, Espinal. Interview by author, September 2004, Colombia.

DeLeon, Col. USAF JAG, U.S. Embassy Bogota. Interview by author, September 2004, Bogota.

DeRouchy, Col. Terry. U.S. Mil-Group, U.S. Embassy Caracas. Interview by author, December 2004, Caracas.

Downie, Dr. Richard. Director of Center for Hemispheric Defense Studies. Interview by author, September 2004, Washington, DC.

Feeley, John. Deputy Political Counselor U.S. Embassy Mexico City 2001–2003. Interview by author, June 2003, Mexico City.

Ferrand, Pierre. International Committee of the Red Cross, Bogota. Interview by author, September 2004, Bogota.

Fiemeyer, Lt. Col. Dennis. Office of Secretary of Defense. Interview by author, July 2003, Washington, DC.

Freitas, Alexandra. Consorcio Justicial, Caracas. Interview by author, December 2004, Caracas.

Gallon, Gustavo. Director International Commission of Jurists. Interview by author, September 2004, Bogota.

Galvin, Jeff. U.S. Embassy Political Officer, Santiago. Interview by author, November 2004, Santiago.

Gillooly, Lt. Col. Bruce. U.S. Army Counterterrorism Program, Bogota, Colombia. Interview by author, September 2004, Bogota.

Gingras, Lt. Col. Mark. Assistant JAG SOUTHCOM. Interview by author, July 2003, Miami.

Gomez, Cpt. Michael. U.S. Army 7th Special Forces, Espinal, Colombia. Interview by author, September 2004, Colombia.

Gomez, Lt. Col. Sal. U.S. Mil-Group, U.S. Embassy Lima. Interview by author, September 2004, Lima

Grissom, Sgt. Barry. U.S. Army 7th Special Forces, Espinal, Colombia. Interview by author, September 2004, Colombia.

Gutierrez, Lino. U.S. Ambassador U.S. Embassy Buenos Aires. Interview by author, December 2004, Buenos Aires.

Harding, Peter. Human Rights Officer U.S. Embassy La Paz. Interview by author, September 2004, La Paz.

Hernandez, Mauricio M. International Committee of the Red Cross, Bogota. Interview by author, September 2004, Bogota.

Hodge, Lt. Col. Timothy. DAO Army Attaché U.S. Embassy La Paz. Interview by author, September 2004, La Paz.

Huizi, Rafael, Adm. Ret. Venezuelan Navy, Caracas. Interview by author, December 2004, Caracas.

Isacson, Adam. Program Director Center for International Policy. Interview by author, October 2004, Washington, DC.

Karol, Col. U.S. Embassy Brasilia. Interview by author, December 2004, Brasilia.

Knutson, Maj. Michael. Office of Secretary of Defense. Interview by author, July 2003, Washington, DC.

Leuer, Joseph. Instructor, Western Hemisphere Institute for Security Cooperation. Interview by author, November 2004, Ft. Benning.

Levinson, Lt. Col. Robert. SOUTHCOM Legislative Affairs, Washington, DC. Interview by author, July 2004, Washington, DC.

Llorens, Hugo. Deputy Chief of Missions, U.S. Embassy Buenos Aires. Interview by author, December 2004, Buenos Aires.

Llorenti, Sacha. President Asamblea Permanente de Derechos Humanos de Bolivia. Interview by author, September 2004, La Paz.

Matos, Col. Jorge. U.S. Mil-Group, U.S. Embassy Bogota. Interview by author, September 2004, Bogota.

McClintock, Cmd. Lowell. U.S. Mil-Group, U.S. Embassy Buenos Aires. Interview by author, December 2004, Buenos Aires.

McFarland, Maria. Human Rights Watch. Interview by author, January 2005, Washington, DC.

Miles, Richard. Political Officer U.S. Embassy Buenos Aires. Interview by author, December 2004, Buenos Aires.

Miller, Col. Commander SOUTHCOM Human Rights Division. Interview by author, July 2003, Miami.

O'Reilly, Kevin. Deputy Political Counselor, U.S. Embassy Mexico City. Interview by author, July 2003, Mexico City.

Olson, Eric. Advocacy Director Amnesty International for the Americas. Interview by author, September 2004, Washington, DC.

Olson, Joy. Executive Director Washington Office on Latin America. Interview by author, November 2004, Washington, DC.

Prieto Silva, Enrique, Gen., Ret. Venezuelan Army, Caracas. Interview by author, December 2004, Caracas.

Raimondo, Maj. Antonio. Human Rights Instructor, Western Hemisphere Institute for Security Cooperation. Interview by author, November 2004, Ft. Benning.

Ramsey, Russell W. Instructor, Western Hemisphere Institute for Security Cooperation. Interview by author, November 2004, Ft. Benning.

Rodriguez, Lt. Col. Humberto. U.S. Defense Attache Office, U.S. Embassy Caracas. Interview by author, December 2004, Caracas.

Ruiz, Alfredo and anonymous assistant, Red de Apoyo, Caracas. Interview by author, December 2004, Caracas.

San Miguel, Rocio, former Venezuela War College Professor, Caracas. Interview by author, December 2004, Caracas.

Schell, Col. W. Jay. U.S. Mil-Group, U.S. Embassy Bogota. Interview by author, September 2004, Bogota.

Schneebaum, Steven M. Chairman WHINSEC Board of Visitors 2004. Interview by author, November 2004, Washington, DC.

Supervielle, Col. SOUTHCOM JAG. Interview by author, July 2003, Miami.

Three Anonymous U.S. Government Officials. Interview by author, July 2003, Washington, DC.

Trimarco, Maria Virginia. Regional Representative, UN High Commission on Refugees. Caracas. Interview by author, December 2004, Caracas.

Trombitas, Col. Simeon. U.S. Mil-Group Commander, U.S. Embassy Bogota. Interview by author, September 2004, Bogota.

Trujillo, Col Alex. U.S. Defense Attache Office, U.S. Embassy Bogota. Interview by author, September 2004, Bogota.

Uribe, Victor. SOUTHCOM Human Rights Initiative Participant. Interview by author, July 2004, Miami.

Vickers, George. SOUTHCOM Human Rights Initiative Participant. Interview by author, July 2004, Washington, DC.

Viscarra, Patricia. Foreign Service National U.S. Embassy La Paz. Interview by author, September 2004, La Paz.

Vivanco, Jose Miguel. Executive Director Human Rights Watch Americas Division. Interview by author, February 2005, Washington, DC.

Zequeira, Maj. Jorge. U.S. Defense Attache Office, U.S. Embassy Caracas. Interview by author, December 2004, Caracas.

Zurita, Audalia. District Prosecutor La Paz, Bolivia. Interview by author, September 2004, La Paz.

Index

About the Author

JERRY M. LAURIENTI works as a Latin America analyst for the U.S. government and writes frequently for top policymakers. He has traveled extensively in the region, where he conducted research for this book. He earned his Ph.D. from the University of Denver, Graduate School of International Studies.